Private Schooling in Less
Economically Developed Countries:

Private Schooling in
Less Economically
Developed Countries:
Asian and African perspectives

Edited by
Prachi Srivastava & Geoffrey Walford

Oxford Studies in Comparative Education
Series Editor: David Phillips

SYMPOSIUM
BOOKS

Symposium Books
PO Box 204 Didcot Oxford OX11 9ZQ United Kingdom
the book publishing division of wwwords Ltd
www.symposium-books.co.uk

Published in the United Kingdom, 2007

ISBN 978-1-873927-85-4

This publication is also available on a subscription basis
as Volume 17 Number 2 of *Oxford Studies in Comparative Education*
(ISSN 0961-2149)

Typeset by wwwords Ltd
Printed and bound in the United Kingdom by Cambridge University Press

Contents

CHAPTER 1

Examining Private Schooling in Less Economically Developed Countries: key issues and new evidence

GEOFFREY WALFORD & PRACHI SRIVASTAVA

In the more economically advantaged world, private schooling has long been associated with privilege and elitism. In practice, this association has always been misleading, for in most countries the sector is very diverse; while the leading schools may well be highly selective, expensive, and likely to lead to high-status universities, there are many that are far more modest.

In the currently less economically advantaged world, the association between private schooling and elitism is even more complex. While most countries still have a highly privileged and exclusive private sector that educates the children of the middle class, there is also a wide diversity of other private schools that serve a much broader range of children. Of particular interest are the 'low-fee' private schools in countries such as India, China, and Kenya that provide schooling for poorer groups. Where the government system is perceived to be inadequate, small-scale entrepreneurs and a range of non-governmental organisations have stepped in to provide schooling for those who cannot afford the high fees of the elite schools, but are able and prepared to spend a significant proportion of income on lower fee schools.

This diversity of private providers raises the immediate question of what is meant by the term 'private'. The range is from small-scale entrepreneurs who enter the schooling market simply because they see the opportunity to make a profit, to those run by individuals, groups and organisations with more altruistic motives. Religious organisations, of course, have been centrally involved in private provision in many countries for decades. They have become so much a part of the educational landscape that they receive substantial support form the state in many countries. The distinction

7

between private and state schools is often blurred, with some well-established private schools benefiting from a range of tax incentives and direct financial support from government.

The state also imposes a range of controls over all schools whether they are run by the government or private agents, and private schools are usually required to obtain recognition from the government at some stage in their development. One of the fascinating aspects of private schooling in less economically developed countries is the large number of unrecognised schools, such that governments may have only a broad idea of the full scale of private provision in their own countries.

With the dramatic growth of private schools in many less economically developed countries, there are important questions that need to be answered about the possible role of these schools in achieving Education for All targets and the Millennium Development Goals. It may already be, as Tooley & Dixon suggest, that the many low-fee private schools that are practically unknown to the governments of, for example, China, Nigeria and India, are actually making a substantial contribution towards meeting those targets. If so, they suggest that some degree of financial and other support from the government or international agencies might be a better investment than similar support given to the government sector. However, in the absence of a funding structure contingent on quality assessed on indicators beyond facilities and achievement, this may contribute to further inequities for the most disadvantaged children.

This book does not set out to answer these important questions, but to provide further research evidence on which answers to such questions might be based. It brings together a series of newly written chapters that provide important evidence on the extent and nature of private schooling in economically developing countries in Asia and Africa.

In chapter 2, James Tooley & Pauline Dixon give an overview of their large-scale international research project that examined private schooling for the poor in India, Ghana, Nigeria and Kenya. In each of these countries, specific low-income regions were selected and a survey was conducted by a team of on-the-ground researchers to discover the extent of private schooling in each region. As many of these schools for the poor are unrecognised, often neither the local nor central government actually knows how many children are attending them or even how many such schools there are. The results are stark. In the low-income areas of India, Ghana, Nigeria and Kenya that Tooley & Dixon studied, they found that a majority of schoolchildren were found in private unaided schools. In slum and shanty towns it was the private sector that dominated provision over government provided and funded schools.

This finding has some fascinating implications, for such children in unregistered private schools are usually not considered to be in school at all. In Hyderabad, for example, they found that inclusion of these children within official figures might reduce the percentage of children not in school from about fifteen to less than six. Thus, according to Tooley & Dixon, the cost of providing schooling for the children of the remaining extremely poor parents would be far less than usually calculated, and the presence of these unrecognised private schools could bring the possibility of Education for All far closer than is commonly argued. Nonetheless, the problem of over-reporting and double enrolment aggravates precise estimations.

In any case, access is only valuable if the quality of these schools is reasonable. As these are low-fee schools where teachers may be untrained and where they are often paid considerably less than teachers in the government schools, one might expect students' levels of academic achievement to be lower than those in government schools. Tooley & Dixon's second stage of research was based on a stratified random sample of students in government and private schools within these low-income areas. Children were tested in English and mathematics in about 150 schools in each of Hyderabad, India; Ga, Ghana; and Lagos State, Nigeria; and 80 in Nairobi, Kenya. They found that, in all cases, children in the private schools did better than those in the government schools. This finding has to be interpreted with care, for the authors clarify that in three of the four cases it was the slightly more wealthy of the poor who were able to pay for private schooling rather than use government schools. But these better levels of achievement were obtained at about a quarter of the cost of those for children in the government schools. From such preliminary analysis, it seems that these schools are not failing, and they raise important questions about the place of private provision in attaining Education for All in poor countries, and for the need of more research in this area.

In chapter 3, Keith M. Lewin presents a less optimistic view than Tooley & Dixon of the possible role of private schooling in helping countries to reach the Millennium Development Goals. He presents data on the extent and nature of private schooling in the whole range of sub-Saharan African countries, and shows that non-government private providers do make a significant contribution in many of these countries. In most sub-Saharan African countries enough school places exist to enrol most but not all primary school-aged children, but across the continent the majority of secondary-aged children, for whom private provision is more common, are excluded. He argues that most non-governmental provision, especially at secondary level, is urban and concentrated in more wealthy areas. This means that the most likely way in which private schooling might increase access is by the more wealthy opting for this provision, leaving spaces in the public schools that the less wealthy can thus occupy. While this may be beneficial overall, there remains a concern for the ultra-poor, or the 'last 20%', who remain unlikely to be able to afford schooling.

Lewin argues that non-governmental schooling, especially that which is truly private and completely unsubsidised, is likely to have limited impact towards universalising access to basic education in sub-Saharan Africa. The state must remain the provider of last resort, especially for the children located in households living on less than a dollar a day per capita. He argues that household income and income distribution between households is such that few of the lowest two quintiles could afford the full economic cost of unsubsidised schools at ·prevailing fee rates. He predicts that the most successful countries in sub-Saharan Africa, in terms of reaching the Millennium Development Goals, will be those that extend the reach of their public school systems and lower the direct costs to the poor. While private schools have a contribution to make, their overall effect is likely to be small.

This is a strikingly different prediction to that of Tooley & Dixon. An important difference is simply that Lewin derives his analysis from official data which he recognises himself are sometimes suspect. Tooley & Dixon claim that many governments simply do not know how many private schools are operating in their countries and that there is often a raft of unrecognised and unknown private schools serving the very poor. Whether these schools are really beneficial or are simply giving parents the illusion that their children are being educated, depends in part on whether their quality is at least as good as (or better than) the quality of the public sector schools. That has still to be determined and will, of course, vary widely both within and between different countries.

Focusing on the implications of private provision on access to schooling for poor communities in Africa, Pauline Rose & Modupe Adelabu's discussion in chapter 4 is a case study of two contrasting states in Nigeria, which they characterise as: one where private provision is small relative to the state sector (Enugu) and another where private provision appears to predominate (Lagos). The study, funded by the United Kingdom's Department for International Development, incorporated analysis of official policy documents, interviews with private school operators of unapproved and approved schools, and interviews with members of two private school associations.

Similar to Lewin and contrary to Tooley & Dixon's argument, they stress that while unapproved unregistered schools serve low-income households, they are unlikely to capture the poorest among these. Rose & Adelabu contend that the poorest households would most likely access schooling in the state sector where provision is free, or not at all. However, similar to Lewin, they acknowledge the lack of data on unapproved unregistered schools, complicating the analysis on a large scale.

According to their study, while fees at unapproved schools were higher than at state schools, facilities were not necessarily better. Nonetheless, teacher absenteeism was reported to be low, discipline was judged to be better, and these schools operated for longer hours, in effect providing childcare for families where both parents worked. These were used as reasons to access the private sector by lower income families who could afford to do so.

Fundamentally, Rose & Adelabu question government regulatory requirements and processes for approval. They state that while some private schools have been operating without formal approval, the government has either been unable to enforce its regulation or has adopted a laissez-faire attitude, ignoring unapproved schools. The authors attribute this to the government's own realisation of its inability to provide on the one hand, and its commitment to universal primary education on the other.

Government regulatory and policy contexts for private provision are the focus of Igor Kitaev's analysis in chapter 5. This macro-review of private provision across a range of Asian countries highlights the diversity of geopolitical and historical contexts within which private sectors have developed and operate. The relatively recent emergence of a small private sector for upper-middle classes in the former centrally planned countries of Central Asia is operating in a context where formal private schooling was historically illegal but enrolment rates were almost universal. The context for private provision in South and South East Asia is very different, with highly heterogeneous client groups and providers from for-profit, religious, to non-governmental organisations (NGOs), and is operating in countries with significantly lower enrolment rates and persistent schooling gaps. This has complicated the very definition of what private provision is and what the private sector constitutes, and Kitaev provides a framework of terms and definitions which may be useful in this regard.

The chapter further outlines the official regulatory requirements and practices for the operation of private sectors around such issues as funding, teacher staffing, and inspection. What makes Kitaev's chapter particularly informative in the context of this book is that it is based largely on official high-level government reports commissioned for UNESCO. The chapter, when compared with some of the field-based studies on Asia in this book (for example, Bangay's on Bangladesh and Indonesia, Caddell's on Nepal, and Srivastava's on India), helps to highlight the importance of a nuanced discourse on private provision taking into account the differences of what is supposed to happen 'in principle' and what happens 'in practice'. Ultimately, the sheer scope of the chapter underscores the need for further context-specific and in-depth field studies on private provision in economically developing countries.

In the next chapter, Colin Bangay examines further the relationship between state and non-state private schools, with a particular focus on Indonesia and Bangladesh. Taking as his starting point the fact that non-governmental providers often make a significant contribution to schooling in economically developing countries, he examines the diversity of provision paying particular attention to private fee-charging schools and schools run by NGOs. Similar to Kitaev, he takes a broad view of private schools as all of the formal schools that are not public, even in cases where the state provides most of the funding and has considerable control over the schools. Bangay's first task is thus to present a framework for the discussion of the spectrum of schools based upon their position with regard to dependence on state funding and the degree of control that the state exerts on them. He examines evidence on teacher accountability, management efficiency and the pressures that often lead to more schools being established in urban rather than rural areas.

Bangay then describes some of the work that has been done by NGOs in Bangladesh to provide schools for particular groups of children. While many of these initiatives have clearly been successful, there are questions about the long-term desirability of such non-state involvement and abut the extent to which such activities are replicable within the government system. However, he argues that the division between state and private provision is likely to blur even further in the future, such that it is essential that the state develops a relationship with the private sector that enables a coherent and high-quality system to be developed.

Chapter 7 by Santosh Mehrotra & P.R. Panchamukhi summarises a survey study of eight Indian states, seven of which account for three-quarters of the children officially recorded as out of school in India. It is a macro-level account of some of the features of private elementary schooling in India, and draws comparisons with government schools. It compares gender and social equity in the coverage of private and government schools, physical facilities and human resources, and outcome and process indicators. Finally, it draws some policy conclusions from the perspective that in order for India to achieve its Education for All targets, the 'efficiency and equity of the entire educational system has to improve – not just that of the public sector'.

The issue of definition brought out in Kitaev's piece resurfaces, as Mehrotra & Panchamukhi's classification of school types in India comprises four types. Typically, the literature on Indian private schooling categorises school types as three: government, private aided, and private unaided, the latter comprising recognised and unrecognised schools.

More fundamentally, Mehrotra & Panchamukhi state that the private unaided sector in India has emerged as a response to a failing state sector. However, similar to Rose & Adelabu's discussion on Nigeria, they describe a context where the existence of unrecognised private schools, often without the knowledge of local education officers, complicates an examination of the private sector and its potential implications. With the inclusion of unrecognised schools in the sample, Mehrotra & Panchamukhi's survey analysis aims to provide some general descriptions of the private unaided sector in India.

In chapter 8, Prachi Srivastava's analysis of private schooling in India takes a more in-depth look at 'low-fee private' schools in Uttar Pradesh. This case study is specifically focused on the sub-sector of recognised and unrecognised private unaided schools that serve socially and economically disadvantaged groups. This qualitative study was based on 10 selected case study schools (where school owners/principals, and 60 household participants were interviewed), and provides a complementary analysis to that provided by the more quantitative studies on India that precede it.

In the first part of the chapter, Srivastava describes the nature of these low-fee private schools in considerable detail. She includes material on the views of the owners/principals about education and their reasons for being involved in school provision, as well as the marketing strategies they use to attract and retain students. This is followed by a discussion of some of the major challenges faced by these schools: in particular, the low levels of pay offered to teachers and related high staff turnover, lack of training of teachers, and problems with fee collection, which seem similar to some of the issues brought out by private school operators in Rose & Adelabu's study on Nigeria.

Finally, Srivastava examines the complicated power relations between the parents and the school owners, and suggests that both groups have a range of strategies that they employ (including fee bargaining and fee jumping on one side and fee concessions, flexi-fees and withholding documentation on the other) in their attempts to gain leverage. She concludes that the low-fee private schools in her study cannot be characterised simply as engaged in philanthropy or exploiting the poor for personal benefit – the patterns of interaction between parents and the schools are far more complicated than either extreme would suggest.

The final chapter in the book by Martha Caddell considers the fate of private schools in strife-torn Nepal, and most overtly highlights the private sector as a space for political struggle. For the last decade or more, Nepal has been in a de facto state of civil war with Maoist forces fighting the state for control. In such a situation schools, and in particular the private schools, have become a site for violent political conflict over the nature of what is taught and their very existence.

Liberalisation of the market in schooling has led to a dramatic growth in private schools of various types, with an estimated 1000 schools in Kathmandu alone. This chapter explores how, at the time of her study, private schools had become a focus of attention for the Maoist forces in their efforts to wage and win a 'People's War' against the monarchy and state forces. The chapter highlights the need for academics and policy makers to engage with a broad range of issues concerning private schools, beyond issues of efficiency and effectiveness.

In essence, the underlying themes of this book centre around the potential implications of an increasingly marketised and privatised schooling arena on disadvantaged groups in contexts that are not only economically constrained and politically charged, but that are struggling with such issues as universal enrolment, retention, gender equity, and adequate quality provision at even the most basic levels of schooling. As such, discussions throughout the book on norms for private school recognition, governing regulatory frameworks, motives of private school operators, equitable access, and quality performance should be understood within this larger context. The hope is that the presentation of new research on the growing phenomenon of private schooling in economically developing countries will provide researchers and policy makers with a more nuanced understanding of the educational challenges that many countries are faced with, and will provide them with the beginnings for more concentrated analysis.

CHAPTER 2

Private Education for Low-Income Families: results from a global research project

JAMES TOOLEY & PAULINE DIXON

Introduction

Can private education help meet the educational needs of poor children in low-income countries? To some, this question may seem strange. Private education is most often perceived to be for the elite and middle classes, not the poor. However, there is a growing body of evidence that challenges this conception.

The *Oxfam Education Report*, for instance, reports 'the notion that private schools are servicing the needs of a small minority of wealthy parents is misplaced', and that 'a lower cost private sector has emerged to meet the demands of poor households' (Watkins, 2000, pp. 229-230). Research in Haryana, India, found that private unrecognised schools 'are operating practically in every locality of the urban centres as well as in rural areas' and are often located adjacent to a government school (Aggarwal, 2000, p. 20). Reporting on evidence from the Indian states of Haryana, Uttar Pradesh and Rajasthan, researchers noted that 'private schools have been expanding rapidly in recent years' and that these 'now include a large number of primary schools which charge low fees', in urban as well as rural areas (De et al, 2002, p. 148). Serving the poor of Calcutta, there has been a 'mushrooming of privately managed unregulated pre-primary and primary schools' (Nambissan, 2003, p. 52).

In Uganda and Malawi, private schools have 'mushroomed due to the poor quality government primary schools' (Rose, 2002, p. 6; 2003, p. 80) and in Kenya 'the deteriorating quality of public education ... created demand for private alternatives' (Bauer et al, 2002). In sub-Saharan Africa and Asia generally, 'the poor and declining quality of public education has led to growing numbers of parents sending their children to non-state schools' and in south Asia 'this amounts to a mass exodus' (Bennell, 2004, p. iv).

In India and Africa private schools for low-income families seem to be flourishing. Why do poor parents send their children to private unaided schools, when government schooling is available, usually free of tuition fees and often providing free midday lunches, textbooks, uniforms or other benefits? Several reasons have been given to explain this 'mushrooming' of the private school sector. These include the deterioration of government schools, the lack of government schools, and (in India) the desire of parents for instruction in English.

Researchers reporting on private and public schools in northern Indian states describe the 'malfunctioning' of public schools for low-income families (Probe Team, 1999, p. 47). The schools suffered from poor physical facilities and high pupil–teacher ratios, but what is most disturbing is the low level of teaching activity taking place. When the researchers called unannounced on a randomly selected sample of schools, they found 'teaching activity' going on in only half of the schools. In 33%, the head teacher was absent. Significantly, the low level of teaching activity 'has become a way of life in the profession' (Probe Team, 1999, p. 63).

These problems, the researchers note, were not found in the private schools serving the poor and low-income families. In the great majority of these there 'was feverish classroom activity' (Probe Team, 1999, p. 102). So much so, that the majority of parents reported that 'if the costs of sending a child to a government and private school were the same, they would rather send their children to a private school' (Probe Team, 1999, p. 102). This deterioration of government school standards has been attributed to the lack of teacher accountability, strong unions (which contribute to teacher complacency and lack of motivation to teach), poor facilities, high pupil–teacher ratios and poor management (Probe Team, 1999; Aggarwal, 2000; Rana et al, 2002; Nambissan, 2003; Habyarimana et al, 2004; Kremer et al, 2005).

Furthermore, in a number of countries public schools have limited spaces, because government spending has not kept up with an increase in the number of school-aged children. In Nigeria 'the inadequacy of the infrastructural facilities to cope with the very rapid rate of expansion in student enrollment is a major source of crisis in the education system'. In the 1990s 'very few new classrooms were built to accommodate the extra three million pupils' (Nwagwu, 1997, p. 91). In Tanzania 'as in many low-income countries, excess demand was sufficient to stimulate the growth of a large private sector' (Lassibille et al, 1998, p. 38).

Finally, the demand for private schools has increased in India, it is reported, because private schools often, ostensibly at least, provide instruction in English, which parents regard as desirable. In most government schools, lessons are taught in the state language and English does not become a subject until approximately the fifth grade (Majumdar et al, 2002; Nambissan, 2003).

But are parents correct in their belief that private schools are superior to government schools? According to two studies, the evidence from Africa is mixed, with one study showing higher academic achievement for private schools (Cox & Jimenez, 1990) and another showing lower achievement (Lassibille & Tan, 2001). However, neither of these studies looked specifically at private schools serving low-income families. Several studies have compared the relative performance of private unaided, private aided and government schools in India – but again none has specifically looked at schools for the poor, and all appear to have considered only recognised private schools. A study in urban Lucknow, Uttar Pradesh, found that after controlling for background variables, students in private unaided schools scored higher on standardised tests in mathematics than in the other school types. When the cost per unit gain in achievement was computed, private unaided schools showed higher achievement results for less than half the cost of the government schools (Kingdon, 1996a). Similarly, a study in Tamil Nadu found that students in private unaided high schools performed better than those in government schools in English and mathematics (Druaisamy & Subramanian, 2003). Children attending private unaided schools in Madhya Pradesh outperformed children attending government schools in maths and Hindi: 'management-type – government or private – emerges as the most significant factor influencing learner achievement' (Govinda & Varghese, 1993, p. 265).

However, until now, the quality of private schools serving low-income families has been unknown, because no quantitative research has been carried out in private schools in low-income areas. It has simply been assumed that the quality of the unrecognised private unaided schools that are serving the poor across Africa and Asia is low.

The *Oxfam Education Report*, for instance, notes that while 'there is no doubting the appalling standard of provision in public education systems', this does not mean that private education is necessarily better (Watkins, 2000, p. 230). As far as private schools for the poor are concerned, these are of 'inferior quality', indeed they 'offer a low-quality service' that is so bad it will 'restrict children's future opportunities'. The *Report* concludes, 'surprisingly, in view of the confident assertions made in some quarters, there is little hard evidence to substantiate the view that private schools systematically outperform public schools with comparable levels of financial resources' (Watkins, 2000, p. 230).

The United Nations *Human Development Report 2003* makes precisely the same claim (United Nations, 2003, p. 115). Similar claims of the low quality of the unrecognised private schools come from other sources, including a study from Calcutta: 'the mushrooming of privately managed unregulated pre-primary and primary schools ... can have only deleterious consequences for the spread of education in general and that among the poor in particular' (Nambissan, 2003, p. 52). The quality of education in the private schools is 'often suspect' (Nambissan, 2003, p. 15, footnote 25).

Significantly, none of these sources offers detailed evidence for the assertion of low quality in unrecognised private schools; indeed, the claim is precisely that no quantitative evidence is available. Poorer achievement has been assumed, in part because of the low-quality infrastructure in the schools, and because such schools often have untrained and low-paid teachers. The 'unrecognised' or 'unregistered' schools are unregulated by the state and are perceived to be of minimal quality. But does being unregulated make for lower quality in the schools? In addition to answering this important question, our research examined the extent to which private unaided schools serve the poor and the relative quality of the private schools in comparison to government schools.

Overview of Research

The current research project, which ran from April 2003 to June 2005, was a large international project, with parallel research going on simultaneously in India (Delhi, Hyderabad and Manbubnagar), China (Gansu Province), Ghana (Ga District), Nigeria (Lagos State), and Kenya (Nairobi Province). In this chapter we report on the findings from India (Hyderabad), Ghana, Nigeria and Kenya only. The research had two major components.

The first component included the administration of a 'Census of Schools' in selected low-income regions and a 'Survey of Inputs' to these schools, aimed to discover the nature and extent of private schools in selected low-income regions, and to compare their inputs with the government schools. The second component of our research used the census from component one as the population frame to compare student achievement in a stratified random sample of government and private schools and also compared the financial resources available to both types of schools. This chapter presents an *overview* of a selection of findings from these two components. (Other papers are under peer review looking at these and other findings in more detail for each country.)

What is the Nature and Extent of Private Education for the Poor?

Research Countries and Method

We chose to do the study in Kenya, as free primary education (FPE – for eight years' primary schooling) had just been introduced. Specifically, we wanted to know how the introduction of free education affected private schools for the poor, should they be found to exist. In this chapter we report on the slum of Kibera, reportedly the largest slum area in sub-Saharan Africa. Parallel research was also conducted in the slums of Mukuru and Kawangware in Nairobi, not reported here, which produced similar findings.

Nigeria was chosen because it is the country with the largest population in sub-Saharan Africa, and its significance to the continent's future is clear. In Lagos State we randomly selected three local government areas for study – one from each of the three senatorial districts making up Lagos State: Surulere, Kosofe and Badagry. Surulere and Kosofe are urban, Badagry is rural. Using official data, areas were classified as 'poor' or 'non-poor', with the former featuring overcrowded housing with poor drainage, poor sanitation and lack of potable water, and prone to occasional flooding. We report on our findings from only those 'poor' areas. We separately looked at the urban shanty town of Makoko, in Mainland local government area, where perhaps 50,000 people live, many housed in houses built on stilts sunk into the Lagos lagoon.

We had conducted research earlier in Hyderabad, India, were familiar with the terrain and had many contacts in government and the private sector, so it seemed sensible to continue the project there. Here, we covered three zones in the Old City: Bandlaguda, Bhadurpura and Charminar. The three zones of Bandlaguda, Bhadurpura and Charminar together have a population of about 800,000 (about 22% of Hyderabad's people) and cover an area of some 19 square miles. We included only schools that were found in 'notified slums', as determined by the latest available census and Hyderabad municipal guides. These were areas that lacked amenities such as indoor plumbing, running water, electricity, and paved roads.

Finally, because of a chance meeting at a conference with the Ghanaian Minister of Education, we were invited to conduct our research in Ghana as well. We chose to conduct our research in the Ga district, which surrounds the country's capital city of Accra and is classified by the Ghana Statistical Service as a low-income suburban and rural area. The Ghana Poverty Reduction Strategy Document (Ga District Planning Coordinating Unit, 2004) suggests that about 70% of the population of 500,000 live on or below the poverty line. Ga includes poor fishing villages along the coast, subsistence farms inland, as well as large dormitory towns for workers serving the industries and businesses of Accra itself; most of the district lacks basic social amenities such as potable water, sewage systems, electricity and paved roads.

In India, we followed the usual definition of school management type as being of three kinds: government, private aided and private unaided (see for example Kingdon, 1996a). Government schools are totally funded and managed by some level of government, state or local. Private aided schools are privately managed, but have teacher salaries paid for by government. Other expenses are partly funded privately and partly by government. Private unaided schools are entirely privately managed and privately funded. Private unaided schools are of two types, recognised and unrecognised: recognised schools have purportedly met the regulatory requirements of the state. Unrecognised schools are in effect operating in the informal sector of the economy. They have either not applied for recognition, or have not succeeded in gaining recognition from the government.

In the African countries, we distinguished between two types of schools, government and private. Government schools receive all of their funding from the state. In some cases they may have private management, for many church schools were nationalised in Ghana and Nigeria and operate now as government schools, but with some vestiges of private management under state regulations. These are rather like the Anglican and Catholic schools in the United Kingdom, funded by the state but managed by the church under state regulations. Private schools are both privately managed and privately funded. Private schools are again of two types. Registered private schools are those that have, purportedly, met state regulations and been inspected. Unregistered private schools are those that either have not applied to be registered, or have not (yet) been said to have met these regulations.

To conduct the research, we collaborated with research teams consisting of four or five senior researchers from each of the University of Cape Coast, Ghana; University of Ibadan, Nigeria; the Inter-region Economic Network and Kenyatta University, Kenya; the Educare Trust, Hyderabad; and the Gansu Yitong Marketing Company, Lanzhou, China. These lead teams, prior to our visit, recruited between 30 to 40 researchers each – chosen after interviewing a large batch of graduate students – to conduct the fieldwork, who were also trained by us. The first component involved weeks combing the selected low-income areas, to find all elementary and high schools serving the population. We visited each of the countries several times during the research, unannounced, to check on progress.

Four important caveats must be made about the results that follow concerning the proportion of private schools and enrolment: First, there is the reported propensity of government and private aided schools to exaggerate enrolment, with clear financial and job security incentives to claim larger enrolment than is actually the case (Kingdon, 1996a; Kingdon & Drèze, 1998). Second, it was reported anecdotally that there may be some double enrolment of children in both government and private schools, for this enabled a child to attend private school during the morning and government school for the free lunch provided; it also would enable a child to take state examinations and gain transfer certificates, which would not be possible in an unrecognised private school. Third, we have no way of checking that all unrecognised/unregistered schools were located by the researchers, for there are, by definition, no official lists with which to compare our findings. For the first and third of these reasons, it is suggested that the data here may be an underestimate of the true proportion of enrolment in private, especially unrecognised or unregistered, schools, although the second caveat has an unknown impact on enrolment.

Finally, it may be the case that some private schools, especially unrecognised or unregistered ones, may be opening and closing fairly quickly. Hence, the figures below must be taken as indicating what was the case only at the time of the census.

How Many Schools are There and What Proportion is Private?

In India, Nigeria and Ghana, we were interested in the same major issues – the proportion of children in private and government schools, gender issues, the respective teacher–pupil ratios, the age of schools, and management of private schools. In Kenya, we were only looking at a small sample of government schools on the periphery of the slums compared to a large number of private schools within the slums, so it was not statistically viable to make comparisons, or to generalise about the overall enrolment in private and government schools. (The same is true of the smaller study in Makoko, Nigeria.)

In the study locations in India, Nigeria and Ghana, government schools were found to be in a minority. In Hyderabad, of the 918 schools in the low-income area schools, 34.9% (320 schools) were government, 5.3% (49 schools) private aided, and 59.8% (549 schools) private unaided. Of these, the largest number is unrecognised (335 schools or 36.5% of the total), while 214 private unaided schools were recognised (23.3% of the total). Hence, not only are government schools in the minority, there are more unrecognised private unaided schools than there are government schools.

Of the 779 schools in Ga, 25.3% (197 schools) were government and the rest – 74.7% of the total (582 schools) – were private (unaided) schools. That is, the large majority of schools are private unaided. Of these, the largest number is registered (405 schools or 52.0% of the total), while 177 private unaided schools were unregistered (22.7% of the total). Here, there are almost as many unrecognised private unaided schools as there are government schools.

	Hyderabad, India		Ga, Ghana		Lagos State, Nigeria	
	n	%	*n*	%	*n*	%
Government	320	34.9	197	25.3	185	34.3
Private aided	49	5.3	N/A		N/A	
Private unaided unrecognised/ unregistered	335	36.5	177	22.7	233	43.1
Private unaided recognised/ registered	214	23.3	405	52.0	122	22.6
Total	918	100.0	779	100.0	540	100.0

Table I. Number and proportion of schools, by school type.
Source: Census of Schools data.

In Lagos State, of the 540 schools in the low-income areas, 34.3% (185 schools) were government and the rest – 65.7% of the total (355 schools) – private unaided schools. That is, a large majority of schools are private. Of these, the largest number is unregistered (233 schools or 43.1% of the total), while 122 private unaided schools were registered (22.6% of the total). Hence, there are more unregistered private unaided schools than there are government schools. These results are summarised in Table I.

What is the Proportion of Pupil Enrolment in Private Education?

In the low-income areas of India, Ghana and Nigeria that we studied, a majority of school children were either calculated or estimated to be in the private (unaided) schools.

In Hyderabad, the total number of children enrolled in the 918 schools was 262,075. Breaking this down by school type, the government schools accounted for 24.0% of that enrolment, the private aided schools for 11.4%, the recognised private unaided schools for 41.5%, and the unrecognised private unaided schools for 23.1%. That is, roughly the same number of children were reported to be in unrecognised private schools as were in government schools. In total, 65% of schoolchildren attend private unaided schools – that is, a large majority of the children in the low-income areas of Hyderabad are reported to be attending private unaided schools.

In Ga, 161,244 children were in 779 schools. Breaking this down by school type, 35.6% of all children were at government schools, 49.1% of children at registered private unaided schools, and 15.3% of children at unregistered private unaided schools. In total, 64.4% of schoolchildren are reported to be attending private unaided school – that is, a large majority of the children in the low-income areas of Ga are attending private unaided schools.

In Nigeria, our Census of Schools gave enrolment figures only for the private schools, so the numbers given here are estimates. The official Lagos State Ministry of Education figures for primary school enrolment in 2002-03 report that the proportion of children in government and private registered schools is 38% and 62% respectively (451,798 in government and 737,599 in private registered schools) (Lagos State Economic and Empowerment Development Strategy, 2004). Our own census figures showed that the proportion of children in private *unregistered* primary schools was 78% of the number in private *registered* primary schools. If the proportions in the three local government areas included in our study were similar to the state as a whole, then we would find a total of 577,024 children in unregistered private schools across the state (i.e. 78% of the official figure in registered private schools of 737,599). Combining these figures gives the estimated percentage of pupils enrolled in the three school types across Lagos State. Adding together children in unregistered and registered private schools, we suggest that about 75% of schoolchildren are in private schools, with a greater proportion in private unregistered than government schools (33% compared to 26%). These data are summarised in Table II.

	Hyderabad, India		Ga, Ghana		Lagos State, Nigeria (estimate)	
	n	%	*n*	%	*n*	%
Government	62,839	24.0	57,374	35.6	451,798	26.0
Private aided	29,976	11.4	N/A	–	N/A	–
Private unaided unrecognised/ unregistered	60,533	23.1	24,738	15.3	577,024	33.0
Private unaided recognised/ registered	108,727	41.5	79,132	49.1	737,599	42.0
Total	262,075	100.0	161,244	100.0	1,766,421	100.0

Table II. Number and proportion of pupil enrolment, by school type.
Sources: Census of Schools data and Lagos State Government (2004, p. 29).

Our surveys of schools in the Kibera slum of Kenya and the Makoko shanty town in Nigeria reveal parallel figures. In Makoko, Nigeria, the team found 30 private primary schools. (The research team also found one private secondary school and one nursery school. These were not included in this survey.) There were also three government primary schools, situated on the edge of Makoko. Total enrolment in the 30 private primary schools was reported to be 3611, while government primary school enrolment was reported as 1709. In the government schools, it was reported that some children came from outside Makoko, although no proportion was given. In the private schools, all children came from within Makoko. Thus, we estimate that at least 68% of schoolchildren in Makoko attend private school. The actual figure is likely to be higher than this.

In Kibera, we found 76 private primary and secondary schools, enrolling 12,132 students (excluding nursery students), together with 59 nursery-only schools. These figures did not include 'non-formal education' centres that are also prevalent. In the five government schools that were reported to serve children from Kibera, we found a total of about 9000 children. It is not known how many of these were from the slum areas, but comments from head teachers suggested about one-half. Hence, it is clear that, if children from Kibera only go to either the private schools in the slums, or the government schools on the periphery, then a large majority of schoolchildren from this slum attend private schools.

Official Versus Actual Enrolment

The fact that so many children go to private unrecognised/unregistered schools that are entirely 'off the state's radar' has implications for the official figures for number of children out of school, and hence for the topical UN

General Assembly deliberations about progress towards the Millennium Development Goal of 'Education for All'. This means that there are likely many more children in school than is recorded in official statistics (although the caveats mentioned above will of course have an impact on these deliberations, so they are offered as estimates only).

In the 'slum' areas of three zones of Hyderabad, we found 79,851 students in private schools that were not on government lists – around 30% of the total number of schoolchildren in those areas. But recent data from the Azim Premji Foundation using official government figures suggested that for the 35 zones that make up Hyderabad District, 129,000 children are out of school, that is, 15.4% of the 837,212 school-age children (aged 5 to 15) in Hyderabad (Azim Premji Foundation, 2005). It is likely that many of these children were located in the three zones we surveyed as we chose them because they were reportedly some of the poorest neighbourhoods. If *all* the 'out of school' children were in the zones we surveyed, then this would reduce the number of out of school children to about 49,000 children – the balance being accommodated in private unrecognised schools that are missed in official figures. Instead of 15.4% out of school, the figure would be sharply reduced to only about 6% (see Table III). More realistically, if some of the officially 'out of school' children are spread over the 32 other zones, then the actual figure of out of school children would be even lower. It is surely easier to bring 6% or a lower percentage of children into school than it is to bring 15%. India's task of achieving Education for All may thus be much easier to reach than official sources claim.

	Hyderabad (official figures)	Worst case scenario (all out-of-school children in the three zones surveyed)
Total number of school-age children	837,212	837,212
Number of children in schools	708,212	788,063
Number of children out of school	129,000	49,149
% of children out of school	15	6

Table III. Hyderabad: official and estimated out of school children.
Sources: Census of Schools data and Azim Premji Foundation (2005).

Similar calculations can be made for the other countries. For instance, a recent report from the Lagos State Economic Empowerment and Development Strategy estimates that 50% of 'school aged' children are out of school, although it doesn't state what ages these cover (Lagos State Government, 2004, p. 29). In the absence of any better estimates, we can compare these with our estimated figures given above. If the 50% of children out of school applies to primary enrolment too, then we would have the official figures given in the second column of Table IV. This shows a total of 1,189,397 out of school, that is, 50% of the total. If we add in our estimates of children in private *unregistered* schools, however, this total will be sharply reduced to 612,373, or only 26% of the total of school-age children. These are indicative figures only, given a number of assumptions that may not be correct (e.g. there may be a lower proportion of primary-age than secondary-age children out of school). Nonetheless, it is worth stating that bringing 26% of children into school may be much easier than bringing 50% into school. Again, Nigeria's task of achieving Education for All may be considerably easier than is currently anticipated. These findings are surely 'good news' for the international development community.

	Official figures	Our estimates
Government	451,798	451,798
Private registered	737,599	737,599
Private unregistered	0	577,024
Total	1,189,397	1,766,421
Estimated out-of-school children	1,189,397	612,373
Total school-age children	2,378,794	2,378,794

Table IV. Lagos State: official and estimated out of primary school children. Sources: Census of Schools data and Lagos State Economic and Empowerment Development Strategy (2004).

How Well Do Children Achieve? Survey of Achievement

How do government and private schools compare in terms of pupil achievement? We explored this by examining pupil achievement in primary schools at a single class or grade (either class/grade 4, 5 or 6), using tests in English, mathematics and (in Africa) one other subject, depending on context, together with other cross-sectional data collected from the school and family. This section describes the methodology used to collect student achievement data and presents the results of the student achievement tests.

Method

Because unrecognised or unregistered private schools are not on any government lists, we used the list of schools obtained from our earlier Census of Schools as the basis to select schools for the second part of our research on student achievement. The student achievement data have been analysed for Hyderabad, India; Ga, Ghana; Lagos State, Nigeria; and Nairobi, Kenya. Further studies are ongoing in Delhi, India; Mahboobnagar (rural Andhra Pradesh), India; and Gansu Province, China. Results of these studies will be reported in later publications. In the Indian study, we excluded the small number of private aided schools. As mentioned above, these made up only about 5% of the schools in Hyderabad, so were too small in number to be a viable option for most children. In the African studies we included all school types.

A stratified random sample of between 3000 to 4000 students was selected for study. Schools were sorted by size and school type so that each sample included a roughly equal number of students in each school type: private unregistered/unrecognised, private registered/recognised, and government. We grouped schools in each of the three management types into 21 size groups, with the aim of ensuring all school sizes were represented within the sample. In the India, Ghana and Nigeria studies we also aimed to restrict the number of children to be sampled in any one school to 30. If classes were larger than 30, the first 30 children (15 boys and 15 girls, or the maximum number of either gender if there were fewer than 15) on the register were selected for testing. Again, this was to avoid the sample being skewed toward pupils from larger schools. The Kenya case was unique in that we had only a small number of government schools, so we had to test a larger proportion of children in the government schools to create a large enough sample. Table V shows the number of government, private unrecognised/unregistered, and private recognised schools in each country.

	Hyderabad, India	Ga, Ghana	Lagos State, Nigeria	Nairobi, Kenya
Government	44 (28.8%)	37 (27.0%)	40 (25.0%)	12 (15.0%)
Private unrecognised/ unregistered	64 (41.8%)	47 (34.3%)	67 (41.9%)	68 (85%)
Private recognised/ registered	45 (29.4%)	53 (38.7%)	53 (33.1%)	
Total	153 (100%)	137 (100%)	160 (100%)	80 (100%)

Table V. Schools in stratified random samples, by management type.

Data on background variables that earlier research on school effectiveness had suggested might be significant for achievement – such as household income and wealth indicators, years of parental education, caste or tribe, religion and parental motivation – were elicited through questionnaires, apart from IQ (innate ability), which was tested for both pupils and teachers using Raven's Standard Progressive Matrices, the results of which were normed using local published norms (Deshpande & Ojha, 2002). Questionnaires were prepared by the research teams in each country and modified to suit local conditions. Questionnaires were prepared for students, families of the students, as well as teachers and school managers/head teachers. The class teacher in grade 4, 5, or 6 was asked to fill out the questionnaire. The total number of valid questionnaires for each survey is shown in the tables below.

The core curriculum subjects of mathematics and English were tested in all countries – English being at least one of the official languages in each country studied. Use of public examination scores was not a viable means of assessing student achievement, as the reliability of these scores has been questioned, particularly in India, where widespread mass cheating, leakage of exam papers, tampering with results, and other unethical practices have been reported (Kingdon, 1996b, footnote 8).

All tests were reviewed by panels of teachers drawn from private and government schools to assure that each test reflected material that should be known to the children in the appropriate grades in both private and government schools. In India, tests in mathematics and English were adapted from standardised tests constructed by NIIT Ltd, Delhi with advice from the State Council for Educational Research and Teaching in Hyderabad. In the African countries, we used mathematics and English tests developed for the US Agency for International Development by the Educational Assessment and Research Centre (EARC), Accra, Ghana. These tests were modified based on discussions with focus groups brought together by the University of Cape Coast (Ghana), the University of Ibadan (Nigeria) and the Inter-region Economic Network (Kenya). A third test was used in the African countries as follows: Ghana: a religious and moral education test developed by EARC; Nigeria: a test in social studies was prepared by educators at the University of Ibadan in conjunction with local teachers; Kenya: a test in Kiswahili was prepared by the Inter-region Economic Network in conjunction with local teachers and university experts. All tests were pilot tested with about 80 children chosen equally from private unaided and government schools. The internal consistency reliability of each test was calculated using the Kuder-Richardson 20 coefficient, which was high in all cases. In order to have a roughly normal distribution of results, a few questions were omitted, and the modified tests were again retested with approximately the same number of children in different schools, and the reliability and distribution checked. None of the children who took part in the pilot testing participated in later tests.

In all countries except Kenya, the data were analysed using the Heckman two-stage procedure, to control for the fact that children were not randomly assigned to schools (Heckman, 1979, 1989; Green, 2000). In Kenya, it was not possible to conduct this statistical procedure due to the way the government schools were sampled. Other literature and anecdotal evidence have suggested that parents are likely to choose private schools for their boys and/or brighter children, and also that wealthier, better educated parents from higher castes are more likely to choose private over government schools (Kingdon, 1996a; Drèze & Sen, 2002). Once this school choice process was controlled for, the data were subjected to statistical techniques that controlled for other variables such as family background and peer-group effects. These results are currently under peer review and so are not reported in this chapter. (For the record, our results so far suggest that the private school advantage found in the raw scores continues after these background effects are controlled for. In the Kenya study, this analysis shows private schools outperforming government schools in all subjects.)

Results: raw test scores and standardised data

Tables VI-XIII show raw test scores and standardised data for all the subjects tested. The number of observations reflect the total number of children tested prior to conducting the statistical analysis outlined above. The results show a similar pattern of achievement for Hyderabad, Ga and Lagos State, with slightly different results for Nairobi, reflecting the differing circumstances under which the student achievement tests were conducted. In Hyderabad, Ga and Lagos State, all of the private and government schools included in our study were located in the low-income areas. In these cases, the data showed that it was the slightly wealthier and better educated of the low-income families that used the private schools. In the Nairobi study, however, the private schools were situated in the slums and served only slum children, whereas the government schools were located on the slum periphery and served middle-class as well as slum children. In this case, the data showed that it was the poorer and less educated parents that used the private schools.

For Hyderabad, mean scores in mathematics were about 22 percentage points and 25 percentage points higher in private unrecognised and recognised schools respectively than in government schools. The advantage was even more pronounced for English.

In Ga, the advantage for both types of private schools was smaller but still large in terms of standard deviations, with average maths scores being about 6 and 12 percentage points higher in private unregistered and registered schools respectively than in government schools. In English the advantage was about 9 and 14 percentage points.

In Lagos State, the mean maths score advantage over government schools was about 15 and 19 percentage points respectively in private registered and unregistered schools, while in English it was 23 and 30 percentage points.

In Kenya, private schools performed at about the same level as government schools in all subjects. In maths and Kiswahili, the private schools were slightly better, while in English, a small advantage lay with the government schools. But this advantage may be because many of the middle-class children in the government schools pick up English outside of school – through watching television, for example.

Subject		Mean % score	SD	Cases
Maths	Government	38.41	26.51	1240
	Private unrecognised	60.78	20.55	1315
	Private recognised	63.38	21.26	1355
	Total	54.59	25.38	3910
English	Government	22.44	20.63	1240
	Private unrecognised	53.64	19.82	1315
	Private recognised	59.48	21.22	1355
	Total	45.77	26.10	3910

Note: SD = standard deviation.

Table VI. Hyderabad – raw scores. Source: Survey of Achievement data.

Subject		Mean score	SD	Cases
Maths	Government	-0.637	1.044	1240
	Private unrecognised	0.244	0.810	1315
	Private recognised	0.347	0.838	1355
	Total	0.000	1.000	3910
English	Government	-0.893	0.790	1240
	Private unrecognised	0.301	0.759	1315
	Private recognised	0.525	0.813	1355
	Total	0.000	1.000	3910

Notes: SD = standard deviation. Scores in this table have been standardised to have a mean of zero and a standard deviation of one.

Table VII. Hyderabad – standardised scores. Source: Survey of Achievement data.

Subject		Mean % score	SD	Cases
Maths	Government	55.60	20.06	1364
	Private unregistered	61.31	19.38	665
	Private registered	67.72	16.90	1521
	Total	61.86	19.42	3550
English	Government	57.15	17.20	1356
	Private unregistered	65.67	17.73	666
	Private registered	71.50	14.83	1517
	Total	64.91	17.56	3539
Religious and moral education	Government	52.65	17.84	1372
	Private unregistered	60.13	16.39	686
	Private registered	63.05	14.46	1536
	Total	58.53	16.86	3594

Note: SD = standard deviation.

Table VIII. Ga, Ghana – raw scores. Source: Survey of Achievement data.

Subject		Mean score	SD	Cases
Maths	Government	-0.323	1.033	1364
	Private unregistered	-0.028	0.998	665
	Private registered	0.302	0.870	1521
	Total	0.000	1.000	3550
English	Government	-0.441	0.979	1356
	Private unregistered	0.044	1.010	666
	Private registered	0.375	0.845	1517
	Total	0.000	1.000	3539
Religious and moral education	Government	-0.348	1.058	1372
	Private unregistered	0.095	0.972	686
	Private registered	0.269	0.857	1536
	Total	0.000	1.000	3594

Notes: SD = standard deviation. Scores in this table have been standardised to have a mean of zero and a standard deviation of one.

Table IX. Ga, Ghana – standardised scores. Source: Survey of Achievement data.

Subject		Mean % score	SD	Cases
Maths	Government	41.36	19.10	1108
	Private unregistered	55.92	19.56	1142
	Private registered	60.68	19.27	1045
	Total	52.53	20.97	3295
English	Government	42.18	20.06	1099
	Private unregistered	65.12	21.02	1134
	Private registered	72.06	20.31	1036
	Total	59.61	24.10	3269
Social studies	Government	58.80	22.99	1081
	Private unregistered	71.46	21.32	1091
	Private registered	76.18	18.37	990
	Total	68.61	22.28	3162

Note: SD = standard deviation.

Table X. Lagos State, Nigeria – raw scores. Source: Survey of Achievement data.

Subject		Mean score	SD	Cases
Maths	Government	-0.533	0.911	1108
	Private unregistered	0.162	0.933	1142
	Private registered	0.388	0.919	1045
	Total	0.000	1.000	3295
English	Government	-0.723	0.832	1099
	Private unregistered	0.229	0.872	1134
	Private registered	0.517	0.843	1036
	Total	0.000	1.000	3269
Social studies	Government	-0.440	1.031	1081
	Private unregistered	0.128	0.957	1091
	Private registered	0.340	0.824	990
	Total	0.000	1.000	3162

Notes: SD = standard deviation. Scores in this table have been standardised to have a mean of zero and a standard deviation of one.

Table XI. Lagos State, Nigeria – standardised scores.
Source: Survey of Achievement data.

Subject		Mean % score	SD	Cases
Maths	Government	69.87	18.34	1713
	Private	70.72	16.80	1335
	Total	70.24	17.69	3048
English	Government	68.00	16.12	1725
	Private	65.90	16.48	1318
	Total	67.09	16.31	3043
Kiswahili	Government	60.97	15.54	1732
	Private	64.18	15.75	1342
	Total	62.37	15.71	3074

Note: SD = standard deviation.

Table XII. Nairobi, Kenya – raw scores.
Source: Survey of Achievement data.

Subject		Mean score	SD	Cases
Maths	Government	-0.021	1.037	1713
	Private	0.027	0.950	1335
	Total	0.000	1.000	3048
English	Government	0.056	0.990	1725
	Private	-0.073	1.010	1318
	Total	0.000	1.000	3043
Kiswahili	Government	-0.090	0.989	1732
	Private	0.115	1.002	1342
	Total	0.000	1.000	3074

Notes: SD = standard deviation. Scores in this table have been standardised to have a mean of zero and a standard deviation of one.

Table XIII. Nairobi, Kenya – standardised scores.
Source: Survey of Achievement data.

How Well are Private Schools Funded?

Pupil Fees

We asked school managers for their fees, checking these against fee ledgers; here we report on the findings from India and Nigeria. In Hyderabad, the private unaided schools charge a range of monthly, term, and admission fees. There is a statistically significant difference in the fees charged in unrecognised and recognised schools, with the former consistently lower than the latter, at each level. For example, for first grade, mean fees in recognised private unaided schools are Rs. 95.60 (£1.22) per month (using £1 = Rs. 78/-), compared to Rs. 68.32 (£0.88) per month in the unrecognised schools. At fourth grade, the same figures are Rs. 102.55 (£1.31) compared to Rs. 78.17 (£1.00).

Minimum wages for Andhra Pradesh are set in the range from Rs. 25.96 to Rs. 78.77 (2001 figures, Government of India, 2005), with workers in Hyderabad (who will be non-agricultural) typically at the higher end. A wage of Rs. 78/- (£1.00) per day translates to about Rs. 1872/- (£24.00) per month (assuming 24 working days per month). That is, the mean fees for unrecognised schools for fourth grade might be 4.2% of the monthly wage for a breadwinner on a minimum wage, while recognised school fees might be about 5.5%.

In Nigeria, private schools usually charge term fees. Again, private unregistered schools charge fees that are consistently lower than the registered schools, at each level. For example, for Primary 1 class, average fees in registered private schools are Naira 4064 (£17.67, using the exchange rate of October 2005, £1 = 230 Naira) per term, compared to Naira 2744 (£11.93) in the unregistered schools. At Primary 4, the same figures are Naira 4362 (£18.97) compared to Naira 2993 (£13.01). Dividing these figures by four (the number of months per term), we find that mean monthly fees in unregistered schools are about Naira 686 (£2.98) per month in Primary 1, and about Naira 733 (£3.19) per month in Primary 4.

We can put these figures into the context of the minimum wage in Nigeria, which was set at 5500 Naira (£23.91) per month (2000 figures, National Minimum Wage (Amendment) Act 2000) – although actual wages may be likely higher in Lagos State, given the greater wealth of this state compared to the rest of the country. That is, the mean fees for unregistered schools are about 12.5% and 13.3% of the monthly wage for someone on the minimum wage for Primary 1 and 4 children respectively.

It is should be noted that not all children pay these fees. In all of the countries we surveyed, we found that a considerable number of places were provided free or at reduced rates (e.g. to orphans and children from large families). We estimated that in Hyderabad 18% and in Lagos State 5% of all children in private schools were provided with free or concessionary places.

Teacher Salaries

We have seen that, in general, student achievement in the private schools serving low-income families is greater than in government schools. Is this achieved because these private schools have greater financial resources available to them?

As part of our research, we tried to obtain information about the financial resources available to the different types of schools, but private school managers were understandably wary of divulging financial details to researchers. However, we were able to gain at least some insight into private and government school financial resources by examining teacher salaries, which are estimated to make up between 80% and 96% of all recurrent expenditure in government primary schools in developing countries (Zymelman & Destefano, 1989; Mingat & Winter, 2002).

It should be noted that although teacher salaries were found to represent the majority of financial resources available to private schools (our research indicated that the vast majority of private schools did not receive income from any other source except pupil fees), they do not represent the total level of financial resources going to government schools. In the case of government schools, funds are also used to fund large state and local bureaucracies. Such administrative bureaucracies will be minimal for private registered and recognised schools and non-existent for private unregistered and unrecognised schools. Data on teacher salaries were obtained from the teacher questionnaire, which was administered to one of each of the sample schools in Hyderabad, Ga and Lagos State. In the Nairobi sample, questionnaires were given to an average of about three teachers in each school.

Table XIV shows average monthly teacher salaries in Hyderabad, India; Ga, Ghana; and Lagos State, Nigeria as well as the ratio of these salaries to those in the private unrecognised or unregistered schools. (These data were collected from one teacher in each of the survey schools.) In all three cases, the salaries in government schools were over three times higher than in the private unrecognised/unregistered schools. In Hyderabad and Lagos State, salaries in government schools were nearly four times the reported private school salaries. Table XV shows the same situation with regard to Nairobi, Kenya, with additional information on the number of teachers surveyed. Again, the average teacher salaries in the government schools were about three times higher than those in the private schools. Based on the assumption that teacher salaries reflect the majority of financial resources available at the school level, we can say that government schools have considerably higher levels of financial resources than do their private school counterparts.

(a) Hyderabad, India

	Average monthly salaries of full-time teachers (Rs.) (Rs. 78 = £1)	Ratio of salaries to private unrecognised salaries
Government	4568 (£58.56)	3.86
Private unaided unrecognised/ unregistered	1182 (£15.15)	1.00
Private unaided recognised/ registered	1964 (£25.18)	1.66
Total	2176 (£27.90)	1.84

(b) Ga, Ghana

	Average monthly salaries of full-time teachers (Cedis) (15,995 = £1)	Ratio of salaries to private unregistered salaries
Government	950,346 (£59.42)	3.39
Private unaided unrecognised/ unregistered	280,333 (£17.53)	1.00
Private unaided recognised/ registered	447,856 (£28.00)	1.60
Total	512,684 (£32.05)	1.83

(c) Lagos State, Nigeria

	Average monthly salaries of full-time teachers (Naira) (231 = £1)	Ratio of salaries to private unregistered salaries
Government	20,781 (£90.75)	3.71
Private unaided unrecognised/ unregistered	5598 (£24.45)	1.00
Private unaided recognised/ registered	6415 (£28.01)	1.15
Total	9389 (£41.00)	1.68

Table XIV. Monthly average teacher salaries, by school type.

	Average monthly salaries of full-time teachers (Ksh.) (130 Ksh. = £1)	Ratio of salaries to private unrecognised salaries	Number of teachers
Government	11,080 (£85.23)	2.99	31
Private	3704 (£28.49)	1.00	200
Total	4694 (£36.11)	1.27	231

Table XV. Nairobi: monthly average teacher salaries in stratified random schools.

Conclusions

Many have expressed concern that the 'mushrooming' of private unaided schools in sub-Saharan Africa and South Asia may be undesirable. It is accepted by some commentators that private unaided schools are now widespread in low-income areas, such as city slums and villages. But there are worries expressed about the quality of education that is provided in this low-cost sector: for if schools charge such low fees, and pay teachers so little, how can they offer a high-quality education?

Concerns are also expressed about the inequity that private education for the poor brings. For as growing numbers of parents take their children from government schools, it is argued that only the poorest are left. This seems unfair to those who are left behind.

Through our detailed two-year research in low-income areas of Hyderabad, India; Ga, Ghana; Lagos State, Nigeria; and Nairobi, Kenya [1] we have found challenges to all of these assumptions. In the context of this paper, the major findings are as follows:

The Majority of Schoolchildren in Poor
Areas Attend Private Unaided Schools

First, we have shown that the private sector is indeed huge, with a large majority of schoolchildren – around 65% or more – enrolled in private unaided schools in the selected low-income areas researched, urban and peri-urban/rural. A large proportion of these are enrolled in unrecognised or unregistered private schools – in some cases the same proportion or more as are in government schools. (We noted that several factors may impinge on these estimates, most of which are likely to lead to the reported figures underestimating the total enrolment in private schools.)

School Enrolment Underestimated

Because many children are in unrecognised or unregistered private schools that do not appear in government statistics, overall enrolment is much higher than figures suggest. This means that Education for All may be much easier to achieve than is currently believed. In Hyderabad, the 80,000 children in private unrecognised schools not counted in official statistics could bring the proportion of out of school children down from 15% to 6% or lower. In Lagos State, the existence of private unregistered schools might reduce the percentage of out of school children from 50% to 26%.

Higher Achievement in Private
Unaided than Government Schools

Children in private unaided schools also usually perform better in terms of raw scores than in government schools in key curriculum subjects, including mathematics and English.

Private Unaided Schools Cost Significantly
Less Than Government Schools in Teacher Costs

The private unaided school advantage is achieved for considerably less expenditure on teachers – which is likely to make up the majority of recurrent in-school expenditures – than in government schools. In general, the average monthly teacher salary in a government school is between *three to four times higher* than in an unrecognised or unregistered private school. Apart from teacher salary costs, government schools are supported by a hugely expensive state bureaucracy, which also needs to be taken into account in any comparison of school costs. These additional costs will either be minimal or non-existent for private schools.

Each of these findings, we believe, has implications for the role that private education can play in moving countries towards Education for All. If large numbers of poor parents are already using private schools that outperform government schools at a fraction of the teacher cost, then this would suggest a possible affirmative answer to the question raised at the beginning of this chapter.

Note

[1] Additional studies of other settings are currently under analysis.

References

Aggarwal, Y. (2000) *Public and Private Partnership in Primary Education in India: a study of unrecognised schools in Haryana*. New Delhi: National Institute of Educational Planning and Administration.

Azim Premji Foundation (2005) Andhra Pradesh Programmes. http://www.indianngos.com/azimpremjifoundation/andhrapradesh.htm (accessed August 2005).

Bauer, A., Brust, F. & Hybbert, J. (2002) Entrepreneurship: a case study in African enterprise growth, expanding private education in Kenya: Mary Okelo and Makini schools, *Chazen Web Journal of International Business*, Fall. http://www0.gsb.columbia.edu/chazen/journal

Bennell, P. (2004) *Teacher Motivation and Incentives in sub-Saharan Africa and Asia*. Brighton: Knowledge and Skills for Development.

Cox, D. & Jimenez, E. (1990) The Relative Effectiveness of Private and Public Schools: evidence from two developing countries, *Journal of Development Economics*, 34, pp. 91-121.

De, A., Majumdar, M., Samson, M. & Noronha, C. (2002) Private Schools and Universal Elementary Education, in R. Govinda (Ed.) *India Education Report: a profile of basic education*. Oxford and New Delhi: Oxford University Press.

Deshpande, C.G. & Ojha, J.M. (2002) *Indian Norms for Raven's Standard Progressive Matrices: a normative study in Delhi and Maharashtra*. Delhi: Manasaya.

Drèze, J. & Sen, A. (2002) *India: development and participation* (2nd edn). New Delhi and Oxford: Oxford University Press.

Druaisamy, P. & Subramanian, T.P. (2003) Costs, Financing and Efficiency of Public and Private Schools in Tamil Nadu, in J.B.G. Tilak (Ed.) *Financing Education in India: current issues and changing perspectives*. Delhi: Ravi Books.

Ga District Assembly (2004) *Poverty Profile, Maps and Pro-Poor Programmes*. Amasaman: Ga District Assembly.

Government of India (2005) *Labour Bureau, Statistics, Minimum Wages*, http://labourbureau.nic.in/wagetab.htm, accessed 10 October 2005.

Govinda, R. & Varghese, N.V. (1993) *Quality of Primary Schooling in India: a case study of Madhya Pradesh*. Delhi: International Institute for Educational Planning, National Institute of Educational Planning and Administration.

Green, W.H. (2000) *Econometric Analysis* (4th edn). Upper Saddle River: Prentice Hall.

Heckman, J.J. (1979) Sample Selection Bias as a Specification Error, *Econometrica*, 47, pp. 153-161.

Heckman, J.J. (1989) Choosing Among Alternative Non-experimental Methods for Estimating the Impact of Social Programs: the case of manpower training. National Bureau of Economic Research Working Paper, No. 2861.

Habyarimana, J., Das, J., Dercon, S. & Krishnan, P. (2004) *Sense and Absence: absenteeism and learning in Zambian schools.* Washington, DC: World Bank.

Kingdon, G. (1996a) The Quality and Efficiency of Private and Public Education: a case study in urban India, *Oxford Bulletin of Economics and Statistics,* 58(1), pp. 57-82.

Kingdon, G. (1996b) Student Achievement and Teacher Pay, Discussion Paper No. 74, STICERD, London School of Economics, August.

Kingdon, G. & Drèze, J. (1998) Biases in Educational Statistics, *The Hindu,* 6 March.

Kremer, M., Mularidharan, K., Chaudhury, N., Hammer, J. & Rogers, H. (2005) Teacher Absence in India, *Journal of the European Economic Association,* 3(2-3), pp. 658-667.

Lagos State Economic and Empowerment Development Strategy (2004) http://www.lagosstate.gov.ng/LASEEDS/LASEEDS%20DOCUMENT.pdf

Lagos State Government (2004) Report from Lagos State to the Joint Consultative Committee on Educational Planning (JCCE) Reference Committee on Educational Planning Holding at Owerri, Imo State between 18th and 23rd April 2004, Ministry of Education, Alausa, Ikeja.

Lassibille, G. & Tan, J. (2001) Are Private Schools More Efficient than Public Schools? Evidence from Tanzania, *Education Economics,* 9(2), pp. 145-172.

Lassibille, G., Tan, J. & Sumra, S. (1998) Expansion of Private Secondary Education: experience and prospects in Tanzania, *Impact Evaluation of Education Reforms,* Paper No. 12, Working Paper Series. Washington, DC: World Bank.

Majumdar, M., Samson, M. & Noronha, C. (2002) Private Schools and Universal Elementary Education, in R. Govinda (Ed.) *India Education Report: a profile of basic education,* pp. 131-150. Oxford and New Delhi: Oxford University Press.

Mingat, A. & Winter, C. (2002) Education for All by 2015, *Finance and Development,* 39(1), pp. 1-6.

Nambissan, G.B. (2003) Educational Deprivation and Primary School Provision: a study of providers in the city of Calcutta, IDS Working Paper 187, Institute of Development Studies, University of Sussex, Brighton.

Nwagwu, C.C. (1997) The Environment of Crises in the Nigerian Education System, *Comparative Education,* 33(1), pp. 87-95.

Probe Team (1999) *Public Report on Basic Education in India.* Oxford and New Delhi: Oxford University Press.

Rana, K., Rafique, A. & Sengupta, A. (2002) *The Delivery of Primary Education: a study in West Bengal.* Delhi: TLM Books in association with the Pratichi (India) Trust.

Rose, P. (2002) Is the Non-state Education Sector Serving the Needs of the Poor?: evidence from East and Southern Africa, paper prepared for Department for International Development Seminar in preparation for 2004 World Development Report.

Rose, P. (2003) From the Washington to the Post-Washington Consensus: the influence of international agendas on education policy and practice in Malawi, *Globalisation, Societies and Education*, 1(1), pp. 67-86.

United Nations (2003) *Human Development Report 2003: Millennium Development Goals – a compact among nations to end human poverty.* New York: United Nations Development Programme.

Watkins, K. (2000) *The Oxfam Education Report.* Oxford: Oxfam in Great Britain.

Zymelman, M. & Destefano, J. (1989) *Primary School Teachers Salaries in sub-Saharan Africa.* World Bank Division Paper No. 45. Washington, DC: World Bank.

CHAPTER 3

The Limits to Growth of Non-government Private Schooling in sub-Saharan Africa

KEITH M. LEWIN

The contribution private non-government schooling can make to achieving the Millennium Development Goals (MDGs) related to education is a matter of widespread debate.[1] Non-government schooling has been growing in many of the poorest countries in sub-Saharan Africa. This growth has been encouraged by state failures in providing greatly increased access to schooling at acceptable levels of quality as a result of Education for All (EFA) programmes, increased opting out of public education by those who can afford to pay, and by liberalised regulatory frameworks that allow non-government providers to offer educational services. These developments have led some to argue that non-government providers in general, and private providers in particular, offer opportunities to extend access to un-served groups and increase the rate of progress towards universal levels of enrolment in primary and secondary schools.

This chapter discusses how plausible these arguments are and identifies a range of constraints and contextual realities that will shape future development. It is organised in six sections. First, attention is drawn to the diversity of non-government private provision and some fundamental issues that shape its possible contribution to enhanced access to schooling. Second, estimates are presented of the numbers currently out of school and their location. Third, data are discussed which illustrate the extent to which exclusion is related to wealth, location and gender, focusing on economic constraints. Fourth, costs related to teachers are modelled to indicate likely minimum operating costs for unsubsidised schooling. Fifth, an analysis is offered of the underlying demographic realities of expanded enrolment to reinforce the need to understand the magnitude of the task of achieving the MDGs and the need to identify mechanisms that expand services to large

41

numbers of school-age children drawn from the poorest households. Finally some concluding remarks draw together the arguments in this chapter.

Mapping the Territory

Non-government school provision comes in many forms (Kitaev, 1999; Lewin & Sayed, 2005). Some is community based and secular, much is faith based and linked to established or fringe groups who share common religious convictions. Some is grant aided and some is financially independent. Some is sponsored by enterprises (e.g. commercial farms, mines, industrial organisations), and some receives external subsidy from parent organisations. There are a myriad of different patterns of beneficial ownership and accountability which range across registered non-government organisations, legally constituted businesses, informally organised associations, and individually or family owned schools. Some pay taxes, others do not. Some are for profit and some declare non-profit status.

The non-government sector is thus not a single entity, but very diverse. The contribution that different types of non-government provision may make to greater access is therefore very varied. Discussion of the roles non-government providers can play in extending access are thus not reducible to crude dichotomies between public and private, or states and markets. Manifestly some non-government providers can and do provide valued services. Private contributions to public schooling can support expanded access. Few doubt that schools should be in partnership with the communities they serve, and that complementary partnerships can and should exist, and that individual and collective contributions to public services can be beneficial.

However, depending on non-government service providers in general, or truly private schooling in particular, to achieve EFA targets or MDGs in sub-Saharan Africa is a flawed proposition for several reasons. This is especially so if wholly private and unsubsidised providers are considered. To simplify the arguments it is this kind of provision that is the focus of this paper.

First, primary schooling is a universal right – only states can make a reality of the delivery rights to populations, especially those marginalised by poverty. Universal free primary education – the EFA commitment – is essentially state responsibility. The for-profit private sector has no essential interest delivering free services, and no obligation to provide education to the poor and ultra-poor, HIV orphans, excluded girls and those with special needs. Not-for-profit providers may address the needs of these excluded groups, but can only do so on a national scale with subsidies from public or quasi-public sources. As soon as the bulk of costs are met through subsidy such provision is public from a resource point of view, though the management of delivery may be subcontracted to publicly accountable community or private entities.

Rights-based approaches to educational access depend on the existence of a 'provider of last resort'. It is states that have made commitments to EFA and the MDGs, it is states that have the responsibilities to protect minorities, promote equity, and diminish exclusion, and it is states (acting with or without external support) that have the most capacity to so do, especially in poor countries. Where they fail there is no simple 'stateless' solution to delivering human rights commitments to access to education, especially to the most marginalised.

Second, unsubsidised providers cannot serve the poor and the poorest if they depend on revenue from the communities they serve. This is a demographic and economic inevitability. It is determined by high dependency rates (simply the ratio of income-earning adults to dependent school-age children); skewed household income distribution whereby 20% of households may receive more than 60% of income; labour market rates for qualified teachers within a developmental career structure; and scarcity of domestic capital and corporate sponsors.

It is essential to recognise that there are important asymmetries between most countries in sub-Saharan Africa and rich countries with private non-government fee-paying schooling. This means that whatever the arguments are for non-government private schooling in rich countries they cannot be seamlessly transferred to low-income sub-Saharan Africa. The 0-14 year-old age dependency rates are between 90% and 100% in Uganda, Malawi, and Tanzania (the proportion of 0-14 year-olds compared to the population of 15-64 years old) and average 85% for sub-Saharan Africa as a whole. In the United Kingdom (UK), USA and Australia they are 30%, 32% and 34% respectively (UNESCO Institute of Statistics data, 2005). The ratio of school-age children to the number in the workforce is therefore very different. The availability of income to support fees is thus much more limited. Moreover the relationship between typical teachers' salaries and gross domestic product (GDP) per capita is also very different. In Malawi secondary teacher salaries are more than six times GDP per capita; in the UK they are about the same as GDP per capita. And finally it is important to remember that domestic revenue (which supports public expenditure) often accounts for less than 15% of GDP in sub-Saharan Africa, whilst in the Organisation for Economic Cooperation and Development (OECD) it averages closer to 40%.[2] Taken together these demographic and cost factors limit the expansion of unsubsidised schooling supported by fees paid from household income.

Third, greater dependence on non-government providers of educational services often presumes that such a strategy would lead to greater efficiency, lower cost, and higher quality and relevance, arising from greater competition and accountability. Though it is true that these potential benefits of marketisation of educational services can be useful in encouraging efficient and effective service provision, this can only be the case where a wide range of conditions are satisfied. These include informed choice, transparent accountability, adequate regulation, and effective legal frameworks. In much of sub-Saharan Africa these conditions are not met. Those currently excluded may have little or no choice of school to attend for reasons of location or income, public accountability is often weak, reflecting local power structures and the interests of providers rather than consumers, regulation is hampered by lack of capacity, record keeping and procedures, and legal redress for malpractice and misrepresentation fragile and inaccessible especially to the poor. Unplanned and uncoordinated growth in service provision is much more likely to be unequally distributed, concentrated in economically favoured areas, and wasteful of scarce resources, than planned growth which links school location to demographic needs, offers economies of scale from shared services (e.g. teacher training, curriculum development), and has the capacity to promote equity and meet special needs.

It may be significant that no OECD country or rapidly developing country (e.g. those in East Asia) has depended on non-government providers to universalise access to basic education. There are many obvious reasons – basic education is a public good with a range of externalities, modernising elites see the value of democratising access which reduces inequalities and enhances national capabilities, and it is widely believed that poverty is caused and perpetuated by lack of access to education. In much of sub-Saharan Africa education policy seeks to promote national identity to overcome the social divisions inherited by post-colonial states composed of disparate groups in competition and sometimes in conflict with each other. It is difficult to see how this goal can be achieved without predominantly public provision of basic education within a common curricula framework, without a developmental national teaching service, and without the publicly supported physical provision of school buildings, textbooks and other facilities in areas where household incomes are less than a dollar a day.

Out of School Children and Enrolment Rates

Current estimates suggest there are about 108 million primary-age children in sub-Saharan Africa, of whom about 91 million are enrolled. At secondary level there are 92 million children and about 25 million enrolled.[3] This means that at a minimum 17 million children of primary school age and 67 million of secondary school age are out of school. In reality the numbers are much greater since enrolment figures include large numbers of over-age pupils and repeaters. Enrolment estimates also fail to capture those who may be registered but not attending. Though reliable estimates of those not attending school across sub-Saharan Africa are not available, it is reasonable to conclude that more than 25 million in the primary age group and 75 million of secondary age are excluded. If private schooling is to have an impact on the achievement of EFA and the MDGs then it must provide access to these children.

Table I shows numbers of children out of school by country. DR Congo, Ethiopia, UR Tanzania, Burkina Faso, and Niger all have more than a million not enrolled in primary school on these estimates. These countries account for nearly 70% of the total unenrolled (considering only those countries where the age group is larger than the number enrolled) indicating that numerically the problem of access in sub-Saharan Africa is very skewed towards a few countries. These are amongst the poorest in sub-Saharan Africa with average GDP per capita of about USD300. The countries towards the lower part of Table I appear to have a surplus of primary school places over the number of primary school-age children and thus gross enrolment rates over 100%. This arises because of over-age enrolment and repetition. It does not mean that all school-age children in these countries are actually enrolled.

	Primary age group	Enrolled	Difference	Secondary age group	Enrolled	Difference
D.R. Congo	8518	4012	4506	7322	1464	5858
Ethiopia	11285	7213	4072	9440	1786	7655
U R Tanzania	6979	4845	2134	5086	323	4763
B. Faso	2127	927	1200	2062	218	1844
Niger	1900	761	1139	1783	124	1659
Mali	2151	1227	924	1801	312	1490
Nigeria	20093	19385	708	17328	6313	11014
Ghana	3177	2586	591	2979	1151	1828
Côte d'Ivoire	2635	2116	519	2891	620	2271
Zambia	2063	1626	437	1261	345	916
Senegal	1590	1197	393	1601	306	1295
Angola	1512	1125	387	2241	242	1999
Chad	1385	1016	369	1316	188	1128
Burundi	1151	817	334	1183	119	1063
Guinea	1294	998	296	1289	301	988
Kenya	6074	5828	246	4222	1362	2860
Eritrea	546	330	216	575	159	415
CAR	621	411	210	617	66	551
Sierra Leone	729	554	175	590	134	455
Congo	614	525	89	589	164	424
G-Bissau	230	150	80	149	26	124
Gambia	204	161	43	176	60	117
Mozambique	2585	2556	29	3128	476	2652
Liberia	524	496	28	401	85	316
Zimbabwe	2561	2535	26	2057	828	1229
Comoros	116	104	12	124	38	85
Seychelles	11	10	0	7	8	-1
Swaziland	211	212	-1	138	62	77

S T+Principe	23	29	-6	19	7	11
Mauritius	126	134	-8	138	100	38
Botswana	319	329	-10	218	153	65
Eq. Guinea	62	78	-16	71	20	52
Cape Verde	73	90	-17	71	48	23
Namibia	376	398	-22	221	138	83
Benin	1107	1153	-46	1131	284	848
Gabon	210	282	-72	212	105	107
Lesotho	334	415	-81	237	81	156
Madagascar	2311	2408	-97	2721	436	2284
Cameroon	2570	2742	-172	2627	669	1958
Togo	787	978	-191	782	335	447
Rwanda	1312	1535	-223	1174	167	1007
South Africa	7052	7413	-361	4917	4109	808
Malawi	1952	2846	-894	1000	176	824
Uganda	5059	6901	-1842	3487	656	2831
Somalia	1772			1073		
	108331	91454	15104	92455	24764	66617

Table I. Sub-Saharan Africa – primary and secondary age group, and enrolments (thousands). Source: UNESCO Institute for Statistics (UIS), 2005, based on 2002 data.

Figure 1 shows gross enrolment rates at primary (GER1) and secondary (GER2) level by country. Figure 2 shows GERs at lower and upper secondary levels. The average (unweighted average of available data) GER1 for sub-Saharan Africa is now about 93% indicating that in many countries there are nearly enough places for universal enrolment if repetition rates and over-age enrolment are reduced to low levels. Secondary gross enrolment rates average about 25% overall and about 40% at lower secondary (unweighted average of available data). Countries which have high values of GER1 and GER2 have little immediate need to increase the quantity of private schooling to enhance enrolment rates. Those with the lowest enrolment rates are characteristically poorer with typically more than half of all households existing on less than a dollar a day and as many as 80% on less than two dollars a day. EFA and the MDGs effectively commit states to universal free primary education, implying that fee-paying private schooling at this level is elective for those who can afford to pay, not a method for expanding access to the poorest. Most sub-Saharan African countries retain fee-paying secondary schooling in which participation is heavily influenced by household income. Secondary enrolment rates are clearly lowest in the poorest countries (Figure 3). Richer sub-Saharan African countries with higher enrolment rates (e.g. Namibia, Botswana, South Africa) all have predominantly public provision at primary and secondary level with a small private sector largely addressing the needs of the relatively wealthy

(Akyeampong, 2005; Bennell et al, 2005; Debourou et al, 2005; Lewin, 2006).

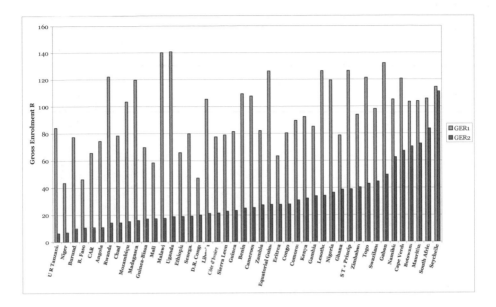

Figure 1. Gross enrolment rates at primary and secondary by country.
Source: UIS (2005).

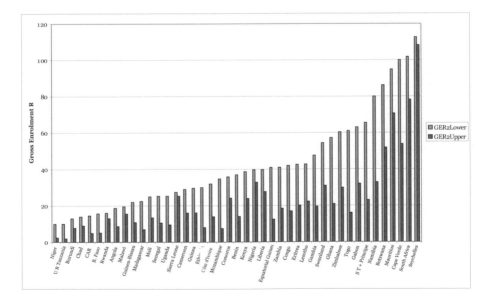

Figure 2. Gross enrolment rates at lower and upper secondary by country.
Source: UIS (2005).

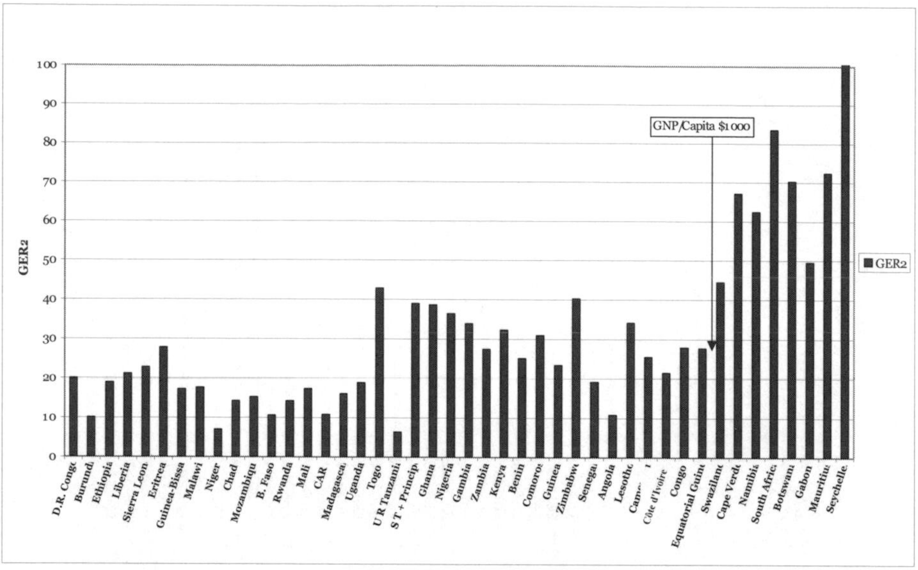

Figure 3. Gross enrolment rate at secondary by countries ranked by GNP per capita. Source: UIS (2005).

The UNESCO Institute of Statistics estimates that less than 10% of primary and about 13% of secondary education in sub-Saharan Africa is privately provided (UNESCO, 2005). Mingat (2004) estimates that 23% (lower secondary) and 29% (upper secondary) is privately financed in a sample of 17 low-income sub-Saharan African countries. (In neither case is it clear what definition of private is being used. This may explain the differences in estimates.) Some sub-Saharan African countries have very little private secondary schooling (e.g. less than 5% in Botswana and South Africa) and others much higher levels (e.g. Uganda and Tanzania over 40%) coupled with fairly low enrolment rates. However non-government private schools are poorly defined and documented and enrolment data are widely incomplete. UIS estimates of private schooling include both publicly financed but privately owned schools (e.g. Mauritius, Lesotho), and those that are wholly private (e.g. Uganda, Ghana).

Unknown but significant numbers of private schools are unregistered (e.g. in Nigeria, Uganda, Tanzania, Malawi, and Rwanda). This is by default (i.e. inadequate and insufficient capacity to register – in 2002 there were two officers responsible for the registration of over 2000 private schools) or by design (i.e. avoidance of registration to evade taxes and meet minimum requirements for registration). For example, in Malawi in 2002 about 50% of private secondary schools captured in a recent survey were unregistered (Lewin & Sayed, 2005), and were overwhelmingly urban or peri-urban, small, household based, and casually staffed. There is plenty of scope for uncertainty about the numbers enrolled in these schools, especially where attendance records are not kept and enrolment fluctuates widely with the availability of cash to pay fees. Analysis of examination entries provides some indication of the numbers completing an educational cycle since most who do will wish to be entered for public examinations. In Uganda and Malawi this leads to the conclusion that there are not large numbers enrolled that are invisible to the national statistical database, though undoubtedly there are some.

Some simple conclusions are that in the majority of sub-Saharan African countries there are not yet enough school places to enrol all school-age children at primary level, and that many more are excluded from lower secondary schooling than primary. Secondary enrolments in lower income sub-Saharan African countries are very low though lower secondary is increasingly seen as part of basic education and EFA. If non-government private schooling is to have much impact on improved access for those currently excluded then it must provide access at primary level to the 'last 20%' who are likely to be from poorest sections of the population. Since the numbers excluded at secondary level are much greater, on average those who are out of school are likely to include children from households with higher levels of income. This means there may be some scope for more private secondary enrolment in some sub-Saharan African countries. However, quality secondary schooling in sub-Saharan Africa is often five times more expensive per pupil than primary schooling and most public systems have substantial private direct costs to households. Expanding fee-paying secondary schooling has equity implications which may result in greater differentiation and polarisation of access than currently exists (Adea-Mensah, 2000). Inevitably, poor communities with the least resources and lowest enrolments will have most difficulty in supporting unsubsidised schooling.

Participation, Wealth, Location and Gender

The characteristics of the 'last 20%' excluded from primary, and the greater numbers excluded from secondary, are predictable. Participation by grade level in sub-Saharan Africa is heavily skewed by household income, location and gender. Using Demographic and Health Survey data from household surveys from 23 sub-Saharan African countries shows that those excluded are disproportionately poor, rural and female (DHS census dates vary but most are from the period 1998-2003). For the 15-19 year-old populations, over 93% [4] of males from the richest 20% of households completed grade 1, but only 50% of girls from the poorest 40% of households did so.[5] About 50% of rich boys completed grade 7, but only 4% of poor girls. Over 90% of urban boys completed grade 1, but only 67% of rural girls. About 50% of urban boys completed grade 7, but only 7% of rural girls (see Figures 4 and 5).[6] Those not enrolled at primary are almost certainly from households with incomes of less than a dollar a day. At secondary level they include a majority from households receiving less than two dollars a day.

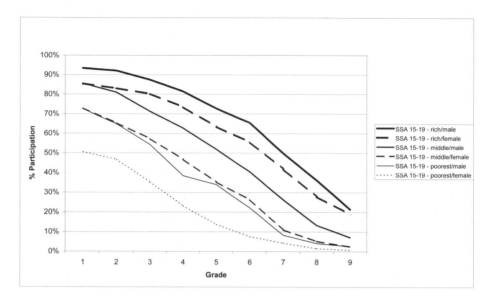

Figure 4. Highest grade reached by wealth and gender – sub-Saharan Africa.
Source: Demographic and Health Surveys, various years.

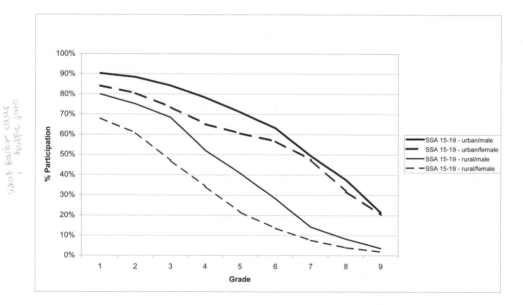

Figure 5. Highest grade reached by location and gender – sub-Saharan Africa.
Source: Demographic and Health Surveys, various years.

Exclusion as a result of location is largely a physical problem that can, in principle, be greatly reduced by increasing the supply of schools in un-served areas. Gendered exclusion is embedded in socio-cultural practices in and out of school that are susceptible to purposeful interventions and changed incentives to enrol girls. Influencing both these factors is exclusion related to low household income and inability to pay the direct and indirect cost of schooling. This needs further discussion. The costs to households can be substantial even for 'free' primary schooling. They are widely exclusionary at secondary level in sub-Saharan Africa both because fee paying is common and because operating costs of secondary schools in sub-Saharan Africa can be five or more times greater than those of primary schools. Most household surveys of expenditure in sub-Saharan Africa show that educational expenditures are below 10% of total household income, and often below 5% amongst the poorest. These levels are widely insufficient to meet the costs of schooling for those in the lowest quintiles of household income, especially where income distribution is heavily skewed towards the wealthy.

Data on incomes, expenditure, and schooling costs at secondary level illuminate the issues that costs raise. Household survey data is generally the best method of profiling consumption expenditure despite its well-known limitations. A recent analysis in Tanzania suggests that households spend at most about 5% of income on average on educational expenditures (Household Budget Survey, 2002, p. 42).[7] The poorest spend less than middle-income households as a proportion of their income, since other basic needs take priority.

Most private schooling in Tanzania is at secondary level where both public and private schools charge fees. Secondary school direct private costs averaged TSh 154,000 (128 USD) a year in 2000 (Education Status Report, 2001, p. 102), or about TSh 13,000 a month across all types of school. In 2003, government schools charged TSh 70,000 for boarding and TSh 40,000 for day schools a year. In addition other fees and contributions totalled at least TSh 56,000 excluding costs of privately purchased books, travel, and so on. The total cost to households of enrolling a child in a government school is therefore between Tsh 96,000 and TSh 126,000 a year. Typical private schools appear to charge fees of about TSh 300,000 a year per student in Dar es Salaam (Lewin, 2003). Low-cost private schools and dwelling-house schools may well charge less than government schools but no data are available on these institutions, many of which are of very poor quality.

The monthly costs to households of public secondary schooling are therefore between TSh 8000 and TSh 10,500. Private schools average about TSh 25,000. Per capita monthly expenditure in Dar es Salaam averaged TSh 24,000 and TSh 3300 for the richest and poorest quintiles. In rural areas the figures were TSh 17,800 and TSh 3000 in 2001 (National Bureau of Statistics, 2002, p. 86). It is clear that households in the highest quintile of income would have to allocate a third or more of per capita expenditure to support one child at a public day school, and the equivalent of their average per capita income for a private school. Few outside the highest income quintile will therefore be able to participate without subsidy. Non-government private secondary schools are highly concentrated in just three districts in Tanzania and few are located in poorer regions (Figure 6). Though their performance is often superior, their location and costs constrain access (Lasibille et al, 2000).

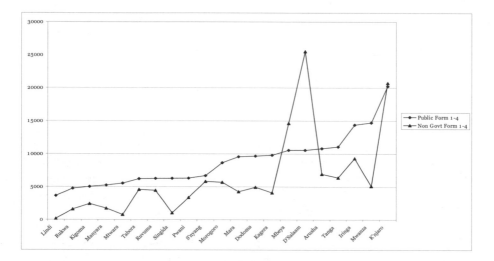

Figure 6. Public and non-government enrolments in Tanzania, Form 1-4 (Ministry of Education, Dar es Salaam, 2004).

In Uganda public primary schooling is fee free. Most costs (over 70%) in public secondary schools are already borne privately by parents and guardians over and above the public contributions (predominantly to salaries and capitation). The Uganda Household Survey (2001) suggests that 60% of household income is below USh 100,000 per month (55 USD) and only 1% is above USh 200,000 (110 USD). Between 5% and 10% of household expenditure is allocated to education. Average household size suggests that typically there are two children of school-going age, and more in poor families. Mean annual expenditure per student at secondary level was over USh 500,000 in urban areas and USh 300,000 in rural areas. To support one child at these levels in rural schools would require 25% of the household income of those below USh 100,000 per month, and over 40% if the enrolment was in an urban school. It is evident that there is a limit to the capacity to pay the direct costs of schooling that is rapidly being approached. The private sector cannot grow much further at the fee levels it charges; nor can public secondary school enrolment unless its direct costs to households are reduced (Lewin, 2002).

In South Africa 80% of households receive income below 50,000 Rands (4500 USD) (Figure 7) per year. If as much as 10% of this is allocated to education expenditure this amounts to no more than 5000 Rands (450 USD) a year, and considerably less for most households. The cost of a secondary school place in Gauteng was estimated to be about 4000 Rands (360 USD) in 2002 for normal public schools. Most private schools charge considerably more than this and provide places for the affluent. Those that are lower cost are subsidised. If they were not, those much outside the top 20% of household income could not afford to purchase private schooling.

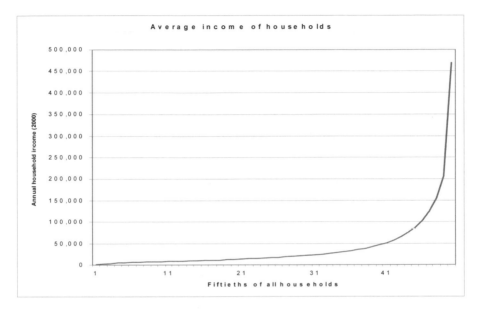

Figure 7. Income distribution in South Africa.
Source: Department of Planning, Department of Education, South Africa.

In sum, non-government private schools which are not subsidised have minimum operating costs which determine fee levels. The main costs, especially in low-fee schools, lie in teachers' salaries. When fee levels and other costs are related to household survey data, many families will be excluded by poverty from participation, especially at secondary level, in full-cost non-government schools. In much of sub-Saharan Africa the effect is so strong that few outside the richest 25% of households can afford to participate. This is clearly the case in Benin, Ghana, Zambia, Uganda, Tanzania, and Rwanda (Lewin, 2006). Non-government schools that access the poor can only do so if they are subsidised, even when they minimise overheads to close to zero and pay teachers much less than in government schools, with unknown consequences for quality. Some schools receive contributions from NGOs and from faith-based communities. The point is that there are limits of affordability to participation determined by costs which will limit effective demand for non-government providers. For-profit organisations will not operate at a loss. Not-for-profit organisations are

53

unlikely to offer schooling opportunities on a national level to large numbers without national or international subsidy. This raises issues of accessibility, quality assurance, equity and the opportunity costs of diverting public finance to private beneficial owners.

Teacher Salaries and School Cost Per Child

The economics of expanded access to schooling are closely related to the costs of salaries for teachers which in most sub-Saharan African systems account for the bulk of recurrent expenditure as noted above.[8] These determine the largest part of the minimum costs at which private non-government schools can operate without subsidy. There are various estimates of the costs of teachers' salaries across sub-Saharan African countries. Table II shows estimates by Mingat (2004) for teachers' salaries as a percentage of GDP at different levels across 17 low-income sub-Saharan African countries. This indicates that on average unit costs are about three times greater than primary at lower secondary level and six times at upper secondary. The reasons lie in a combination of lower pupil–teacher ratios, higher salary costs, boarding subsidies, and larger numbers of non-teaching support staff. Non-teaching costs at secondary level can account for more, as much as 40% of total cost per pupil.

		Teacher salaries (per capita GDP)	% Recurrent spending for other than teachers	Unit costs (% per capita GDP)
Primary	Average	4.6	27.4	11.4
	Variation	(2.4-6.8)	(15-43)	(4-20)
1st secondary cycle	Average	6.6	37.4	31.2
	Variation	(3.6-13.1)	(24-56)	(13-64)
2nd secondary cycle	Average	9.3	39.5	63.4
	Variation	(3.8-19.8)	(18-53)	(22-157)

Table II. Unit costs for different educational levels. Source: Mingat (2004).

If these actual ratios of teachers' salary costs to GDP are used to model the fee levels necessary to support the salary costs of private education in a hypothetical sub-Saharan African country, the result is the following (Table III).[9] In the poorest countries fees of 61 USD and 160 USD would need to be levied to cover salary costs of teachers. Other costs (ancillary staff, learning materials, equipment and furniture, etc.) could increase these figures by 30% or more. From the analysis of household income above it is clear that these levels of fees would exclude the great majority of children from poor households.

Scenario 1: Sub-Saharan Africa Typical Data	Primary	Lower Sec	Upper Sec	Other Ed. Exp
Pupil–teacher ratio	44	30	20	
Teacher salaries/GDP/capita	4.6	6.6	9.3	
Non-teaching salaries/GDP/capita	0.4	1.5	2.7	
Non-salary expenditure/GDP/capita	0.4	1.5	2.7	
Teacher salaries as % of total recurrent	85%	69%	63%	
Total unit cost % GDP/capita	12%	32%	74%	
School-age pop as % total pop	18%	9%	7%	
% school-age pop enrolled (GER)	85%	26%	13%	

GNP per capita (USD)	Fees needed at different levels of GNP per capita		
	Primary	Lower Sec	Upper Sec
500	61	160	368
1000	123	320	735
1500	184	480	1103
2000	245	640	1470

Table III. Fee costs needed to pay teachers'
salaries in private schools in sub-Saharan Africa.

The argument can of course be made that these typical teacher salary levels are too high and that costs per pupil could be reduced by either increasing pupil–teacher ratios or by lowering salary rates. The former would need increases in pupil–teacher ratios well above the 44:1 modelled for primary and 30:1 at lower secondary to make much difference to costs. There would seem little scope for this at primary level but some at lower secondary. The latter can only be judged in the context of particular labour markets for teachers. Most sub-Saharan African countries have shortages of teachers and reducing wage rates might damage both recruitment and motivation. This is especially so in relation to rural areas and difficult postings which are those most likely to be in places that reach out to the 'last 20%'. Even if salaries could be reduced to 3.5 times GDP per capita, viable schools with normal staffing practices would still need to charge fees in the order of 50 USD or more which would still be double or more the affordable limits of those in 'dollar a day' poverty.

Demography and the EFA Challenge

Achieving and sustaining higher rates of participation in primary and secondary schooling in sub-Saharan Africa is a challenge which is partly determined by demographic realities. Demographic transition to low growth has occurred in some sub-Saharan African countries (Seychelles, Mauritius) but high growth has remained in others (Eritrea, Uganda). Most countries have high dependency rates that are only reducing slowly. In some cases HIV/AIDS is responsible for exacerbating already high dependency rates.

Figure 8 shows data on the rate of growth of the school-age cohort in different sub-Saharan African countries. It shows that the number of school-age children is growing on average at about 2% with a variation of between minus 1.4% to over 5%. The school-age population represents different proportions of the total population in different countries from below 20% to nearly 40% (Figure 9).

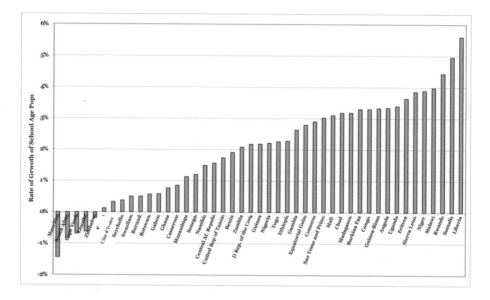

Figure 8. School-age population growth rates. Source: UIS (2005).

The growth rates for the primary school-entry age group have been used to estimate overall growth in school-age children to 2015. The result is that the primary-age population (defined by the official number of years of schooling and official entry ages) appears set to increase from about 108 million to 146 million. Lower secondary-age children will increase from 49.2 million to 66.2 million, and upper secondary from 45.1 million to 60.9 million (defined by the official number of years of schooling and official entry ages).

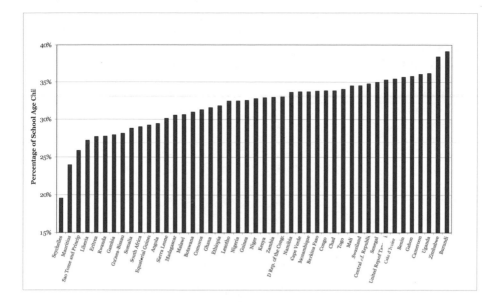

Figure 9. Percentage of school-age children in the population
(primary and secondary). Source: UIS (2005).

Where GER1 is in excess of 110%, total primary enrolment should stabilise
and may even fall for a period as repetition and over-age entry are eliminated.
Where GER1 is less than 100%, total primary enrolment will need to
increase more rapidly than growth in school-age children if all children are to
be enrolled. In both cases the numbers completing primary school will
increase as greater proportions of those who enter primary successfully reach
the last grade of primary. The number of new secondary places needed
depends on a range of policy choices, for example, how fast to expand
primary, how quickly to reduce repetition and drop-out at primary which
determines the numbers completing, how to select pupils into lower and
upper secondary school, how to manage the primary/secondary transition
rates, and how to reduce repetition and over-age enrolment at secondary.

The growth needed in school places to achieve GER1 of 110%
(assumed to be a level that can provide universal enrolment with low levels of
repetition and over-age enrolment) averages about 1.8 times current
enrolments. A quarter of the countries in sub-Saharan Africa would have to
increase enrolments to three times current levels to achieve this goal by 2015.
At lower secondary level an increase of 5.6 times would be needed on average
for all countries to achieve universal enrolment (GER = 100%), and for the
25% with the lowest enrolment rates, increases of nearly 12 times would be
needed (Table IV).

	Increase for GER1 = 110%		Increase needed for GER2L 100%		Increase needed for GER2U 100%	
	2001	2015	2001	2015	2001	2015
Seychelles	1.0	1.0	0.9	1.0	1.0	1.0
South Africa [10]	1.1	1.0	1.2	1.0	1.9	1.6
Cape Verde	0.9	0.8	1.2	1.1	2.5	2.2
Botswana	1.1	1.2	1.2	1.3	1.7	1.9
S T + Principe	0.8	1.2	1.4	2.2	4.9	7.7
Namibia	1.1	1.4	1.4	1.8	3.8	4.7
Mauritius	1.1	0.9	1.5	1.2	2.1	1.7
Togo	0.9	1.3	1.8	2.5	6.9	9.7
Ghana	1.4	1.5	1.8	2.0	6.7	7.5
Zimbabwe	1.2	1.2	1.9	1.9	18.3	17.7
Swaziland	1.1	1.2	2.0	2.2	3.6	3.8
Gambia	1.4	2.1	2.2	3.2	5.5	8.1
Eritrea	1.8	3.1	2.3	4.0	4.8	8.2
Congo	1.3	2.1	2.5	4.1	8.8	14.3
Lesotho	0.9	0.8	2.5	2.3	5.0	4.6
Nigeria	0.9	1.3	2.6	3.6	3.2	4.4
Equatorial Guinea	0.9	1.3	2.6	4.0	16.5	25.0
Comoros	1.5	2.4	2.9	4.4	4.4	6.7
Zambia	1.4	2.0	2.9	4.0	7.8	10.7
Benin	1.1	1.4	3.1	4.1	11.6	15.5
Côte d'Ivoire	1.4	1.5	3.4	3.5	7.0	7.3
Cameroon	1.1	1.2	3.5	3.9	6.8	7.8
Guinea	1.5	2.0	3.8	5.3	9.0	12.4
Kenya	1.2	1.2	4.0	4.1	4.3	4.4
Rwanda	0.9	1.7	4.3	8.2	7.6	14.7
Ethiopia	1.7	2.4	4.5	6.3	8.5	11.9
Madagascar	1.1	1.7	4.7	7.5	13.1	21.0
Senegal	1.5	1.8	4.8	5.7	10.1	12.0
Guinea-Bissau	1.7	2.8	5.0	8.3	12.2	19.9
Malawi	0.9	1.6	5.1	9.2	6.4	11.6
Mali	1.9	3.1	5.8	9.1	N/A	N/A
Uganda	1.1	1.5	7.6	9.9	31.3	40.5
Burkina Faso	2.5	4.1	7.9	12.9	26.8	43.5
Burundi	1.6	1.7	8.1	8.7	23.7	25.6
Chad	1.4	2.3	8.2	13.1	14.5	23.3
U R Tanzania	1.2	1.9	9.3	15.3	44.5	73.6
Mozambique	1.4	1.7	9.5	11.3	27.3	32.3
Niger	2.8	4.9	11.3	20.1	40.6	71.9
Unweighted average	1.3	1.8	4.0	5.6	10.9	15.5

Table IV. Growth needed in school places for
different enrolment levels. Source: Lewin (2006).

It is clear that in the lowest enrolment countries these increases are very large. This raises several questions about the role that private, non-government providers might play. These include:

- Is it likely that private providers have the capacity to increase their enrolments by the magnitudes needed?
- If they have the capacity how likely is it that they will direct expansion towards areas where there are the greatest shortages of school places?
- Even if they do how would such additional capacity be financed if not from public funds in economies where annual per capita expenditure on all goods and services averages no more than about 400 USD?

Concluding Remarks

Non-government private providers, both for profit and not for profit, do make a significant contribution to enrolments in many sub-Saharan African countries (Kitaev, 1999). However most non-government private provision, especially at secondary level, is urban and concentrated in wealthy districts. Where private secondary schooling is rural it often serves urban clientele through boarding schools. There are exceptions. For example, Rwanda has rural private secondary schools which enrol poor children; however these are currently heavily supported from the Genocide Fund (Lewin & Akyeampong, 2005). Higher income sub-Saharan African countries appear to have lower rates of non-government private enrolment.

Clearly, non-government private schools can contribute to expanded access. The most likely way in which this can happen is where differentiated demand grows and is reflected in increased numbers of the relatively wealthy opting for fee-paying schooling, releasing places in the public system that can be occupied by others from lower income households. Whether in fact this does happen is an empirical question that may have different answers in different systems. It is at least possible that when government elites opt out of public schooling, increased private spending may be accompanied by reduced public subsidies and/or falling costs per pupil directed at mass public schooling. Where the growth of low-cost (and often low-quality) non-government providers reflects state failure to serve low/middle income households it is not clear that this constitutes a systemic solution to extending the educational franchise, nor is it likely to reach the ultra-poor and the 'last 20%'. Rather it is an indictment of the gaps between public policy priorities and successful implementation.

Two other issues remain of concern. The first concerns the possible destructive interference between public and private systems. Local competition for pupils, competition for and sharing of teachers, and the use of public facilities for private gain are some possible sources of conflict and inefficiency in providing basic services. The second concerns the consequences of weak regulation and oversight which open possibilities for rent seeking, excessive profits, malpractice and fraud. Neither are easy to resolve but they have to be considered as possible consequences of a laissez-faire approach to the contribution non-government private providers can make to expanded access.

This chapter has argued that non-government schooling, especially that which is truly private and completely unsubsidised, will have a limited impact on progress towards universalising access to basic education in sub-Saharan Africa. The case made is that servicing rights to universal free primary schooling (and increasingly lower secondary) cannot be transferred by states to third parties not least because it is only states that can act as providers of last resort and because of commitments to services free at the point of delivery. Unsubsidised providers cannot service the poor and the poorest en masse and remain solvent. Marketised solutions which outsource service delivery may have some attractions in principle, but in practice few of their presumed advantages are likely to be easily realised when addressing the educational needs of the vulnerable, marginalised and excluded.

The analysis has shown that:

- In the majority of sub-Saharan African countries enough school places exist to enrol most but not all primary-age children, and that the largest numbers out of school are concentrated in a small number of countries. Across sub-Saharan Africa the majority are excluded from secondary schooling, where private non-government provision is more common.
- Those excluded – the last 20% at primary and many more at lower secondary – constitute the populations that non-government private schooling would have to reach if it were to have major impact on expanded access.
- This excluded population of children is disproportionately poor, rural, and female with many located in households living on less than a dollar a day per capita.
- Household income and income distribution between households is such that few of those in the lowest two quintiles could afford the full economic cost of unsubsidised schools at prevailing fee rates.
- Teachers' salary costs – the main determinant of costs – are such that much lower operating costs per pupil at primary level will be difficult to achieve, except where these are exceptionally high. In general there may be more scope at lower secondary for efficiency gains to reduce costs and related fee levels. Even with such efficiency gains the unsubsidised direct costs of schooling would exceed the ability to pay for those in the 'last 20%'.
- Demography indicates that a further constraint on the contribution unsubsidised providers can make is that dependency ratios remain high (i.e. ratio of school-age children to income earners is high) thus limiting the availability of disposable income especially where income distribution is heavily skewed. The poor also characteristically spend less on educational services than the less poor since their other basic

needs take precedence, further limiting their capacity to support private direct costs of schooling.

- The growth needed to realise and sustain universal levels of enrolment is striking in low-enrolment countries – many will have to more than double the number of primary places and vastly increase lower secondary access. The organised non-government private sector often constitutes no more than 10% of the labour force in poor sub-Saharan African countries and not much more of economic activity. This raises questions about the capacity of non-government agents to respond to such large needs to increase access.

Arguments about the role non-government providers can and will play in increasing access to basic education generate different degrees of heat depending on the prejudices of their proponents and their willingness to confront economic realities. They are also coloured by ideology transposed from well-developed, professionalised, regulated, and partly marketised education systems in rich countries to partly developed, poorly professionalised, largely unregulated systems in which educational market places only exist for the relatively wealthy, not the poorest and excluded.

It may be that the issue is less of a policy question, than a practical one. Since regulation is widely ineffective in sub-Saharan Africa, and in an increasing number of countries there are now de facto few barriers to non-government private schools operating, their growth will be self-determined and self-locating in terms of where they are and who they serve. It will be limited by the factors explored in this chapter, and is unlikely either to service the needs of the majority, or to reach to poor and ultra-poor effectively by 2015. At primary level there should be no dependence on non-government private schooling as a strategy since free education should indeed be free for those who cannot or choose not to elect out into the non-government private sector. Governments will remain the providers of last resort and will remain challenged to live up to their obligations to those they govern and to the commitments they have made to universalise access. At secondary level, much provision in poorer but not richer countries in sub-Saharan Africa is already private, or financed substantially from private direct costs. But most of these services are consumed by economic elites. Substantially increased secondary access will be impossible without lower direct costs to households.

If the policy debate is really about the possibilities of capturing domestic or international public finance for private benefit through a raft of possible mechanisms – 'public–private partnerships' to construct schools, charitable status, exemption from VAT and import taxes, construction subsidies, support for teachers' salaries in non-government private schools, low-interest unsecured loans, and so on – then it seems to have limited merit and high opportunity costs. Whatever the benefits and the risks, they come with an opportunity cost that redirects public finance away from supporting basic services and their extension to those with little or no access to basic education.

61

The prediction this analysis leads to is that by 2015 those countries in sub-Saharan Africa most successful in approaching the educational Millennium Development Goals will have achieved this through extending the reach of public school systems and lowering their direct costs to the poor; in these cases the amount of non-government private provision will reach a plateau and then may fall back. Those least successful in progressing will see some growth in non-government private provision but it will be insufficient to have much impact on the achievement of the MDGs and will fail to provide access to most of those currently excluded.

The short answer to the original question posed – what contribution can private non-government schooling make to achieving the education-related Millennium Development Goals – is a little but not a lot. If it were a priority for private non-government providers to reach out to the 'last 20%' this would already be happening on some scale. If it is not happening because providers need publicly financed incentives and substantial subsidy, it remains to be demonstrated that this would be more effective than continuing to extend the reach of the public system, as has been done in all higher enrolment sub-Saharan African countries close to achieving the educational Millennium Development Goals.

Notes

[1] See for example James (1991), Colclough with Lewin (1993), Lockheed & Jimenez (1994), Bray (1996), Colclough (1996), Crouch (1998), Kiernan et al (2000), Lewin & Caillods (2001), Sayed & Rose (2001), Tooley (2001, 2004), Hofmeyr & Lee (2004), Rose (2006).

[2] The detailed implications of this are beyond the scope of this chapter. Simply put low rates of revenue collection constrain public finance for educational development; they are not a reason to increase dependence on private financing especially in the delivery of services to the poorest.

[3] UNESCO Institute of Statistics data, 2005, relating to 2002.

[4] Median values are used across the sub-Saharan African data set. These indicate the proportions completing a grade in the 15-19 year-old age group at the time of the census.

[5] Household income was divided into the top 20%, the middle 40% and the poorest 40%. This is appropriate given the shape of the income distribution curve with a small number of households receiving the majority of household income.

[6] These aggregates conceal radically different patterns in different countries – see Lewin (2006) for more detailed disaggregation of patterns of participation within countries.

[7] Five per cent may seem low to some readers. It is what the household survey indicates and is consistent with typical allocations across different countries. Even if this were raised to 10%-15% it would not substantially change the nature of the problem.

[8] This is true for all systems operating day schooling. Boarding schools, which are common in some sub-Saharan African countries at secondary level, can have large non-teaching and non-salary expenditure. Expansion of access to near universal levels will reduce the proportion of locations where boarding is essential. Elective boarding could then become subject to cost recovery from those able and willing to pay.

[9] All assumptions derived from sub-Saharan Africa data sets to determine typical values.

[10] South Africa's projected growth may be anomalous since its crude transition rate from primary to secondary grades appears to be greater than unity as there are more pupils in grade 8 than in grade 7 in the USI database.

References

Adea-Mensah, I. (2000) Education in Ghana: a tool for social mobility or social stratification? J.B. Danqah Memorial Lecture, Ghana Academy of Arts and Sciences.

Akyeampong, K. (2005) Cost and Finance of Secondary Education in Ghana: a situational analysis. Commissioned Report for the Financing of Secondary Education in Africa Research Project (FINSEC) based at the Centre for International Education, University of Sussex, for the Secondary Education Initiative in Africa Programme of the World Bank.

Bennell, P., Bulwani, G. & Musikanga, M. (2005) Costs and Financing of Secondary Education in Zambia: a situational analysis. Commissioned Report for the Financing of Secondary Education in Africa Research Project (FINSEC) based at the Centre for International Education, University of Sussex, for the Secondary Education Initiative in Africa Programme of the World Bank.

Bray, M. (1996) *Privatisation of Secondary Education: issues and policy implications*. Hong Kong: Comparative Education Research Centre, University of Hong Kong.

Colclough, C. (1996) Education and the Market: which parts of the neo liberal solution are correct? *World Development*, 24(4), pp. 589-610.

Colclough, C. with Lewin, K. (1993) *Educating All the Children: strategies for primary schooling in the South*. Oxford: Oxford University Press.

Crouch, L. (1998) Public vs Private Education: why South Africa needs a healthy public education system, in *Education Africa Forum*, 2nd edn. Gauteng: Education Africa.

Debourou, D. & Gnimadi, A. with Caillods, F. & Abraham, K. (2005) Costs and Financing of Secondary Education in Benin – a situational analysis. Commissioned Report for the Financing of Secondary Education in Africa Research Project (FINSEC) based at the Centre for International Education, University of Sussex, for the Secondary Education Initiative in Africa Programme of the World Bank.

Education Status Report (2001) *Education Status Report*. Dar es Salaam: Ministry of Education.

Hofmeyr, J. & Lee, S. (2004) The New Face of Private Schooling, in L. Chisholm (Ed.) *Changing Class: education and social change in post-apartheid South Africa.* Cape Town: Human Sciences Research Council.

James, E. (1991) Public Policies towards Private Education, *International Journal of Educational Research,* 15, pp. 359-376.

Kiernan, M., Latham, M., Macrae, M. & Read, T. (2000) The Development of Private Secondary Education in Malawi: towards a public–private partnership. The Power of Learning. Report to CfBT and Danish International Development Agency, Malawi.

Kitaev, I. (1999) *Private Education in sub-Saharan Africa: a re-examination of theories and concepts related to its development and finance.* Paris: International Institute of Educational Planning, UNESCO.

Lassibille, G., Tan, J.P. & Samra, S. (2000) Expansion of Private Secondary Education: lessons from recent experience in Tanzania, *Comparative Education Review,* 44(1), pp. 1-28.

Lewin, K.M. (2002) *Options for Post Primary Education and Training in Uganda, Increasing Access, Equity and Efficiency – a framework for policy.* Ministry of Education and Sports, Kampala for Educational Funding Agencies Group/Department for International Development. http://www.sussex.ac.uk/education/1-4-7-3.html

Lewin, K.M. (2003) Projecting Secondary School Expansion in Tanzania: the art of the possible. Conference on Secondary Education Development, Arusha, Ministry of Education and Culture and Washington, DC, World Bank.

Lewin, K.M. (2006) *Seeking Secondary Schooling in sub-Saharan Africa: strategies for sustainable financing.* Washington, DC: World Bank, Secondary Education in Africa Programme.

Lewin, K.M. & Akyeampong, K. (2005) *Mapping Ways Forward: planning for nine year basic education in Rwanda.* Kigali: CfBT/Department for International Development.

Lewin, K.M. & Caillods, F. (2001) *Financing Secondary Education in Developing Countries: strategies for sustainable growth.* Paris: International Institute for Educational Planning.

Lewin, K.M. & Sayed, Y. (2005) *Non-government Secondary Schooling in sub-Saharan Africa. Exploring the Evidence in South Africa and Malawi.* London: Department for International Development.

Lockheed, M. & Jimenez, E. (1994) *Public and Private Secondary Schools in Developing Countries: what are the differences and why do they persist?* Washington, DC: World Bank.

Mingat, A. (2004) *Questions de Soutenabilité Financière Concernant le Développement de l'Enseignement Secondaire dans les pays d'Afrique Subsaharienne.* Secondary Education in Africa Background Paper. Washington, DC: World Bank.

Rose, P. (2006) Private Post Basic Education: evidence from East and Southern Africa, in K.M. Lewin & Y. Sayed (Eds) *Non-government Secondary Schooling in sub-Saharan Africa: exploring the evidence in South Africa and Malawi.* London: Department for International Development.

Sayed, Y. & Rose, P. (2001) Private Education in South Africa: forging new partnerships? Paper presented at the conference on 'Siyafunda: Partners in Learning'. London: Institute of Education.

Tooley, J. (2001) Serving the Needs of the Poor: the private education sector in developing countries, in C. Hepburn (Ed.) *Can the Market Save Our Schools?* Vancouver: The Fraser Institute.

Tooley, J. (2004) Private Education and 'Education for All', *Economic Affairs*, 24(4), pp. 4-7.

UNESCO (2005) *Education for All: the quality imperative.* EFA Global Monitoring Report. Paris: UNESCO.

CHAPTER 4

Private Sector Contributions to Education for All in Nigeria

PAULINE ROSE & MODUPE ADELABU

Introduction

As emphasis has been placed on expanding access to primary schooling particularly since the 1990 Jomtien World Conference on Education for All (EFA), it has become evident that private provision at relatively low fee levels has been growing in many developing countries (Rose, 2005). Given that such private schools are potentially contributing to the achievement of EFA goals, questions arise of the ways in which private providers could collaborate with government to ensure that poor children are not denied access to a basic education. This chapter aims to identify the contribution that private provision makes to achieve EFA, and considers in particular the ways in which government and private providers engage with each other with a focus on two states in Nigeria: Enugu, where private provision is small relative to the state sector, and parts of Lagos where private provision appears to predominate.

There is extremely limited existing literature on private schooling in Nigeria. The literature that does exist mainly discusses private schools as a homogenous group, without differentiating between approved (registered) and unapproved (unregistered) schools.[1] This chapter will highlight the importance of recognising the different roles each of these types of provider plays, and how they engage with each other as well as with government.

The chapter begins by tracing some of the early developments in government intervention in private provision in Nigeria. This is followed by identifying the current status of private provision in the country, focusing particularly on Enugu and Lagos states. It then considers the engagement amongst private providers, and between them and government, with respect to regulation and policy dialogue in particular.

Research Context

The chapter arises from research commissioned by the United Kingdom Government's Department for International Development (DFID). The purpose of that work was to identify whether, how and under what conditions governments can work with non-state providers (including profit-motivated private providers, as well as non-governmental organisations, faith-based organisations, and community-based initiatives) to support and improve non-state provision of basic education (together with healthcare, water and sanitation) in six countries in sub-Saharan Africa and South Asia. The focus was on identifying and analysing forms of engagement between government and non-state providers rather than on measuring the effectiveness of different forms of provision.[2]

This chapter relates to the aspect of the work undertaken with respect to private schooling in Nigeria. Here, the research focused on two states selected by DFID – Lagos and Enugu. The analysis in the chapter mainly derives from a review of policy documents, and semi-structured interviews with key informants in government in the two states as well as the Federal Capital, Abuja. We also carried out group and individual discussions with chairs and committee members of organisations associated with these – namely, the Association of Formidable Educational Development (AFED) representing unapproved schools, and the Association of Private Proprietors of Schools representing approved schools. These discussions were extremely valuable both in giving insights into the role that their associations play, as well as the characteristics of schooling provided by a range of proprietors.

Where possible, visits were made to private schools (particularly unapproved ones), and semi-structured interviews were carried out with their proprietors. Given that these schools are not recognised, purposive sampling was undertaken as no sample frame was available. In Lagos, this was relatively straightforward as the Chair of AFED was able to assist us in identifying schools based on our criteria of including ones across a range of fees being charged. The involvement of the Chair of the Association facilitated our access to these schools. We visited five unapproved schools and two approved schools in the state.

However, in Enugu, where such an association of unapproved schools did not exist, locating schools was more problematic as they are often not visible, since they often operate in rented premises or proprietors' houses with no signs outside (in part to avoid recognition by government). Where we were able to identify schools, in part with the assistance of members of the community, proprietors were often unwilling to talk as they were concerned that we would report them to the Ministry of Education. We were able to visit three approved and three unapproved schools in this state.

In terms of the context in which the research was undertaken, Nigeria has the highest population in Africa – estimated at around 130 million people. In 1999, it returned to civilian rule with the introduction of a federal constitution. However, it has not achieved anticipated progress towards pro-poor change (Heymans & Pycroft, 2003). Despite being rich in terms of oil, it has relatively low human development indicators – ranked at just 158 out of 177 countries in the United Nations Development Programme's (2005) Human Development Index. An estimated 70% of the population lives on a dollar a day, and a third survives below the national poverty line. As such, Nigerians refer to their country as 'poverty amongst plenty'. Nigeria is considered to have a vibrant entrepreneurial energy (Larbi et al, 2004), which is particularly evident in Lagos.

Lagos was once the Nigerian capital and remains the nation's economic and commercial capital. Lagos State is one of the smallest states in the country but has the highest population density and largest population of around 12 million (equivalent to approximately 5% of the total population, according to national estimates). Around 85% of the population in the state reside in Lagos city.

Enugu, located in the east of Nigeria, is an industrial and commercial centre with the majority of the economically active population, particularly men, involved in commercial business. Enugu State has a population of about two million, also with a relatively high population density, with most of the population concentrated in urban centres.[3]

Historical Development of Government Relations with Private Providers of Education

As in many other sub-Saharan African countries, non-state provision in formal schooling in Nigeria preceded state involvement in the pre-colonial era, and was initially associated with missionary endeavour (Fafunwa, 1995). This section indicates that attempts at collaboration between non-state providers and government are apparent from an early stage in the development of the formal education system. Forms of collaboration developed in the early 1900s are still in evidence today, with problems associated with such collaboration already perceptible a century ago.

The British colonial government's direct involvement in education dates from 1882 when the first Education Ordinance was promulgated, marking the promotion of government assistance to missionary schools (Fafunwa, 1995). At this stage, there were four main types of primary school: government, government-assisted mission, unassisted, and Koranic schools. Government primary schools were established and maintained from public funds. Assisted mission schools were given grants, based on criteria set by government, with the deficit met by school fees and church collections (Fufunwa, 1995). Unassisted schools were either mission schools which did not choose to receive assistance from government because of rules on teaching of religion that would have to be complied with. The other group of unassisted schools were those failing to meet the criteria, or those which were purely private enterprise (for-profit venture schools).

In the 1916 Education Ordinance (amended in 1919), inspectors were given authority to inspect both assisted and non-assisted schools, allowing the Board of Education to close down those that were not performing on the recommendations of inspectors. The Ordinance stipulated that schools, whether controlled by government or by missions, should operate with a common object and, as far as possible, by similar methods of discipline and inspection:

> 'Unassisted' schools are independent of government control, but I hope that they will be induced to conform to the principle and policy laid down by government, and supported and approved by the principal education agencies. Those, which do so conform – and invite inspection – will naturally be justified in expecting a greater measure of encouragement from government. (Cited in Fafunwa, 1995, p. 119)

Despite the government's desire to assist schools, there was still a plethora of unassisted schools of low quality. By 1922, 122,000 children were enrolled in these schools, compared with just 28,000 in government and assisted schools. This led to a further Education Ordinance of 1926, following the Phelps-Stoke Commission Report, aiming to provide a better quality of education through increasing direct government control and supervision, increasing subsidies to schools and training institutions, and attempting to improve the quality and status of teachers in these schools. Another significant aspect of the Ordinance was that missions were permitted to appoint their own supervisors, thus leading the missionaries towards autonomy in the management of their schools. These changes led to an increase in total enrolment, at the same time as an overall decline in unassisted schools (Fafunwa, 1995).

Attempts to implement free primary education were first introduced half a century ago with the aim of moving towards universal primary education (UPE), although this goal still remains elusive in the context of the more recent international drive to achieve Education for All. In 1955, following the findings of the Dike Commission report of 1951, the Western regional government introduced free and compulsory primary education. As a result, school fees were abolished and state grants covered the cost of education. The Eastern region followed in 1957, and the Northern Legislature also decided to plan for free primary education on a provincial basis in 1958. However, shortfalls were already evident in areas of quality and funding (Adelabu, 1990; Fafunwa, 1995).

For-profit private schools began to be established by individual entrepreneurs mainly after independence in 1960. Since then, education policies of successive Nigerian governments have changed according to prevailing political and economic conditions. According to Adelabu (1990), after the fee abolition in the 1950s, the government gave more room to private participation in education as it could not cope financially. The system of grant-aided mission schools with some for-profit private schools continued until the early 1970s. Only after the end of the civil war of 1967-70 and beginning of the oil boom in the 1970s, was the Federal Government able to enforce more uniform educational policies. At this time, the Federal Government was able to launch a federally initiated and financially supported free education scheme throughout Nigeria. Other policies included the public takeover of grant-aided schools in most states, and the publication of a comprehensive National Policy on Education in 1977 (Adelabu, 1990; Federal Ministry of Education, 2003). In 1972, the Federal Government directed each state government to take over non-state schools within its jurisdiction, because it felt that the private sector was making excessive profits and it was concerned about losing control of the education sector.

In 1976, the UPE scheme was launched, which stated that primary education would be free and universal throughout the country from that date, and would become compulsory from 1979 (*Daily Times*, 1976). This resulted in the doubling of primary enrolment within a decade. However, the growth was again marred by inadequate planning and financing. In reality, the takeover of schools did not last long because the Federal Government could not afford to run its free primary education policy. Some private school proprietors, including missionaries, resisted the takeover, as a result of which some private schools remained private, especially in the Southwest and the North-central states (Ibrahim, 2002). The government chose to ignore these schools, as it needed them to augment its inadequate provision. Despite this, by 1979, the government of the states in Western Nigeria decided to extend its free education policy up to the secondary level for political reasons. This free education policy also did not last because of financial constraints on the part of the state government (Fafunwa, 1995).

According to Adesola (2002, p. 24), the weakness of the state system provided an opening for private entrepreneurs to operate 'remedial schools' for those who could afford to pay to prepare pupils for entry to better quality secondary schools:

> The new 'schools' had no government approval to open, and government did not seriously attempt to moderate their quality or regulate their fees, which were so high that only the rich could afford them. Consequently, only the children of the rich could have some assurance of gaining access to good secondary schools and tertiary institutions thereby frustrating the very principle of equality of access, which the policy of free education was intended to promote.

With the growing dissatisfaction with public primary schools, private schools began to grow at a fast pace during the 1970s. The economic downturn of the 1980s brought an end to the expansion of government-funded primary education resulting in unpaid teachers' salaries, the degeneration of educational facilities at all levels, and associated strikes in schools and

71

universities (Federal Ministry of Education, 2003). These factors contributed to a further proliferation of private provision which has continued to grow by default, with limited government control, to the present time (Francis et al, 1998; Urwick, 2002).

Current Status of Private Schooling in Nigeria

The current National Policy on Education continues to support the objective of free and universal primary education referring to the 1976 UPE scheme mentioned above, and proposing to make it compulsory 'as soon as possible' (Federal Republic of Nigeria, 1998, section 15.1). Alongside a commitment to fee-free primary schooling, the policy also supports opportunities for private sector involvement in education, with apparent concern for minimum standards, recognising its own inability to provide:

> Government welcomes the contributions of voluntary agencies, communities and private individuals in the establishment and management of primary schools alongside those provided by the state and local governments as long as they meet the minimum standards laid down by the Federal Government. (Federal Republic of Nigeria, 1998, section 15.13.2)

As further stated in the Lagos State policy:

> Government regards private participation in education as a way of providing variety and allowing for healthy competition between private and public sectors education. Government also believes in cost-sharing for the funding of education with genuine voluntary agencies and individuals who, like government, should not run private schools essentially for monetary gains but purely as a humanitarian/social service. Government therefore, welcomes the contributions of all interested organizations and agencies. (Section 5.4.1)

This raises an apparent contradiction between 'healthy competition' and private provision motivated by non-monetary objectives. In any case, in practice, the private sector supported by local 'edupreneurs' has expanded in parts of the country regardless of government policy.

Given problems in obtaining accurate estimates of enrolment, it is difficult to know how many children are currently denied access to primary schooling in Nigeria (Federal Ministry of Education, 2003; World Bank, 2003). However, estimates suggest that while overall net enrolment rates for Nigeria are similar to the average in sub-Saharan Africa, just one-third of those in the poorest quintile are in school (Table I). There are also considerable regional differences, with enrolment rates generally lower in the north of the country. More recent estimates also indicate a more skewed distribution of primary enrolment in Nigeria compared with other developing countries (UNESCO, 2005), with the overall net enrolment rate remaining relatively low at 67% (UNESCO, 2006).

	Poorest	Second	Middle	Fourth	Richest	Overall
Nigeria	33.1	42.6	63.0	76.0	84.0	58.6
SSA	37.1	45.4	52.7	61.4	75.6	56.9

Table I. Net Enrolment Rates, 1999. Source: World Bank (2003).

Unfortunately, data do not exist to assess changes in the size of private sector involvement in schooling over time. It would appear that the private sector provides schooling for a significant number of children. Available estimates indicate that three-quarters of children in school are enrolled in registered and unregistered private schools in Lagos (Tooley, 2005) compared with around one-fifth in Enugu (Hinchcliffe, 2002). The Ministry of Education in Lagos estimates that there are twice as many unapproved schools as approved ones, and that, of 2.5 million children in school in Lagos, one million of these are in unapproved schools (i.e. 40% of those in school). Even so, some estimates indicate that around one-quarter of children in Lagos are not attending primary school at all (Tooley, 2005). This highlights the role that private schools are playing in filling the gap in inadequate government provision even for those living in slum areas on relatively low incomes.

However, it is likely that the poorest children will continue to be excluded from any form of primary schooling. An important reason is the inadequate resource allocation to education, and to primary schooling in particular, in Nigeria. In the National Budget, education, on average, has received below 12% of the Federal Government's budget between 1997 and 2002, with a downward trend apparent over this period (Federal Ministry of Education, 2004). It is difficult to obtain accurate figures on the proportion of the government budget spent on education across the different tiers of government, including both federal and state allocations. However, based on a comprehensive review of state expenditures across the country, estimates suggest that around 14.3% of the total government budget was allocated to education in 1998 (or 2.4% of gross domestic product, GDP). This is somewhat lower than the average for sub-Saharan African countries, where Hinchcliffe (2002) estimated allocations to education at around 19.6% of total government budget, or 4.7% of GDP. Furthermore, the proportion allocated to primary schooling is considerably below average (35% in Nigeria compared with around 48% in sub-Saharan African countries), with a higher proportion allocated to tertiary institutions in Nigeria (Hinchcliffe, 2002).

Despite teacher salary increases in 1999 resulting in an increase in absolute education expenditure, the proportion of government budget allocated to education has not changed significantly (World Bank, 2003). Moreover, given the limited resources allocated to primary education, government is unable to cover costs beyond teacher salaries in the recurrent budget and, in reality, public schooling is not free.

As a result, parents with children in government schools pay parent–teacher association contributions, development levies, and buy books, and so on (Adelabu, 2002; Hinchcliffe, 2002; Urwick, 2002). Even so, school charges are, on average, higher in private schools where schools are free to decide on fee levels (Table II). The difference between private and government schools is less apparent in Lagos where charges in both types of schools are considerably higher. Not surprisingly, school charges in both government and private schools are higher in urban areas where more income-earning opportunities are available, so households have a greater ability to pay. In addition, households incur other costs (e.g. uniform, exercise books, and textbooks), which have also been estimated to be considerably higher in private schools compared with public schools (Urwick, 2002).

	1993/94		1998	
	Plateau Urban	Plateau Rural	Lagos Urban	Lagos Rural
Public	50	36	8705	4652
Private	1494	649	22,762	14,808
Public/private	3%	6%	38%	31%

	2002				
	Ekiti	Enugu	Borno	Rivers	Benue
Public	442	403	106	553	102
Private	12,920	3305	3982	10,619	8018
Public/private	3%	12%	3%	5%	1%

Table II. Fees and school charges in private and public schools (Naira, 1990 prices). Sources: 1993/04 – Urwick (2002); 1998 – Okebukola & Olaniyonu (1998), cited in Federal Ministry of Education (2003); 2002 – Hinchcliffe (2002). GDP deflator – UN statistics.

Unapproved schools are not registered, and therefore are not recognised by government, and so have no legal status. These schools serve low-income households; although probably not the poorest, who would either be in fee-free government schools where available, or out of school. Data do not usually indicate whether information on unapproved private schools is included, and there is no systematic attempt by government to collect such information.

From the findings of our study, fees of unapproved private schools are lower than those of approved schools (particularly in Lagos). However, they are likely to be considerably higher than contributions to public schools, where teacher salaries (which are the largest cost) are paid by the government. In parts of Lagos, proprietors reported that fees of unapproved schools ranged from around Naira 800 per term (£3.50) to Naira 4000 per term (£16.70), while fees of approved schools were estimated to start from

Naira 7000 per term (£29) in low-income areas, reaching as high as Naira 30,000 per term (£125) or even higher in other areas.

In Enugu, there was less diversity between the lower end of fees for approved schools compared with those for unapproved schools. These started at around Naira 1300 per term (£5.40) for approved schools (similar to the upper end of unapproved schools), with the highest fees charged being Naira 6000 (£25) for a long-established private school. Thus, fees of approved schools in Enugu are closer to those of unapproved schools in Lagos. This is no doubt partly a reflection of the relative socio-economic status of the two states. However, where 70% of the population are estimated to live on less than $1 per day (World Bank, 2006), even the lower end of these fees is likely to be inaccessible to many households.

It is evident that class size is considerably smaller and there is better discipline in private schools (including those that are unapproved). From our discussions with proprietors, one reason they felt that parents preferred to send their children to these schools rather than government schools, was that teachers are available until late hours. Thus, outside of school hours approved and unapproved private schools can serve as a childcare centre, for example for mothers working as market traders in low-income urban/peri-urban areas. Most of the unapproved or approved schools had a nursery school attached. In fact, some started as nursery schools and later expanded to the primary level. In addition, proprietors suggested that, unlike government schools, their schools were not affected by teacher absenteeism resulting from strikes or moonlighting.

In particular, teacher strikes in the 1980s were an important reason for the establishment of private schools, some of which are still operating (including as unapproved ones). Proprietors of private schools are concerned about ensuring that they receive a return on their investment, so monitor the teachers closely. They claim that if teachers are not performing, they will be sacked. However, most of the teachers are unqualified. Not only are proprietors unwilling to pay the salaries demanded by qualified teachers, they also feel that unqualified teachers are more pliable since they often do not have an alternative source of employment if they lose their job, and are not protected by unions. Thus, while proprietors claim that teachers in private schools are more 'motivated', this motivation is likely to be a consequence of the threat of losing their job rather than related to job satisfaction.

Moreover, it was evident from visits to schools that the infrastructure was in extremely poor condition, often with flimsy partitions between classes (if any), and a lack of water and sanitation facilities. Although such poor conditions are also evident in government schools, there is clearly a need to address the circumstances in which children are learning, if EFA goals regarding access and quality are to be met. In order to address problems identified in private schools, the government has a potential role to play in regulating their provision. This gives rise to questions about the nature of the relationship between private providers and government, as explored in the following section.

Collaboration between Government and Private Providers

Undoubtedly, the role that the private sector is playing in supporting Nigeria's drive to achieve EFA cannot be ignored. As Obanya (2002) indicates, there are important reasons to involve private sector provision in the country, especially since the providers are often from powerful sections of society, thus having the potential of being strong stakeholders in education. Furthermore, small-scale informal private proprietors are very often active members at the grassroots level. Thus, Obanya suggests there are possible arenas for intervention between government and the private sector with respect to policy articulation, strengthening capacity, targeting resources (financial, human, and material), and broadening opportunities for education, especially for disadvantaged and other marginalised groups. As the following sections indicate, some experience of such interaction is evident.

While Lagos has a government department responsible for private schools, in Enugu (where the proportion of private schools is lower) responsibility for private schools has been integrated within the activities of the Ministry of Education. Collaboration between government and private providers needs to take account of the relationship amongst private providers themselves. Two membership organisations have been established to represent the interests of different groups of proprietors. The Association of Private Proprietors of Schools (APPS), established in 1977, mainly serves higher fee-charging schools, with a network of associations across the country operating at the local, state, and national levels, and appears to be well established. The Association of Formidable Educational Development (AFED) was set up in Lagos in 2000 in response to the threat to close down unapproved schools, as explored below. AFED is registered with the Corporate Affairs' Commission and has legal status, even though its member schools do not.

Registration and Regulation

Regulation remains the key arena through which government interacts with private providers. These regulations have not changed significantly since their introduction in the 1980s and, as in other developing countries, are mostly related to issues of school inputs, with no explicit specifications for pro-poor service delivery.

In 2002, the Federal Inspectorate Service established Guidelines on Minimum Standards in Schools Nationwide, which are used in principle as the basis for state guidelines to register private schools. Through its Inspectorate Division, the state is responsible to ensure compliance to these minimum standards. In Lagos, for example, the state guidelines stipulate that:

> The state government encourages private individuals to establish private primary schools, it is highly essential that the establishment of such schools should be subject to certain conditions which must be fulfilled and strictly adhered to by the proprietors of such schools. (Lagos State Government, 1988, Section 5.4.1, p. 38)

Furthermore, the Lagos State guidelines note that: 'A private primary school shall not be run as a commercial enterprise or as a limited liability company' (1988, p. 6), thus not permitting for-profit provision in principle. The document sets out procedures for approval, which include:

1. Name Search;
2. Application Letter;
3. State inspection;
4. Application Form;
5. Pre-approval Inspection;
6. Subject recognition Inspection;
7. Pre-approval;
8. File documents submission.

The process for gaining approval is supposed to begin prior to the establishment of a school, starting with inspection of the site and plans of the proposed school. In reality, the process often starts after the school is already operating. While the process varies between states, proprietors are expected to contact the state Ministry of Education to initiate the process. Inspectors from the Ministry should then visit the school to assess whether the standards have been met. Criteria include those related to infrastructure and facilities, number and qualification of teachers, and availability of records and documents. Where there are shortfalls, proprietors are supposed to be advised of the gaps remaining. This is followed up with periodic inspections to assess progress made in the school, until full accreditation is reached. As such, some schools can operate in a semi-legal state.

The criterion of ownership of a plot of land is particularly unattainable for many small providers in Lagos, due to high population density and associated high costs of land which can cost as much as Naira one million and above for a small plot. Proprietors do not have the capital to cover this nor do they have access to a bank loan. In addition to land ownership, schools are expected to be purpose built (rather than conversion of property initially built for other purposes, as is often the case), and have at least a 12-classroom structure. Once again, the cost is likely to be prohibitive, and does not seem feasible for local schools operating on a small scale, even if there were sufficient space to build such structures. These regulations are no longer considered appropriate by proprietors because they were set in the

1970s when land was in greater supply and relatively cheap. However, the government has not been willing to reconsider the criterion.

In addition to approval of schools, all teachers are supposed to be registered with the Teacher Registration Council. The Council aims to ensure that all teachers have appropriate qualifications and stipulates a 61-point code of conduct for teachers. In practice, the vast majority of teachers in unapproved schools (and some in approved schools) are under-qualified suggesting that enforcement of informal providers is difficult. It is unlikely that unapproved schools could operate if they recruited qualified teachers as they would demand higher wages, even though there is not a shortage of qualified teachers in the country since graduates from teacher training colleges exceed the recruitment of teachers in government schools. Moreover, unapproved schools usually have to pay for rent on property, in addition to paying teacher salaries. It would, therefore, appear that the profit margins of some of the smaller private unapproved schools are likely to be quite narrow. One way proprietors are able to increase profit margins is to pay unqualified teachers relatively small amounts (as low as Naira 5000 or £20 per month), and only for the months they teach rather than for the whole year. Given the extent of unemployment amongst secondary school graduates, there is a pool of people willing to work under these conditions.

In practice, there appears to be some overlap between the lower end of approved schools and unapproved schools in terms of meeting requirements for registration. For example, according to Ministry of Education officials, in Enugu, only 20% of schools are estimated to have met the requirement of owning of a plot of land. In addition, some approved schools do not have sufficient number of qualified teachers in both Enugu and Lagos. Proprietors suggested that some schools are able to gain approval by temporarily 'buying in' qualified teachers during the process of approval. The Ministry of Education in Lagos also noted that it is sometimes flexible in its application of the criteria, recognising that it would be impossible for schools serving low-income areas to achieve these standards, as this would mean that fees would become too high for the communities they serve. As a result, they are unlikely to refuse an application outright, as they are aware that children are benefiting from the school. Instead, they are likely to keep the application in process until the desired standards are met even if it appears that they will be unattainable.

In other cases, schools do not contact the state Ministry to gain approval, and remain unknown to the government. Ministry officials in Enugu indicated that they have decided to ignore or turn a blind eye to these unapproved schools, recognising that they are filling a gap. It is evident that some schools put up signs to indicate 'Approved School', even if they are unapproved, while others have no visible sign, making it difficult to identify where these schools exist. It was also apparent from our attempted school visits that some schools and their proprietors are 'protected' by the neighbourhood, who do not identify them for fear of school closure. Some schools have been operating without approval since the 1980s when these schools began to proliferate. Others which have recently been established might not continue to operate beyond a few years because low student numbers and movement of students between schools mean that they face difficulties in covering their costs (including payment of teacher salaries).

Although some schools have been operating without full approval for a number of years, the government has not been able to enforce its regulations. In principle, unapproved schools cannot register children for examinations, which should act as an incentive to gain approval. However, schools get around this by paying approved schools to register their pupils on their behalf. The government has the right to fine and/or imprison proprietors who are operating illegally, as stipulated in the Education Law:

> If a proprietor is ordered to close down and fails to do so, [he/she is] guilty of an offence and liable on summary conviction to a fine of Naira 2000 and additional N40 for each day after the order during which the institution is opened, or imprisonment for one year, or to both fine and imprisonment. (Federal Government of Nigeria, Education Law, p. 1286)

As discussed below, while the government has threatened to enforce this in Lagos State, it has not followed through in practice.

The cost of registration in Lagos in particular is a deterrent for small-scale providers, who are only able to charge relatively low school fees. The total official cost of the process of gaining approval in Lagos is Naira 55,000 or £230 (Table III). This is approximately equal to annual fees of seven students in a middle-range unapproved school (compared with around one student in an approved school), or the annual salary of one teacher in such a school. While this might appear relatively modest, such schools claim that they are already stretched to cover teacher salaries and other costs.

	Lagos		Enugu	
	Naira	£	Naira	£
Name search	5000	21	0	0
Purchase of form	15,000	63	2000	8
Pre-inspection fee	5000	21	0	0
Approval	25,000	104	5000	21
Annual renewal	15,000-100,000	62.50-416.67	2000-3500	8.58-15.33

Table III. Official costs of approval and renewal of registration, Ministry of Education (2005). Source: Fieldwork data.

Moreover, in addition to the official costs, proprietors of unapproved schools in Lagos complained that there are often additional unofficial 'fees' which have to be made to government officials in order to gain approval. Proprietors suggested, for example, that purchasing a form can incur an additional unofficial fee of as much as Naira 50,000. They also claimed that the name search has an additional cost of up to Naira 15,000, which is over three times the official cost. Multiple layers of accountability are also evident as, in addition to charges by the Ministry of Education, schools have to pay official fees to the Environment Agency and Ministry of Health, to show that health and safety and water and sanitation standards have been met.

One unapproved school in the study paid these fees and got the necessary certificates, even though it was apparent from the school's conditions that standards were extremely poor with no water and sanitation facilities. This implied that payment of the fee was more important than complying with standards. Other obstacles to approval included the requirement that schools submit three years' tax clearance, and their ability to cover the costs for a period of three years. This might be impossible if proprietors were unemployed previous to setting up the school, and where they are reliant on fees to cover the costs of provision.

In situations where parents are unable to pay fees, proprietors of unapproved schools reported that they sometimes allowed parents to keep their children in the school and pay in small instalments when they could. Tooley & Dixon (2005) claim that this is an indication that such private school entrepreneurs also have philanthropic aims. However, proprietors in our study noted that they allowed children to stay in their schools in order to project a good image of the school and so that it would appear popular. They claimed this would help to attract other students. Additionally, it would ensure that their schools fulfilled the requirement of the minimum number of pupils required by the guidelines. Thus, this strategy made good business sense, rather than fulfilling philanthropic purposes. Even so, informal providers operating with relatively small class sizes (e.g. up to 15 children in a class) are vulnerable when fees are not paid, given their outgoing costs. Thus, they cannot sustain this over a long period of time and are likely to have to close down if they cannot attract sufficient fee-paying students.

Even though the education system in Lagos is heavily dependent on the private sector, it appears that the process of gaining approval is both considerably more cumbersome and more costly than in Enugu. For example, officials in the Ministry of Education in Enugu commented that they do not undertake a name search, as they know the names of approved schools since there are fewer private schools in the state and they can easily find out whether the proposed name for a new school already exists. The higher costs in Lagos are partly due to the higher fees that schools can attract, but act as a further disincentive for schools to seek approval.

After registration, proprietors are expected to pay an annual renewal fee. In Lagos, this fee is set according to the location and population of the school and the fees charged. The Ministry of Education in Lagos sends out a renewal notice for fees at the beginning of every year and schools are given three to four months to pay. If they do not comply, proprietors do not receive a clearance letter enabling them to register their students for examination. Renewal charges in Enugu are based on the number of pupils (below 500 = N 2000; 501-1000 = N 3000; over 1000 = N 3500). The gradation of fees shows some attempt at setting charges according to ability to pay, although this sliding scale is not apparent for the approval phase. The lower renewal charges in Enugu compared with Lagos (see Table III) again reflect the lower school fees charged.

Once registered, government school inspectors from Local Boards of Education are saddled with the responsibility of daily administration, management, and quality control of the schools within their jurisdiction (both government and private). These Local Boards are, in turn, expected to give feedback to the state and federal ministries with respect to curriculum, materials, development, and teaching techniques. However, in practice, there is lack of clarity about how the responsibilities of different levels of government are organised, and how they relate to each other. A recent institutional analysis of the education sector in Nigeria indicates that there are overlaps between different parts of the education system, which can cause confusion about respective roles and, in some cases, result in gaps in responsibility being fulfilled, which leads to:

> split responsibilities with little or no coordination [which] make it difficult to integrate systems. They open the door to duplication and waste. At the same time, the lack of clear leadership makes it impossible to hold anybody accountable for any function.
> (Orbach, 2004, p. 16)

Another recent report has also criticised the inspectorates at state and federal levels for ineffective performance, which is attributed to inadequate funding and training (NPC/UNICEF, 2001, cited in Federal Ministry of Education, 2003). These problems affect inspection of both government and private schools, with the process of inspection potentially even more complex for private schools. For example, within Lagos State, there are two types of inspection of private schools: one based in the Directorate of Private Education, and the other in the Inspectorate arm of the Ministry of Education. Given the complexity, not only is the government not particularly successful in regulating the entry of schools into the education market, it is even less effective at ongoing monitoring of the quality of approved schools. Furthermore, there is no attempt at monitoring the accessibility of different groups (including the poor) to the services provided. In Lagos, some proprietors indicated that inspectors preferred to go to their private schools (including unapproved ones), as they feel that private school proprietors have the resources to pay for favourable reports.

Policy Dialogue

As in other sub-Saharan African countries, formal policy dialogue between government and private providers appears to have improved over the last decade. This seems partly in response to the EFA agenda, which has united different providers with a common purpose, and partly as a result of developments around sector-wide approaches encouraging the involvement of different stakeholders in policy design. In Nigeria, AFED and APPS have initiated dialogue, with the aim of providing a voice to their members by strengthening the influence of individual providers through collective action in order to pressurise governments to recognise their role and address their problems.

APPS was first established in order to have a common voice with respect to dialogue with government, allow mutual interaction of members, and work towards the harmonisation of standards among its members. In addition, the Association aims to protect its members from undue interference from government. In practice, much of the 'dialogue' is around disputes with the government. For example, APPS has lobbied the government on issues of multiple taxation (e.g. to pay charges to the Environment Agency, Ministry of Health, Fire Brigade, Water Corporation, as well as to the Ministry of Education), and in relation to renewal of fees which they feel are too high (with particular concern about higher charges for higher fee schools). In 2001, APPS in Lagos took the government to court over this issue. They were asked to withdraw the case without a resolution, and renewal fees are still charged.

Even so, the relationship between the government and APPS is reported to be two-way, and in most cases, cordial. This is not unexpected since APPS schools represent the elite in society, and membership includes government officials. APPS reported that it often invites the government to its activities such as sports days and carnivals. Similarly the government invites members of the Association to activities it organises for government schools since, according to one government official, 'their children are our children'.

As APPS appears to have a relatively constructive relationship with the government, in recent years it has used its influence to act against the interests of low-budget unapproved private schools serving poorer communities by lobbying to close them down. Its stated motives are to preserve quality, as it considers these schools to be offering sub-standard education. However, proprietors of unapproved schools raised concerns that a motive is also to control competition from lower fee-charging schools, given those attending such schools indicate willingness and some level of ability to pay to some extent. When discussing the reasons behind why they felt that unapproved schools should be closed, proprietors of approved schools cited the guideline that schools should not be within one kilometre of each other. While apparently concerned with self-regulation of their own members to ensure quality standards are maintained, they would rather see the closure of unapproved schools, thus limiting access to lower income groups who would not be able to afford the fees in approved schools in Lagos.

From our discussions, AFED's view of APPS is that it is an association for rich people who are responsible for the problems faced by schools supporting the less privileged. AFED membership, by contrast, is more grassroots, and as such has the potential ability to mobilise mass support for and against government policy. Since the Lagos government does not interact directly with proprietors of unapproved schools as they are not recognised, a group of proprietors established AFED in order for unapproved schools to have a voice, and lobby the government as one body to prevent the closure of unapproved schools. AFED has tried to influence policy through lobbying for a change to the criteria for regulation, making them more relevant and the process more affordable for small-scale entrepreneurs providing education to low-income groups. Given that the Ministry of Education in Lagos is dominant in the policy arena since it wants to be seen to be committed to addressing popular demand for primary schooling (even if it does not fulfil this commitment through its own actual provision), it has continued to adhere to strict regulations in principle, while not being able to enforce them.

AFED has succeeded in preventing school closure in part due to the strength of its leadership, as well as its ability to organise local support. The threat of political insecurity due to grassroots mobilisation has enabled the Association to delay school closures which would otherwise result in large numbers of children not having any school to attend. The inability of government to enforce its legal framework is not new, and is in part due to its own inability to provide schooling of acceptable quality, despite a longstanding commitment to free primary education. Unapproved schools have been able to capitalise on the economic and political instability of the country which has allowed proprietors to establish such schools in the first place. Since proprietors of the schools have a strong local political force, government has to listen to avoid a potential uprising which could result in instability. This threat of instability has enabled the Association to put pressure on government to delay school closures.

In an attempt to achieve their goals, AFED has written letters to the government and has met with traditional rulers, community leaders, and the Commissioner of Education. It has also hired a lawyer for legal advice. At one time, AFED took the government to court over threatened closures of its member schools but, like APPS, was asked to withdraw the case if it wanted government cooperation regarding their demands. As a result, the government extended the deadline for closure by six months and has continued to grant extensions since then, albeit with a constant threat of closure.

In Enugu, while AFED does not yet exist (although APPS is active), individual proprietors of unapproved schools also have had political influence which they have been able to exert to avoid school closures. However, the government and approved schools have not applied the same level of pressure for closure as in Lagos, so the need for an association to resist government has not yet arisen to the same extent.

Conclusion

Overall, the experience of private education provision in Nigeria indicates that it has been expanding over several decades, and has become established in response to state failure. Although the National Policy on Education supports the involvement of the private sector in principle, the expansion has largely been by default rather than as a result of conscious action by government to encourage such provision.

Government intervention is mainly in the form of control of entry through guidelines for the establishment of private schools and associated fees. However, many schools continue to operate illegally. From our research and other studies (Tooley, 2005) it would seem that unapproved schools outnumber those operating legally in Lagos. This is partly because the criteria are unrealistic for small providers, and partly due to the inability of the government to enforce its regulations. Problems of enforcement are associated with inadequacies in its own provision. This makes it difficult to deny access of children to unapproved schools given that they are filling an important gap in provision. Thus, given that small informal providers are unlikely to achieve the current standards, the only options for government are either to force closure which it is either unable or reluctant to do, or to allow them to continue to operate illegally.

In reality, the government has let such schools operate illegally in Lagos and Enugu, albeit with constant threats of closure in Lagos since 2000 in particular. There is little incentive for private schools to register other than to avoid the threat of closure, since the benefits they receive from government are extremely limited (if they exist at all), while the disincentives in terms of cost and bureaucratic procedures are evident. Moreover, government schools themselves often do not meet the guidelines for minimum standards, suggesting that there is a need to consider their revision to make them more appropriate to prevailing conditions.

As highlighted in the chapter, it is apparent that the diversity of private schools creates tensions not just between government and private providers, but also amongst different types of providers. It seems that the more established seek to restrict competition of those schools that are likely to be more accessible to the poor. This reinforces arguments that market forces are unlikely to work effectively in situations where parents do not have access to sufficient information about different types of providers (see, for example, Colclough, 1996), and suggests that collaboration between government and private providers, as well as amongst private providers themselves, needs to take the complexity of the relations between these different providers into account.

Since unapproved schools are likely to exist and fill a gap for the foreseeable future, large-scale closures are not a solution. This would result in large numbers of children, particularly those from low-income families, with no access to schooling which would have wider ramifications. The study indicates a need to review the criteria for approval through constructive dialogue between the government, AFED and APPS to ensure that they are realistic and do not compromise teaching and learning standards (which in any case are extremely low, even in government schools). There are legitimate concerns that some unapproved schools are taking advantage of the gap in the market. Only by having realistic criteria which are mutually agreed and can be enforced, will it be possible to distinguish between unscrupulous providers and those genuinely providing a service.

Notes

[1] Tooley (2005) is an exception to this and focuses on private provision in one part of Lagos State. It is also discussed in the chapter by Tooley & Dixon in this book.

[2] For an overview of this work, including other countries involved in the study, see http://www.idd.bham.ac.uk/research/Projects/service-providers/nonstate_service.htm, and Rose (2006) with respect to the findings relating to education in particular. This chapter reflects the views of the authors, not DFID nor others involved in that research.

[3] See http://www.ngex.com/nigeria/places/states/enugu.htm and Mbagu (2000).

References

Adelabu, M.A. (1990) Politics of Decision-making Process in Education with Reference to South Western Nigeria, 1955-1985. Unpublished Doctoral Dissertation of Obafemi Awolowo University, Ile-Ife.

Adelabu, M.A. (2002) State/Community Partnership Strategy for the Implementation of UBE Programme in Nigeria, in T.E. Ajayi, J.O. Fadipe, P.K. Ojedele & E.E. Oluchukwu (Eds) Planning and Administration of Universal Basic Education in Nigeria. Ijebu Ode: Lucky Odoni (Nig.) Enterprises.

Adesola, A.A. (2002) The State of Education in Nigeria, in H.J. Charles & E. Iheme (Eds) Nigerian Private Sector and Education for All. A Report on the Private Sector Round Table. Abuja: UNESCO Abuja Publications.

Colclough, C. (1996) Education and the Market: which parts of the neoliberal solution are correct? World Development, 24(4), pp. 589-610.

Daily Times of Nigeria Limited (1976) No. 21,337, 7 September.

Fafunwa, A. (1995) History of Education in Nigeria. Ibadan: NPS Educational Publishers.

Federal Ministry of Education (2003) Education Sector Status Report. Abuja.

Federal Ministry of Education (2004) *Education Sector Analysis*. Sector Diagnosis Draft Report. Mimeo. Abuja.

Federal Republic of Nigeria (1998) *National Policy on Education* (3rd edn). Lagos: Nigerian Educational Research and Development Council Press.

Francis, P., Agi, S., Alubo, S., Biu, H., Daramola, A., Nzewi, U. & Shehu, D. (1998) *Hard Lessons: primary schools, community and social capital in Nigeria*. Washington, DC: World Bank.

Heymans, C. & Pycroft, C. (2003) *Drivers of Change in Nigeria. A Preliminary Overview*. Draft. London: Department for International Development. http://www.grc-exchange.org/docs/DOC27.pdf (accessed 26 April 2006)

Hinchcliffe, K. (2002) *Public Expenditures on Education in Nigeria: issues, estimates and some implications*. Washington, DC: World Bank.

Ibrahim, A.J. (2002) The Nigeria National EFA Forum: facilitating consultation and participation in the realisation of the EFA goals, in H.J. Charles & E. Iheme (Eds) *Nigerian Private Sector and Education for All. A Report on the Private Sector Round Table*. Abuja: UNESCO Abuja Publications.

Lagos State Government (1988) *Lagos State Education Policy*. Lagos: Lagos State Government.

Larbi, G., Adelabu, M., Rose, P., Jawara, D., Nwaorgu, O. & Vyas, S. (2004) *Nigeria: study of non-state providers of basic services*. International Development Department, University of Birmingham. http://www.idd.bham.ac.uk/service-providers/stage2.htm (accessed 26 April 2006)

Mbagwu, T.C. (2000) Enugu State, in A.B. Mamman, J.O. Oyebanji & S.W. Peters (Eds) *Nigeria: a people united, a future assured*. Vol. 2. Abuja: Federal Ministry of Information and Calabar: Gabumo Publishing Company.

Obanya, P. (2002) *Revitalizing Education in Africa*. Ibadan: Sterling-Horden Publishers.

Orbach, E. (2004) *The Capacity of the Nigerian Government to Deliver Basic Education Services*. Washington, DC: World Bank.

Rose, P. (2005) Decentralisation and Privatisation in Malawi – default or design?, *Compare*, 35(2), pp. 47-64.

Rose, P. (2006) Collaborating in Education for All? Experiences of Government Support for Non-state Provision of Basic Education in South Asia and sub-Saharan Africa, *Public Administration and Development*, 26(3), pp. 219-230.

Tooley, J. (2005) *Is Private Education Good for the Poor?* EG West Centre Working Paper. Newcastle: Newcastle University.

Tooley, J. & Dixon, P. (2005) Is There a Conflict Between Commercial Gain and Concern for the Poor? Evidence from Private Schools for the Poor in India and Nigeria, *Economic Affairs*, 25(2), pp. 20-26.

UNESCO (2005) *Children out of School: measuring exclusion from primary education*. Montreal: UNESCO Institute of Statistics.

UNESCO (2006) *Education for All Global Monitoring Report: literacy for life*. Paris: UNESCO.

United Nations Development Programme (2005) *Human Development Report.* New York: UNDP.

Urwick, J. (2002) Determinants of the Private Costs of Primary and Early Childhood Education: findings from Plateau State, Nigeria, *International Journal of Educational Development*, 22, pp. 131-144.

World Bank (2003) *School Education in Nigeria: preparing for universal basic education.* Washington, DC: World Bank.

World Bank (2006) *World Development Report: equity and development.* Washington, DC: World Bank.

CHAPTER 5

Education for All and Private Education in Developing and Transitional Countries

IGOR KITAEV

Introduction

Attitudes towards private education have been ambiguous and controversial, and subject to changes in different countries' contexts and priorities. The case of developing and transitional countries is of particular research interest because of dramatic developments in their educational systems in recent times.

According to the Dakar Forum on Education for All established in 2000 and subsequent international initiatives, private education should be seen as complementary to government efforts to cope with the ever-growing demand for quality education. Government efforts and resources should be concentrated on compulsory levels (primary, basic, and lower secondary depending on context), while other levels (pre-school, upper secondary, tertiary, continuing) may be subject to various alternatives for management and financing. For example, these can be cost sharing, cost recovery, income generation, and the expansion or development of private education. From this perspective, private education can be seen as a support to provision of public education even at compulsory levels when it absorbs children who, for the reasons given below, prefer to attend them. In this case, private schools can lessen the burden on enrolment in public schools.

It is worth recalling that the first schools in many developing countries were religious and set up by missionaries. After independence, the new governments often wished to put education systems under their control. In many developing countries, private schools were nationalised, and in extreme cases, private education was not allowed by law. These decisions followed the then 'role model' of the former Soviet Union and other centrally planned economies, where private activities in all sectors, including education, were considered illegal for ideological reasons. In these countries education was a state monopoly at all levels.

However, while better resourced, centrally planned economies achieved high enrolment rates and an acceptable quality of education (e.g. in the former Soviet Union and Eastern Europe 10-year primary and secondary education became universal and compulsory in the 1980s), many developing countries in Asia and Africa who used the same model failed to achieve adequate access and participation even in primary education. Market reforms and economic liberalisation of the late 1980s and 1990s reversed government policies in these countries towards tolerating and even supporting private schooling.

Nonetheless, results of the international macro-level review by UNESCO of private education in Asia show that there is no uniformity in the policies of different countries on private education. In many instances, former colonial powers shaped the organisation and content of many developing countries in South and South East Asia, whereas the metropolitan centres of the former Soviet Union influenced many transitional countries in Central Asia. Nonetheless, despite the similarities in different regions due to shared histories and modern context, there are examples of both similar and contrasting policies in neighbouring countries.

Methodology

This chapter is based on macro-level findings of research conducted by the UNESCO International Institute for Educational Planning (IIEP) in Paris to review the development of private education in Asian countries. We were particularly interested in the issues of government regulation of private (or non-public) education. For this research, UNESCO adopted the broad definition for private education as non-public education – that is, all institutions that were managed by bodies/individuals other than public authorities were considered non-public. This included cases even where institutions may have been owned and financially supported by public authorities. The chapter is mainly concerned with primary, basic and secondary levels of instruction, and reviews the main findings for South, South East and Central Asia.

The main sources of data were high-level official reports and studies by the national ministries of education, donor agencies, and researchers. Key government officials at the ministries and departments of education were asked to complete a set format of questions regarding the development and operation of private education systems in their countries. Questions covered the following areas: history of private education development; government regulations and legal aspects; financing and management; and staff and teacher issues. Furthermore, school visits in particular countries were made in an attempt to learn more directly from school operators and school clientele (parents). The IIEP organised a series of seminars and studies on this topic in collaboration with the UNESCO Offices and the National Commissions for UNESCO reporting on the results.

Fundamentally, this chapter is intended to relay how these official reports characterised the systems of private education in different regions of Asia. As Walford & Srivastava note in the introductory chapter of this book, given the scope of this research exercise, it is important to note the limitations that such official data can have – differences 'in practice' may be quite stark to those 'in principle'. Nonetheless, the findings can provide a very useful starting point for the analysis of private education systems in a range of Asian countries.

The Issue of Terms and Definitions

In this chapter, UNESCO's definition of private (non-public) schools is used even where national legislation differs on criteria and terms used. To reiterate, those schools that are managed by independent (non-public) bodies will be considered private even if they receive funding support from public authorities.

Whether they are distinguished according to management, source of income, autonomy, or ownership, it is misleading to talk of the public and private sectors as if each is comprised of a homogeneous set of schools. In many respects there is as much variation within the sectors as there is between them. For the purposes of this analysis it is helpful to view schools according to their function.

The following set represents 'pure types'. Very few schools would correspond exactly to a type, but in most cases one or at most two of the characteristics prevail. Generally, a particular type is found mainly in either the conventional public or the private sector but there is usually some overlap:

- Academically selective schools for pupils of above-average intellectual attainment.
- Socially selective or elite schools which, because of their location, their high fees or their selection practices, recruit children from families of greater than average social status.
- Religious or denominational schools which cater for the children of particular religious or ethnic sub-sectors of a society.
- Community or municipal schools which are open to all children in a particular neighbourhood.
- Alternative schools which espouse some particular educational or social philosophy.
- For-profit schools run by their owners as a business enterprise.
- Charity or special schools sponsored by philanthropic organisations, or the state, for children with disabilities (physical, social, or intellectual).

According to the definition commonly used by UNESCO for comparative analysis, educational institutions are classified as either public or private, according to whether a public agency or a private entity has the ultimate power to make decisions concerning the institution's affairs. Naturally, each country has its own regulations and terms which correspond to its context and specifics. The spectrum of terms used to qualify private schools is vast and often confusing. To name a few frequently mentioned as synonyms: private schools, non-public schools, non-state schools, non-government schools, independent schools, privately managed schools, privately administered schools.

An institution is classified as *public* if it is: 1. controlled and managed directly by a public education authority or agency; or 2. is directly controlled and managed either by a government agency or by a governing body (e.g. council, committee, etc.), most of whose members are either appointed by a public authority or elected by public franchise. An institution is classified as *private* if it is controlled and managed by a non-governmental organisation (e.g. church, trade union, business enterprise, etc.), or if its governing board consists mostly of members not selected by a public agency.

In general, the question of who has the ultimate management control over an institution is decided with reference to the power to determine the general activity of the school and to appoint the officers managing the school. From this perspective, the extent to which an institution receives its funding from public or private sources does *not* determine its classification status. Likewise, the issue of whether or not a public or private body owns the buildings and site of a school is not crucial to the classification status.

The terms 'government dependent' and 'independent' refer only to the degree of a private institution's dependence on funding from government sources and not to the degree of government direction or regulation. A *government-dependent private institution* is one that receives more than 50% of its core funding from government agencies. An *independent private institution* is one that receives less than 50% of its core funding from government agencies.[1]

The most common definition of a private school is one that is not managed by a state or public authority. The distinction is used by UNESCO in its statistical surveys of education. Private schools are those not managed by or within the government sector; government-aided schools are classified with the private sector if they are privately managed. However, this definition avoids a number of questions that are of interest to policy makers and scholars: whether, for example, funding is from public or private sources, whether individual or specialised schools within the public sector are exempted for some reasons from policies applying to most schools, and whether the school is owned by public or private owners.

Private School Rationale in
Developing and Transitional Countries

Apart from shifting the costs from the public purse to the user, supporters of privatisation claim that the benefits will include greater effectiveness, greater efficiency, and enhancement of parents' freedom to choose. Reform programmes vary in the emphases which are placed on each these objectives. Whereas effectiveness and efficiency are capable of being evaluated empirically, freedom to choose is ultimately a matter of value preference. Nevertheless it is regarded to be of central importance, particularly in countries where there is a pluralism of religious and ethnic communities. Advocates of market solutions to replace managed school systems view freedom of choice not so much as an end in itself, but as a mechanism for causing schools to become more efficient and effective.

Educational reforms in developing and transitional countries are often designed by donor agencies and consultants who use the experiences of their countries as background. This is particularly visible in countries that were inexperienced in private sector regulation and management in education because it was not historically allowed. Nonetheless, various economic and social reasons caused governments in different regions of the world to become interested in forms of privatisation of schooling, in some cases leading to changes in what has been a delicate balance between the public and private sectors. Financial constraints of the state budget are one factor. In some countries, a strong private sector is a response to excess demand as central and local governments are unable or unwilling to find the resources to build the additional schools that are needed and to staff them with trained teachers. In other countries, pressures from religious and ethnic minorities are a reason for renewed interest in private schools, as organised religious and ethnic subcultures come to regard public education as an ineffective means of transmitting group identity to a new generation.

Managerial and cost-efficiency preferences are a third reason for encouragement of the private sector. Following the global economic downturn starting in the mid-1970s, belief in the efficacy of market forces as superior to state regulation and planning led a number of countries to consider privatising management of public institutions, including education. Private schools may also be regarded as 'lighthouse' institutions, increasing the diversity of the country's stock of schools, and as a safety valve, releasing the pressure from those who may be disaffected with their government schools. Furthermore, some countries are devolving authority from central government to regions and to individual schools in a way which may blur the public–private boundary. In that sense privatisation means rolling back the power of the state. These changes imply that the management of schooling is being privatised.

Finally, the concept of vouchers has been discussed a great deal since it was first suggested by Friedman in 1962, but there are still only a few places where it has been tried in practice. Nonetheless, since the 1980s, the terms 'vouchers', 'choice', and 'devolution' have become popular in the vocabularies of school reformers, especially in Anglo-Saxon countries and Chile, and were deemed to represent desirable organisational arrangements, more likely to be associated with private than public schools. One variation of the voucher idea would allow schools to charge tuition fees in addition to the state-funded voucher entitlements. Fee-charging private schools, which also receive per capita government subsidies, represent this form of voucher funding with each additional child entitling the school to a grant.

The following sections present results of UNESCO's review on the private education system in selected countries of the South, South East, and Central regions of Asia.

Experiences of Developing and Transitional Countries

Private Education in South Asia

Overview. For research on this region, the comparisons were made between Bangladesh, Bhutan, India, Nepal, and Sri Lanka. The experiences in this region were more contrasting than in other regions of the world. This is a combination of several factors: demography, economic growth, and traditional beliefs in the predominant role of the state in all sectors, including education. The explanations given by the reports and interviews are that there is a conflict between the traditional strong role of the state in education and the new opportunities created by the Indian economy which have a spill-over effect into the neighbouring countries. This region shows an example of the demand-side development of private education.

The economic boom in India caused vast income disparities, hence more demand for diversity in schooling and upgraded teaching and learning conditions. Given the demographic and regional problems, public education alone in India cannot cope with the growing enrolment. Mushrooming private for-profit schools may offer a solution for those ready to pay fees. According to official reports, high and growing fees mean better teacher salaries (compared to public schools) and preferable learning conditions for pupils (see Srivastava in this book for contrasting evidence from low-fee private schools in India).

Neighbouring Nepal could not follow this trend because of its many internal political problems and relatively sluggish economy. However, being economically linked to India, the country feels the stratification between the rich and the poor and the demand for better schooling. Nonetheless, the majority of the population is not yet ready to accept the division of families not only by income, but also by learning opportunities. In recent years, there have been active demonstrations against private education in Kathmandu (see Caddell in this book). The demonstrators asked for more government and popular control over private schools, including control over the level of tuition fees. Some private schools were literally locked by the demonstrators. Similar sentiments, although not as violent, were reported in Bangladesh and

Sri Lanka, where private education is still considered an exception to mainstream public schooling at primary and basic levels.

According to official reports, if new for-profit private schools are readily welcomed by authorities and the wider public in India, they are violently resisted in Nepal, and have no government endorsement in Bangladesh and Sri Lanka. From our reports, it seems that the majority of the population in these countries does not feel the need for schools outside the public system of education. It seems that the economic momentum and demand based on income growth has not yet arrived unlike in, for example, India. To what extent and how quickly the Indian model of private education development could spread to the other countries of the region remains to be seen. Clearly, the decisive factors will be the changing role of the state under decentralisation and the potential growth of family income.

An interesting case is Bhutan, where the government realised its shortcomings and mobilised private and community initiative to support Education for All goals. Unlike other countries where private schools are at the periphery of government decision making and exist and develop on their own, in Bhutan the government adopted a clear policy approach. The government policy is a prudent compromise – private schools appear where the government cannot deliver. One example is in areas where children have to walk eight hours to school and back. Here, the government clearly demarcated potential locations, specifically rural locations of private schools based on school mapping.

The analysis showed quite clearly that in all five countries, the demand for private schooling is growing, sometimes with unexpected speed. In general, the demand comes from all social levels, with a predominance of wealthier people, but not exclusively. Thus, in countries with mountainous geography and uneven population distribution such as Bhutan or Nepal, private (or non-public) schools cater for that part of the population which lives too far from any state schools. Prestigious private schools in Nepal are, however, mostly urban.

Bangladesh's government is more concerned with maximising coverage and the promotion of Education for All, rather than with any particular *kind* of education (religious or otherwise) to be provided by private institutions. India, in a similar manner, with its massive population and very large geographical area, is more concerned with offering every child the chance of schooling, whether at a public or at a private school. However, in India, there are some private schools of extremely high standard, modelled on the British 'public schools', which charge high fees and enjoy great prestige. These, obviously, have a very different and distinguished clientele.

Among more specific reasons for which parents choose to send their children to private schools is the use of the English language as medium for teaching in Sri Lanka, India, and Bangladesh. In Bhutan and Nepal, the location of the school plays the most important role. Also in Nepal, however, private schools seem to have the reputation of providing more individual attention, better facilities, and a broader range of extracurricular activities. This is also the case in Sri Lanka. According to official reports, custodial service for working parents was available at some private schools in Nepal. In Bhutan, private schools exist more to supplement the action of government schools, to which they are similar in many respects, rather than to offer alternative kinds or standards of education.

Private schools in all five countries fall into two broad categories: those that are aided by the government and those that are entirely financially independent. Typically, unaided schools charge higher tuition fees. The situation is different in Sri Lanka, where, for historical reasons, some schools are both unaided and non-fee levying. These schools are run and funded by religious communities. Bhutanese private institutions, on the other hand, are essentially profit-making business enterprises. Another distinction common to all five countries is between religious and non-religious schools. Finally, private schools can either be registered with or approved by the government or not. In Bhutan and Nepal, only schools that are registered are allowed to operate. In India, Bangladesh, and Sri Lanka registration with the government or 'approved' status signifies higher standards of teaching and better facilities in principle.

There is a great variety of private schools in all the countries studied. Some examples are presented to get an idea of this variation. Bangladesh seems to have the greatest variety of private schools with community schools, satellite schools, schools run by non-governmental organisations (NGOs), independent and *madrasah*-attached non-registered private schools, and kindergartens. This is in addition to the standard, registered non-government type of private schools. India also counts caste-specific and language-specific private schools in addition to religious schools. International schools in Sri Lanka have been established for children of expatriates. The clientele for those schools is almost entirely composed of foreign citizens.

The conditions of schooling at private schools vary greatly. In Bhutan, they are very much the same level as public schools. In Bangladesh and India, the standard of private schools may be considerably higher or lower than that of state schools, depending on the location, size and type of school. In Nepal in particular, and to a certain extent in Sri Lanka, public schools usually offer a better level of education.

There is a distinction between those schools, on the one hand, that are meant to supplement the government action for Education for All and those offering a diversity of provision. The first kind do not necessarily provide a higher standard of education than public schools, and mainly target populations living in remote areas, for example, or in over-populated areas where government schools are not available in sufficient number. There have been reported cases of this in Bangladesh, India, and Bhutan, and to a lesser extent, in Sri Lanka. On the other hand, there are schools that aim to offer an alternative to public education, whether in terms of absolute quality (e.g. better academic achievement, better facilities, etc.) or in terms of variety (e.g.

for different social backgrounds such as in religious or caste schools; different atmosphere in terms of stricter discipline; alternative subjects of study not normally offered at public schools, etc.). These tend to be prestigious, 'top quality' schools and are more numerous in Nepal and India.

Regulation. With the exception of Bhutan, all countries have a precise legal basis regulating the establishment of private institutions. It must be noted, however, that in Sri Lanka these regulations actually *forbid* the establishment of new private institutions and merely serve to regulate the functioning of those already in place. This kind of legal situation leads to a 'burgeoning' of already existing private schools, which continue to expand themselves by establishing branch campuses and expanding their main campuses to increase intake. In Bangladesh, the regulations are very flexible, aimed at encouraging the setting up of new schools and a broader coverage of the population. Nevertheless, one government official is supposed to be incorporated into the school's governing body for monitoring purposes in Bangladesh.

Some sort of agreement between the school and the government is signed in all the countries. In principle, in most cases, the applicant wishing to open a new private school must officially apply to the relevant department of the Ministry of Education. After the application has been reviewed, the department organises an inspection to verify the suitability of the proposed premises and other various aspects. A letter of recommendation from local authorities is required to apply in Nepal, as well as a security deposit. A feasibility study is carried out by the relevant department in Nepal before the agreement is granted. Similarly, a government inspection is required in India before permission to open the school is granted and periodical inspections are then supposed to be carried out by the government.

All countries have a set of minimal standards that private institutions should observe (in principle), concerning issues such as facilities and buildings, hygiene, and academic matters. The strictness of these conditions depends largely on the situation of the state school system. In countries such as Bhutan, Nepal and Sri Lanka which have a school system that is not too badly developed, conditions are stricter. As previously stated, in Bhutan, regulations are aimed at encouraging the establishment of schools in remote regions of the country where public schools are insufficient in number. According to our data, in India and Bangladesh, the development of private schools is greatly encouraged and conditions are less strict. Some schools in India thus prefer to remain unregistered and unrecognised to avoid excessive control from the government, and conversely, some of the recognised schools are unable to keep up with the minimum standards prescribed for them, but nevertheless continue to keep their recognised status.

Curriculum and examinations. As far as the curriculum is concerned in these countries, it is aligned on the official curriculum established by the state and is followed in public and private schools alike. However, private schools are allowed to broaden their curriculum and offer additional courses, which they do in most countries. In Bhutan, government agreement is required to introduce optional subjects.

Rules concerning examinations at private schools differ, with the exception of end-of-school examinations, which are set by the state and result in the award of a school-leaving certificate. Lower level exams are organised by the schools themselves in Nepal, which are also free to organise annual or other exams at their discretion. In the other countries, private school examinations are set and taken in a similar manner to public schools.

Supervision and monitoring. According to official reports, the governments of all five countries make a point of closely supervising the activity of private schools, and of regularly inspecting them so as to check that they are still suitable for the responsibility of delivering education, both in terms of academic standards and in terms of facilities available to pupils. In Bangladesh, state supervision must be performed through local educational committees. In Bhutan and India it is controlled through a state representative commissioned to sit on the school's management board.

In addition, Bhutanese teachers are encouraged to participate in discussions of educational policy and to provide feedback on current regulations to the Ministry of Education as well as to suggest ways of improving them. Thus, in principle, they have the chance to participate in the forming of new regulations. In India, schools can choose whether to be affiliated to regional (state) or national boards for education. Furthermore, according to official reports, the accounts of Indian private schools must be audited by an external auditor every year. Government control is strict in Nepal. A government official is assigned to sit on the school's managing committee and teachers of private schools must have a teaching licence issued by the government to ensure that there are no ghost appointments.

Funding and support. The different governments support private schools, to a greater or lesser extent. In Bangladesh, a considerable percentage of schools receive grants from the government, as is the case in India. As in the other countries, these grants are most often directed towards teachers' salaries. This is also the case in Sri Lanka, except that only non-fee-levying schools receive grants towards teachers' salaries, books, and uniforms. The other schools may only hope for an occasional one-off grant towards infrastructure improvements. The most varied forms of support seem to be provided to private schools in Bhutan, which receive free textbooks, enjoy the use of educational materials developed by the government education departments, and may take advantage of land lease availabilities to build schools in remote areas difficult to access otherwise. Two of the five countries had rather restricted governmental aid: Nepal had no aid and in Sri Lanka, schools levying fees received no support.

Original funding for the establishment of private schools comes from private sources in all five countries. The specific origin of the funds may differ, that is, they may be from religious missions, non-profit non-religious institutions, NGOs, or else from profit-making companies. Furthermore, private schools in all five countries rely mostly on tuition fees to cover their operating costs. This income is in most cases (with the exception of Nepal and in some cases in Sri Lanka) supplemented by grants from the government. On the other hand, Nepali private schools seem to be the recipients of private charitable donations which come from religious bodies or NGOs. External and NGO assistance also plays an important role in the functioning of private schools in Bangladesh. Similarly, in Sri Lanka, where the government's aid is rather scarce, parental donations are more frequent. Tuition fees are usually determined by individual schools. It is only in Bhutan that the level of tuition fees is restricted by the government.

Management and teacher staffing. According to official reports, the school management structure in all five countries is through a managing committee or governing board. There are, however, variations in the membership of the committee. In Bhutan, the parents' representative, principal, and senior teachers sit on the committee alongside an official state representative from the Department of Education. In India, the management committee also must include a government representative, but only in cases where the school receives aid from the government.

In Nepal, the principal has greater authority, whereas the managing committee plays a more supervisory role. In all cases, however, regardless of whether or not the state is represented by an official incorporated in the managing committee, this committee has the right to inspect private schools and to verify that they are appropriately run and are conforming to minimum standards as laid out in the relevant regulations.

Various rules apply as far as the training of teachers is concerned. Mostly, a minimum level of training is a prerequisite for teaching at a school, private or public, at any level. In India, hiring untrained teachers is contrary to the rules. In Bangladesh, the same level of training is required from teachers as at public schools. In some schools, however, training is sometimes conducted after the candidate's appointment. In Bhutan, untrained teachers are not uncommon in private schools, whereas in public schools teachers are required to have a minimum qualification.

Officially, at primary level, the minimum qualification required is a secondary school certificate. At secondary level, especially upper secondary, teachers are mostly trained university graduates in Bhutan, India, Nepal, and Sri Lanka. In Nepal, all teachers must be accredited, that is, holders of a state-issued teaching licence. Some additional restrictions in gender or nationality may apply. In Bangladeshi satellite schools, teachers are exclusively female, and in Bhutan, at the primary level, 50% of the teaching staff must hold Bhutanese nationality. This ratio is decreased to 30% at the secondary level.

Teachers' status is in most cases equivalent to that of civil servants, but not always. This is the case in Bangladesh and Nepal, and sometimes in India, but not in Bhutan. Contracts are most often permanent and teachers are well protected by the law, especially so in India where there is strong legal and constitutional backup. Recruitment, promotion, and retirement are governed by official rules thus leaving the teacher relatively well protected. Nepal constitutes an exception, where teachers are often under temporary contracts and where terms and conditions of appointment are very loose. Legal backup there is weak and rules differ from school to school. According to our data, a probationary period of one year is necessary in Bhutan and in India before a permanent contract is signed with the teacher.

Salaries vary considerably between countries, and within a given country, between schools. In Bhutan, private school salaries are considerably lower than in public schools at primary level, but considerably higher than in public schools at secondary level. In both Nepal and India the level of salaries should be guaranteed by a government scale – paying teachers below that level is illegal, though in practice this is not upheld. A state law also guarantees a decent level of salaries in Sri Lanka which applies to all categories of schools. In Nepal, there are three separate sets of regulations for staffing at different school types: government schools, private schools, and Buddhist schools. These affect issues of salary, training, enrolment, retirement, and various benefits. Bangladeshi schools offer monthly bonuses and rewards to their teachers as well as a bonus and gratuity at the time of retirement.

According to official reports, working conditions are basically the same in all the countries included in the analysis, and do not differ considerably between public schools and private schools. Reports also say that more often than at public schools, teachers must carry out additional duties such as organisation of and participation in cultural or sporting activities, and other duties related to the care of pupils.

Generally, the recruitment of teachers falls under the direct responsibility of the schools and should be organised through open competitions, publicly advertised, which are followed by interviews with the short-listed candidates. In Bangladesh, India and Sri Lanka the recruitment process is indirectly supervised by the government, inasmuch as Bangladeshi teachers follow the same procedure of recruitment as civil servants. Nepali teachers must be titular of a teaching licence issued by the state. In Sri Lanka, strict regulations are laid out regarding the recruitment of teaching staff. According to official reports, no direct supervision of recruitment exists in Bhutan and India. No government regulations actually cover the topic as far as Bhutan is concerned – schools have full authority to hire and dismiss teachers.

Private Education in South East Asia

Private education appears to appeal to all social classes in the five countries observed in South East Asia. These were: Brunei, Malaysia, Indonesia, the Philippines, and Thailand. In Thailand, Malaysia, and the Philippines children of foreign citizens and expatriates generally go to international schools. As expected, the clientele for international schools and the most prestigious private schools are elites.

The reasons for choosing private over public schools vary considerably. The quality of education stands first in the list of choice factors. Prestige and a better quality of education are common to all five countries. Private schools are seen to be better relative to public schools, and in some cases, 'good' in absolute terms. According to our study, religion is the second most important factor in this region. Children are sent to private schools for religious reasons, particularly in Thailand, Indonesia and the Philippines. This signifies an emphasis on religious education, history of religion, and quite often stricter discipline, which is also mentioned as a reason for choosing private schools in Thailand and Indonesia. In Indonesia, this aspect is further emphasised with 'moral values' being seen as characteristic of private schools. Another reason for private school choice is the possibility of learning different languages, particularly the use of English as a medium of instruction, such as in Thailand and Indonesia. In Malaysia, private schools appear as providers of alternative choices and special programmes not available at public institutions. Proximity to home is mentioned as a criterion for choice only in the Philippines.

Financial reasons would usually stand against the choice of a private school given the practice of fee charging, with the possible exception of some religious schools and those set up by charitable institutions. The fees may be lower if the schools are aided by the government. This is the case in Thailand, Indonesia, Malaysia, and the Philippines. However, Brunei constitutes an exception inasmuch as the government encourages parents to send children to private schools through financial incentives.

Private schools fall into several different categories. Firstly, there are international schools which exist in all the countries under survey, with the exception of Brunei. Although they must respect a number of rules and come up to the minimum standards established by the government, they mostly follow a different curriculum and prepare students for different examinations than those taken in the host country. They also teach in a language different from the local language. Thus, they are somewhat outside the focus of this study.

Religious schools exist in Thailand, Indonesia, and Malaysia. They are usually founded by religious bodies and place an emphasis on the teaching of the history of religion and a core set of moral values specific to the religion in question. No specifically religious schools exist in the Islamic monarchy of Brunei since the official curriculum contains religious subjects anyway. A further category of private schools includes vocational and technical schools, and schools for pupils with special needs. Vocational private schools exist in Thailand, Indonesia, Brunei, and the Philippines. Special needs are particularly catered for in Thailand and Brunei. The greatest variety of schools, thus, appears to exist in Thailand and Indonesia.

The conditions of schooling in private schools are, as a rule, better than in public institutions, especially as far as international and private prestigious schools are concerned. These schools, in all countries, offer better facilities, a better level of teaching, and a more personalised approach and other advantages. Quite logically, the school's facilities and level of academic achievement are directly proportional to the fees charged by the school. High fees allow the school to afford lavish facilities, hire teachers to teach minor or optional subjects even to small groups, and pay higher salaries, thus attracting better or more qualified specialists. Schools with high fees can also hire a greater number of teachers, thereby having smaller study groups and, as a consequence, a more individual approach to teaching. They can also hire additional education personnel that contribute to the non-academic side of education, by, for example, inculcating a set of particular 'good' manners and social skills, and supervising and encouraging sporting activities. The reputation of these schools, once it has been established, also leads to higher parental demand allowing the school to be selective in its intake. The result is greater competition between pupils and more intense intellectual exchange leading to higher academic achievement.

However, in Indonesia, Malaysia, and Brunei the study stresses that private schools are not *necessarily* better than public ones and can occasionally be of a lower standard (see chapter by Bangay in this book for further analysis on Indonesia). The general conclusion, nevertheless, seems to be that private schools in these five countries provide a better alternative to public schools.

Curriculum. The schools in all five countries usually provide education in accordance with the curriculum prescribed by the ministries of education, at least at the elementary and secondary levels. Similarly, as a rule, students have to sit national examinations – the only difference to public schools is the administrative body in charge of organising examination sessions. In the Philippines, however, schools that have been granted academic deregulation may modify the curriculum. In Malaysia, some private schools also offer additional subjects and organise additional examinations for them. Finally, in Brunei, one of the requirements is that every private academic educational institution must teach the Malay language/Malay Islamic Monarchy as one of its subjects, in addition to any other subject or course of study taught in the schools.

Regulation. The establishment of a private school, its registration, and accreditation are governed by law in all five countries. The person or organisation proposing to set up a private education institution must submit an official application to the appropriate department in the ministry of education. Nationality restrictions apply in Thailand and the Philippines where the owner must be a national of the respective country. Religious bodies and missions are exempted from this requirement in the Philippines.

According to official reports, the application is then reviewed and evaluated. Generally, the establishment of a private school is most often based on the community's need for education, and must be in line with the local, regional, and national development plans. Unless there is a demonstrable need for a private education institution of a given kind in a given region, the application for the establishment of a private school will not be accepted by the authorities. The individuals or organisation proposing to establish a school must usually also be able to demonstrate that they have sufficient funds for the enterprise and that the grounds and buildings or planned buildings suit the minimum official requirements laid down by law. After being granted permission to open the school, the owner has the option (or the obligation, depending on the country) to register the school. Registration or accreditation means an official recognition of the fact that the school has reached a set of standards in various areas, and provides education services of recognised quality.

The official process and conditions of registration or accreditation and registered accredited status differ somewhat in each country from the process described above. Private schools must be registered in Thailand by the Private Education Commission. The same applies to Indonesia, where all private schools must be accredited by the Board of School Accreditation. Accreditation is not conducted in private primary or secondary schools in Malaysia, but is reserved for higher education. In the Philippines, it is voluntary in nature and is considered a reflection of the initiatives taken by individual private institutions to achieve standards beyond the minimum qualifications required by government regulatory agencies.

Inspection. In all five countries, regulations establishing the minimum standards regarding academic aspects and the infrastructure of a school apply. According to official reports, regular inspections are made to ensure that schools comply with the standards, except in the Philippines. In Thailand, a school is first to be inspected prior to opening. In Indonesia, the district government rather than the central government is responsible for monitoring schools' suitability and performance. However, the regulations establishing the standards are issued by the central government. In Malaysia, schools are required to establish their own quality assurance department to monitor the standards and quality of education. In addition to that, a trimestrial inspection of schools by government officials from the Ministry of Education is compulsory. Supervision is centralised in Brunei and performed by the Ministry of Education, through the Department of Schools. Similarly, basic education programmes are under the responsibility of the Department of Education in the Philippines.

According to our reports, there is regular supervision of private schools by the government in all five countries. This consists of periodical inspections, the frequency of which depends on the particular country. Inspections are conducted by inspectors from the ministry of education and are mostly concerned with the academic side of running the school, that is, qualifications of teachers, following the prescribed curriculum, availability of textbooks, and so on. In Thailand, supervision falls under the responsibility of a specific commission, the Private Education Commission. In the Philippines, a particular agency is entrusted with the supervision of each particular level of education: basic, technical and vocational, and tertiary/higher. A manual of regulations for private schools is devoted to general regulations pertaining to the operation of private schools specifically. In Malaysia, once a school has been granted approval, monitoring and government supervision are more concerned with academic aspects such as the curriculum and teachers' qualifications, rather than with facilities.

Funding and support. Governments provide support to private establishments in the form of various subsidies granted to schools. The situation in each country is different.

In Thailand, the subsidies might take the form of grants, loans, lease of property, and supply of teachers. In Indonesia, the government assigns civil servant teachers to private schools, providing teaching staff to private schools on a contractual basis. In Malaysia, government support through tax exemptions is given to private schools. Brunei's government subsidises schools by providing Malay language/Islamic religious education teachers to private schools. It also gives allowances to parents working in the government sector who send their children to private schools. In the Philippines, government support is provided by helping students enrolled in private schools. Private schools themselves almost entirely depend on fees charged to students.

Initial funding for the establishment of private schools generally has private origins, with money sometimes being invested by companies or funds coming from religious organisations. Operating costs, on the other hand, are met from two main sources: government subsidies and tuition fees. Whereas in Indonesia, Brunei, and the Philippines, funding comes from both sources, in Thailand, the majority of costs are covered by subsidies. On the other hand, in Malaysia, schools rely mostly on fees. In the Philippines more subsidies go to primary than secondary schools. In Thailand, private schools are subsidised to 60% of their operational costs, and charitable and religious schools are fully subsidised, meaning that 100% of their operational costs are taken over by the government.

Management and teaching staff. The management of private schools is independent in all five countries. The responsibility of running the schools is shared between an administrative board and an executive board or board of trustees. In Thailand, nationality restrictions apply to the management of private schools – executive managers must be Thai nationals. Teachers can be nationals of the country or expatriated foreigners. In the Philippines, nationals are treated more favourably.

Other restrictions set by the school may apply, where it is independent in establishing selection criteria for teaching staff. For example, these can be of a religious nature. An Islamic school in Indonesia will usually demand that the teacher should be Muslim, with sufficient knowledge of the Koran and of established 'good' moral character. Academic qualifications are not sufficient in this case to gain appointment.

In terms of qualifications, a bachelor's degree is usually required to teach at primary or secondary level. According to our reports, requirements are slightly lower in Brunei, where the British 'O level' certificate (awarded on successful completion of compulsory education) is required to teach up to lower secondary level. Teachers above secondary level are required to have a postgraduate degree. It is interesting to note that in Brunei requirements for overseas teachers are stricter: they must have a university degree, and preferably a master's degree. In addition to the required qualifications one year's teaching experience is demanded in Brunei and in Thailand.

Our reports show that teachers in all countries except Indonesia are appointed to a permanent position after a successful probationary period, which varies in length between six months (in Brunei) and three years (in Malaysia and the Philippines). Employment in Malaysia and Thailand, however, is subject to good performance. The situation in Indonesia is different for government civil servants who are appointed to teaching posts at private schools, and for teachers from outside the system working on a contractual basis and unlikely to achieve the permanent, civil-servant status. The latter work under a five-year contract. All countries have a pension plan for teachers of the private sector. It must be noted that there is no set retirement age in Thailand for private school teachers.

Monthly entry-level salaries varied from around US$200 in Indonesia to around US$550 in Malaysia. Salaries of teachers at mission schools located in rural areas of the Philippines were lower at US$100 per month. A bonus may be often paid, corresponding to one or two months of regular pay. This is the case in Indonesia, Malaysia, and the Philippines. Finally, there is a considerable difference in salary (more than double) in Brunei for teachers with a university degree. This may be a major incentive to improve one's qualifications as a teacher.

It is reported that teachers in all five countries enjoy a comprehensive set of various benefits and social protection. Teachers in Thailand, Malaysia, and the Philippines are provided with health insurance. In addition, life insurance is provided to Malaysian teachers and accident insurance is provided in the Philippines. Further advantages comprise loans towards various expenses incurred by teachers in relation to their job, such as housing and maintenance in the Philippines, transportation in Indonesia and the

Philippines, and computers in Malaysia. Free allowances towards uniforms are also offered in Indonesia and the Philippines. In addition, systematic training programmes designed to improve teachers' professional qualifications are organised by most schools, independently or in conjunction with the government and public schools. In the Philippines teaching staff have access to development funds to this end. Indonesia and the Philippines come out as the countries with the most developed benefits systems for private school teachers. Thailand and Malaysia offer fewer benefits, but still have a sound and developed system of social protection and benefits as regards private school staff. Very little information is available about Brunei.

Workload at private schools amounts to about 25 periods per week, which is similar to the workload at public schools, and is sometimes less. On the other hand, private school teachers may have additional workload in the form of supervision or organisation of extracurricular sporting or cultural activities in which they may be asked to take part. Teachers at well-established private schools enjoy excellent working facilities, usually better than at public schools. It is reported that pupils' performance is also usually better at private schools. The pupil–teacher ratio is usually lower at good private schools, which could make the teacher's job easier and more rewarding.

Recruitment is through open competition and is entirely the responsibility of the school's management committee. More specifically, Malaysian policy is geared towards the recruitment of foreign teachers. The recruitment of foreign teachers in Brunei, on the other hand, is more strictly monitored by the Ministry of Education.

Private Education in the Transitional Economies of Central Asia

The so-called transitional countries (former centrally planned economies), ranging from Eastern Europe and stretching across the former Soviet Union as far as Mongolia, China and Vietnam, had no traditions of private education for many decades for ideological reasons. Private schools that existed in the distant past (most often religious) were closed or nationalised by public authorities during the twentieth century. No new private schools were allowed as education became, and was, the state monopoly.

Only with market reforms and the transition to a market economy in the 1980s did private education become legally accepted by the authorities due to the public demand for more diversity. Started from scratch, its development was chaotic and context specific. The processes and developments that took place in these countries are not investigated much in the literature and require more attention.

The coverage and quality of education was already high and generally sufficient at primary and secondary levels. Primary and secondary education was free from tuition fees and totally state controlled in terms of curricula and teachers. These levels became universal and compulsory by the 1980s.

While minimal standards were respected, the curricula and teaching became too uniform and conservative, resisting experiments, innovations and improvements. The collapse of the centrally planned economic model caused rapid degradation of teaching and learning conditions. For example, school buildings required repairs and maintenance, and existing furniture, libraries, and equipment became inadequate and obsolete.

It seems that the main reason for emerging private education was not the physical conditions of schools but demand for new improved and updated curricula. Public education authorities were slow in revising the ideologically biased courses and in retraining ageing teachers. Thus, these remnants of the past Soviet model were bound to stay throughout the 1990s before a new generation of courses and teachers appeared.

Under these circumstances, private education intervened and occupied the space left by public education in terms of Westernised modern courses on demand (e.g. more emphasis on anthropology, sociology, management, law, foreign languages, informatics), while better teaching and learning conditions were an additional factor (e.g. less crowded rooms, better remuneration and more motivated teachers).

In the 1990s, the obsolete laws did not allow charging fees for compulsory primary and secondary education. Operators of private institutions had to find loopholes in legislation and get registered by district and provincial authorities. The problems with garnering starting capital were widespread. Many times, in the beginning, school spaces were rented and the teachers were those who had retired from public schools. Support from public authorities was nil or limited. By definition, these schools had to be profit making even when some had religious or alternative affiliations. In most cases, private schools had to depend exclusively on their own income generation via private sponsors and tuition and other fees. Without any previous experience or training, school operators experienced problems in marketing and management.

The correlation between family income and school choice was evident, and these schools became considered 'elitist'. Some schools could not survive a hostile environment and were closed or turned into 'fly-by-night' operations. New private schools preferred to open in areas without direct competition with existing public schools. Some of these schools, in particular at the secondary level, became a suburban phenomenon with boarding and extracurricular facilities.

The main difference between transitional economies and developing countries is that the former had almost a 100% net enrolment rate in primary and secondary education before market reforms. The issues of access and equity were not as dramatic as elsewhere. Thus, priorities for parents choosing private schools were for Westernised curricula, good discipline and, increasingly, security.

As they started from 'ground zero' in the 1990s, private schools in transitional economies looked for rapid expansion and marketing. A typical scheme involved kindergarten-primary-secondary schooling with affiliation to prestigious universities. The first cohorts paved the way to subsequent expansion. Although the number of these schools is still growing, the system has become more and more stable due to negative demographic trends in many of these countries. If private schools were competing with existing public schools, in the beginning with the saturation of demand, they have now started competing with each other.

Generally, the share of enrolment in private schools is very low, pupil–teacher ratios are favourable, and the unit costs are very high. A large number of non-teaching staff and investments in facilities add up to higher unit costs, and consequently, higher fees. The cost of fees is often out of reach even for middle-class families.

From a strategic perspective, the factors of tolerant government policy, economic growth, and related family incomes became decisive for private education development in many countries. In countries with favourable market environments and a high growth of family incomes (i.e. Russia, Kazakhstan, Kyrgyzstan, Georgia, Armenia, the Baltic States, Mongolia, and Vietnam) the developments resembled India. In countries with more centralised policies, a slower pace of market reforms, and less pronounced income disparities (i.e. Byelorussia, Uzbekistan, Turkmenistan, and Moldova) private schools had more difficulties emerging.

For example, within the last decade some private schools in Vietnam expanded from two dozen pupils to an enrolment of 1500 pupils and several campuses. The Vietnamese case is illustrative but exceptional as it can be explained by demography and previously unmet demand due to insufficient supply of public provision. Other transitional economies with high enrolment rates are still looking for an appropriate model for private education development and regulation.

Lessons Learned from the Experiences of Developing and Transitional Countries

Private education is a reality and its impact is growing around the world together with globalisation. The situation in every region and every country is so context-specific that comparisons and aggregations are extremely difficult. In South Asia, the economic boom created demand for diversity and better schooling in India. This seems to be evident by the mushrooming of for-profit private schools. However, the private sector's potential has not yet reached the neighbouring countries. In transitional countries the emergence of private education after many decades of prohibition was chaotic and is only now becoming structured and regulated.

The triangle of government policy vs. demography vs. family income seems to be decisive in the environment for private education development. It seems to be mostly an urban phenomenon targeting, so far, mostly wealthier segments of populations. It found its niche where the demand was not met by public education in terms of diversity of curricula, language of instruction, quality, or new information technologies. However, there are exceptions. Unfortunately, often there is no distinction in legal treatment by authorities between religious schools providing welfare, and for-profit schools.

The explanation for families' demand for private education is mostly diversity of courses with better links to the global education market, traditional values (often religious) linked to better discipline, and better teaching and learning conditions due to well-established infrastructure. Legal conditions for private education development were established due to demand, but this development is not financially supported by government authorities in most cases. Tuition fees and self-income generation are the sole funding sources for private schools in many cases. It seems that the market for private education development is directly linked with economic growth and family income in terms of fees.

The legislation on private education is still unclear, and in some instances, private schools are closed by the authorities for good reason. The role of the governments through respective ministries of education and other authorities should be to ensure law enforcement against corruption and mismanagement, transparent procedures for registration and accreditation, quality control and, possibly, fair competition. In the spirit of the Dakar Education for All consensus, government efforts and resources should be concentrated on provision of primary, basic, and secondary education. Other levels (e.g. pre-primary, i.e. 0-3 years old, and post-secondary, i.e. beyond 18 years old) can be subject to cost sharing and cost recovery through fee-paying educational services, either by public or private operators.

Private education is becoming a challenging segment of the education sector worldwide, and cannot be ignored. Stakeholders agree that government regulation of private education is needed. Issues such as registration, accreditation, inspection, supervision, recognition of diplomas, taxation, status of teachers and their benefits are not resolved in many countries. Even if direct government support to private education may be a sensitive subject for various reasons, a certain strategic demarcation of its role in the overall policy of education development will be essential for all parties involved (government, civil society, the private sector).

Note

[1] *Core funding* refers to the funds that support the basic educational services of the institutions. It does not include funds provided specifically for research projects, payments for services purchased or contracted by private organisations, or fees and subsidies received for ancillary services, such as accommodation and meals.

CHAPTER 6

Cinderella or Ugly Sister? What Role for Non-state Education Provision in Developing Countries?

COLIN BANGAY

Introduction

Private/non-state education has been around a long time. Indeed for most industrialised countries the evolution of state provision has drawn from the form and approaches of non-state precedents. Despite this shared heritage, there has, in recent times, been considerable debate regarding the appropriateness of private/non-government involvement in public service delivery in general and education in particular (see Tooley, 2001; Grindle, 2004). In development spheres much of this debate revolves around issues of equity and whether governments are failing in their responsibility to provide education as a basic human right through over-reliance on non-state provision.

This chapter takes as its starting point the fact that, official or unofficial, non-state provision (NSP) of education exists in all developing countries; in many it is a significant provider, and seems set to grow further as a result of an increasing and differentiated demand for education. In the light of this, an overview of the extent and diversity of NSP is provided, paying particular attention to two areas: private fee-charging schools and provision by non-governmental organisations (NGOs). The chapter explores the particular nature of these two types of delivery, and reviews their potential to contribute to national educational delivery programmes through complementary state/non-government provision with specific reference to Indonesia and Bangladesh.

The Problem of Definition

A first stage in engaging in debate is the ability to define what is meant. Obtaining clarity of what is private or non-state provision has proved problematic. Two basic parameters are evident in the majority of definitions, namely where funding is derived from and the degree of non-state managerial control. A third more intangible descriptor is also often implied, that is, the raison d'être for the school, for example, for profit, community, religious, and so on. The difficulty with applying any one of these parameters is that there are seldom absolutes, it being more a matter of degree. This is true in both the managerial and financial spheres. Across the spectrum from 'for profit' private, through faith based and secular non-government, the state either directly or indirectly exerts influence. Administratively this can take the form of minimum requirements, be they physical, financial or regarding teacher qualifications through to specification of curriculum and examinations. Financially, state contributions to the NSP encompass tax breaks and direct support to schools through mechanisms such as budgetary assistance, secondment of government teachers to non-state schools, provision of free books, and so on. The fact that the training of the majority of teachers working in the private sector is commonly paid for in part or in full by the state could also be regarded as a state subsidy of a key input into the NSP sector. Government can also exert indirect influence on NSPs via parents through initiatives such as mandatory disclosure of school performance indicators into the public domain and government-funded voucher or stipend programmes.

In the face of this heterogeneity, Kitaev has resolved the issue of definition of NSP through use of a 'catch all' contrast, defining what he terms private education as 'all formal schools that are *not* public, and may be founded, owned, managed and financed by actors other than the state, even in cases when the state provides most of the funding and has considerable control over these schools' (Kitaev, 1999, p. 43). The strength of this definition is that it encompasses the breadth of NSP in its many forms, however it does not provide a conceptual framework from which to make comparisons between individual schools or the prevailing nature of national provision. This can however be achieved through locating schools within a matrix defined by two common characteristics of managerial control and finance (see Figure 1).

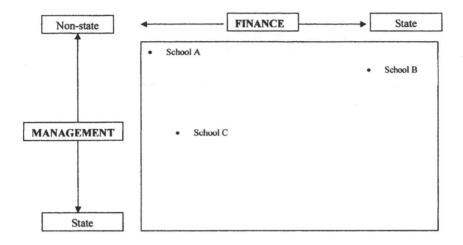

School A = High degree of financial and managerial independence (e.g. British elite private schools, Indian private unaided schools).

School B = Significant state financial support but minimal government managerial intervention (e.g. Bangladesh secondary schools).

School C = Predominant non-state finance but medium levels of government managerial regulation (e.g. Indonesian Yayasan schools, Schools in Democratic Republic of Congo).

Figure 1. Matrix to determine the nature of non-state provision.

Non-state Provision – scale and diversity

The conceptualisation above serves to illustrate the diversity that characterises every aspect of NSP. Businesses, NGOs, international NGOs, faith-based organisations such as church and *madrasah* schools, as well as individual enterprises all fall within the gamut of NSP. The motivations of providers are similarly diverse incorporating profit, philanthropic, cultural and spiritual drivers. Collectively these institutions serve throughout the community from elite private schools through to 'last/only chance schools' providing for those denied access to government provision through geography, economics and selection policies. Such diversity clearly presents problems for the development of standardised international classification of NSP. For this reason and the fact that many NSP schools do not make it onto government records it is likely that NSP is under-recorded in various international statistical digests. The significance of NSP becomes more apparent when viewed at a national level.

Throughout the developing world, country studies reveal NSP as a prominent feature in overall educational delivery – whether this be as a result of national failure of state provision such as in Haiti (Salmi, 1998) and the

113

Democratic Republic of Congo (World Bank, 2005a), unmet demand such as in Nigeria (Larbi et al, 2004, p. 11) or a combination of historic legacy and dissatisfaction with government provision and the aspirations of an emerging middle class such as in Malawi (Rose & Kadzamira, 2004, pp. 46, 48) and India (De et al, 2002, p. 134; Tooley & Dixon, 2003). It seems evident from the country examples provided that NSP warrants careful consideration in overall planning for national educational delivery. To illustrate the scale and diverse role that NSP can provide within national systems, an overview of private fee-funded schooling in Indonesia and Bangladesh is provided by way of introduction.

Private Secondary Schools in Indonesia and Bangladesh: contexts and contrast

Both Indonesia and Bangladesh rely heavily on private fee-funded schooling (legislated as not for profit in both countries) in the delivery of secondary education. World Bank figures for 2003 report the percentage of private schools in these countries at 42.9% and 96.1% respectively (World Bank, 2005b). These high levels of NS representation in part reflect a historical legacy which developed an expectation amongst the populous that education would come at a cost. Post-independence, both countries have 'nationalised' primary education. However at secondary level NSP remains significant with state government supporting NS delivery through various financing arrangements both to secular and the faith-based *madrasah* schools.

Bangladesh

Secondary education provision in Bangladesh is almost exclusively delivered by the non-state sector. However the government provides the bulk of financing through payment of 90% of teacher salaries in all recognised non-government schools (Asian Development Bank, 2004, p. 1). A clear benefit to government of this system is the reduced cost of secondary provision. As the *Bangladesh Education Sector Review* notes:

> The cost to government of one student year in a non-government school is estimated to be only about 40-45 percent of that in a government secondary school. The fact that non-government institutions enrol about 95 percent of the students at secondary level, and government pays for only between 50-70 percent of total costs, means that public funds can cover more students than if the government financed 100 percent of the costs. (World Bank, 2000, p. 61)

Another feature of this system noted in the sector review is that it facilitates local management (including the hiring of teachers) thus making it more responsive to local conditions. It could be surmised that the doubling in secondary enrolment from 3 million in 1991 to 6.1 million in 1997 (World Bank, 2000, p. 61) was in part enabled by the NS sector's 'fleet of foot' response to rapidly growing demand.

Indonesia

Indonesia has a long history of NSP, and since 1989, official policy has advocated educational delivery through a partnership between government and non-state providers. However, in contrast to Bangladesh, the nature of government support to NSP varies considerably (Bray & Thomas, 1998; Bangay, 2005). This manifests itself in a greater heterogeneity amongst Indonesian NS schools: some have national coverage (through franchise-type arrangements), a sound funding base, and manage numerous schools as well as a range of other enterprises. Others are small, localised 'family run' foundations managing one school on a 'shoestring' budget. Perhaps the most important point to note about NSP in Indonesia is that, unlike Bangladesh, for many parents there is 'choice' between private and state schooling and, as such, there is competition between the two providers. This choice is however the preserve of the more privileged in society with NSP predominantly catering for those denied access to government schooling. As an Asian Development Bank report on junior secondary education in Indonesia notes:

> Isolated rural and economically depressed areas of the country are frequently under-served by the public system. Many private SMP [junior secondary schools] were developed either to provide opportunities for further education for those unable to gain admission to, or living in areas not served by, public SMPs. Private SMPs are often the only means to provide access to junior secondary education to the poorer communities. (Asian Development Bank, 1995, p. 3)

Private Education: panacea or Pandora's box?

In a *Financial Times* article of 2003, James Tooley bemoaned the orthodoxy amongst development agents who, while recognising the contribution and performance of private schools catering for the poor, retained a position that blanket state provision was the only means to achieve education for all and did little or nothing by way of support for private schools (Tooley, 2003, p. 15). In recent times the performance of private schools has attracted growing interest and enthusiastic support in some quarters:

> Private schools can be both profitable and provide good education to students of all income levels, including the poor. They accomplish this by: (i) responding to the boom in demand for education; (ii) differentiating the product and pricing it according to the client's ability to pay; and (iii) achieving a higher degree of

115

efficiency than public schools. (Karmokolias & van Lutsenburg Maas, 1997, p. 19)

Such claims can be supported by a body of academic research from both developed and developing countries that finds in favour of private provision: Chubb & Moe (1990); Jimenez & Lockheed (1995); Berger (1996); Kingdon (1996); Tooley & Dixon (2003); Hanushek & Rivkin (2004). However, the body of existing literature is at present relatively small and as such caution is required against drawing hasty conclusions. There are many issues which require further investigation such as: the underlying conditions that may account for enhanced performance of private schools, the degree to which such findings are 'school based', and whether such findings would stand when extrapolated to a system of mixed national provision in which the dynamics of interaction between private and state schooling would come into play. Drawing on research from Indonesia and Bangladesh, the following section reviews two determinants commonly cited to explain the differences in performance of private schools over state provision: firstly, direct accountability, and through this, responsiveness to the parents; and secondly, greater cost-effectiveness. It also explores how commercial and political imperatives can influence the pattern of school expansion with particular implications for equitable access and systems efficiency.

Teacher Accountability

The case for teacher accountability is strongly made by Tooley & Dixon (2003) in their work on private schools for the urban poor in India. Citing official Indian government reports as well as the work of Drèze & Saran (1993), they identify the issue of teacher accountability as a key element in enhanced performance (Tooley & Dixon, 2003, p. 7). In essence they argue that, unlike government counterparts, private school teachers operate within a performance-related working regime and as such are parent responsive and results motivated. There is little evidence available in Indonesia to review comparative levels of teacher accountability in Indonesia. What is evident however is that constrained budgets necessitate a much higher use of part-time teachers in Indonesian private schools. These teachers are required to utilise rapid 'in and out' teaching strategies that can compromise the teaching–learning dynamic (Bangay, 2005, p. 172).

Evidence from Bangladesh does appear to support the proposition of greater teacher accountability in private schools with lower paid teachers in non-government schools being reported as more motivated than their government counterparts (Hossain et al, 2002, p. 21). However, as a counterpoint, a Government of Bangladesh report quoted within the *Bangladesh Education Sector Review* suggests community participation in school management has been marginalised by the high levels of government subsidy – which has both weakened teacher accountability to school management committees and had detrimental effects on school management committee activity (World Bank, 2000, p. 70). Of perhaps greater concern in the Bangladeshi context is the impact that the widespread practice of private tuition has on teacher performance. The lucrative nature of this work does little to encourage teacher efforts to maximise learning achievement during school time. Rather it creates an incentive amongst those teachers who undertake after-hours private tuition to ensure students under their tutorage outperform their classmates as a means of demonstrating the value of household investment in such services.

Management Efficiency

A number of studies have concluded that private schools have a comparative advantage in terms of efficiency, cost-effectiveness and responsive management. In a multi-country study, Jimenez & Lockheed report lower unit costs in private schools compared to state counterparts (Jimenez & Lockheed, 1995, p. 6). Berger's comments on private primary schooling in Indonesia support this contention (Berger, 1996). A further observation from Indonesia is that the pattern of expenditure between private and state schools also differs with private schools investing a greater proportion of total costs on non-salary inputs into the teaching process (Bray & Thomas, 1998, p. 59). In both Indonesia and Bangladesh it would also seem safe to conclude that day-to-day school management – particularly in relation to staff recruitment – is more streamlined in private schools. However, while initial findings suggest that there are beneficial lessons to be learned from the management processes occurring within private schools, the existing body of knowledge is still limited and fragmentary. Caution is required in assuming that identified positive features of private educational management and efficiency hold true in all cases. A case in point is Bangladesh, where the lack of a clear linkage between receiving government funding and enhanced school performance combined with minimal scrutiny of teacher recruitment, has encouraged the ascendancy of nepotistic and financial motivations (job purchase) above the meritocratic.

School Location

In schools in which fees play an important component of school budget the relationship between student numbers and overhead cost is crucial. In both Bangladesh and Indonesia financial dependence on school fees is widespread. In effect fee income determines the ability of private schools to be both commercially viable and exploit cost advantages to deliver quality education. A 'catch-22' relationship comes into play. That is, low enrolment results in higher per student cost to achieve a minimum level of quality; however, raising fees to improve quality runs the risk of inducing drop-out, reducing enrolment, and therefore, income. Thus, ensuring that the school catchment area has the necessary threshold of student numbers and parents with requisite disposable income to sustain schools at the desired level, becomes critical.

The impact of this relationship can be seen clearly in both Indonesia and Bangladesh. In Bangladesh, though efforts have been made to enforce regulations regarding school establishment, decisions over school location remain with the school owner. Their decision making is logically governed by the combination of number of students and ability of parents to pay fees. This has resulted in inequitable provision particularly in rural areas. Conversely in the commercially more promising areas a government report quoted in the *Education Sector Review* states: 'It has been observed in recent years that new high schools are being established in areas which are already served by similar other institutions. This has resulted in a proliferation of non-viable sub-standard institutions' (World Bank, 2000, p. 65).

Indonesia also faces challenges with school location and equitable access. However in comparison to Bangladesh the situation is further complicated by competition between state and non-state schooling and the political exigencies of the ongoing decentralisation process. To recap on pertinent points previously detailed: 1. Indonesian national government policy is to share the financial cost of educational provision between government and private provision; 2. the private sector is a major provider of post-primary education; 3. in general government schooling would be the first-choice option for the majority of parents.

There is an evident tension in this combination of factors. While urban areas offer the best potential for private schools, pervasive parental aspirations are to send their children to government schools. This is brought into sharp focus in the current period of rapid decentralisation and democratisation. It appears that the areas of greatest potential for private schools, that is, densely populated urban and suburban areas, are also the areas where the greatest political pressure for increased government school provision is being exacted. Any resulting urbanised expansion of government schooling could be expected to undermine the viability of urban private schools as students move from private to government schools, the end result being state investment funding a transfer of students between private and state schools without making any impact in expanding educational provision, most particularly in less well-served rural areas (see Bangay, 2005). The phenomenon of 'crowding out' of private schools is not solely confined to Indonesia. Sakellariou & Patrinos (2004, p. 27) also identify its occurrence in Ivory Coast and cite the Philippines as another example of its incidence. Suggesting it is a broader consideration for those seeking to ensure the relative contributions of both sectors are managed for the national good.

In looking at the various research studies on private schooling the issues of performance accountability and school location converge. For many of the research studies identified as "pro-private", the underlying driver identified as accounting for positive attributes such as enhanced levels of accountability and efficiency. This, in turn, infers that parents have a degree of choice in school selection. Unfortunately this is seldom the case, but where it does occur it is predominantly found in urban areas. On this point, it is interesting to note that the majority of studies into private education provision in developing countries have been conducted in urban locations. (This is not surprising given that for private schools fee income is a major determinant of commercial viability and consequently the urban environment is more attractive both in terms of demographics and economic stratification.)

While not wishing to detract from the undoubted achievements of private schools in developing countries, it does not seem unreasonable to infer from the available evidence that private schools do require specific environments to thrive. Such conditions are most commonly found in urban areas. Conversely, in the absence of subsidy, the potential of private schools to fund quality improvement over the long term in low-population-density rural areas will be constrained by their low enrolment. If found to hold true, this presents some interesting policy dilemmas for governments seeking to share the financial burden of educational provision through greater participation of the private sector in educational delivery.

NGOs' Schooling – supplement or complement?

As is clear from Kitaev's (1999) definition, NSP is not limited to private fee-dependent schooling. NGO provision constitutes the second broad form of NSP. Like private schools there is great diversity in NGOs in terms of size, scope, approach, funding, and so on, however what distinguishes NGOs in developing countries from private provision is that: firstly, they generally operate in a programmatic way rather than running individual schools and secondly, they are able to offer education at a subsidised monetary cost (though they may require contributions in kind). As with private fee-dependent schools there are interesting questions that emerge regarding NGO provision including the nature of the relationship between NGO and state provision and to whom NGOs are accountable. Again Bangladesh provides an interesting example to explore these questions as NGOs play a significant role in the primary sector.

Bangladeshi NGOs and in particular the Bangladesh Rural Advancement Committee (BRAC) have a distinguished record in the innovative provision of education services to large significant percentages of the nation's poor (Wils et al, 2005, p. 41). As Hossain et al (2002) note: 'In terms of coverage and presence in rural areas in the early 1990s, then BRAC was comparable to the state education system. There were points during the early 1990s when there were quite possibly more NGO schools than there were state schools' (Hossain et al, 2002, p. 11). Commenting on BRAC's education work, Manzoor (1993) identifies the following as determinants for the NGO's success: a simplified curriculum focused on learners' needs, paraprofessional teachers selected from the local community (but provided with a comprehensive and ongoing teacher training programme), active community and parental involvement engendered through: flexible timetabling, reduced cost and cooperative planning (Manzoor, 1993, p. 123). He notes that while BRAC and government per student costs are equivalent, the achievement and retention rates amongst BRAC students were higher (Manzoor, 1993, p. 116). The explanation provided for this outcome was that in contrast to government investment, BRAC spent less on salaries but more on management, supervision and training.

The combination of BRAC's broad coverage and proven results have clearly not gone unnoticed by government, citizenry or the donor community. How this success has influenced the behaviour of these actors is very different and has generated interesting speculation. For the donors the response to BRAC's performance has been to increase funding levels to a point where BRAC could be regarded as in direct competition with the government for aid dollars. The fact that BRAC schools outperform those of the government must also be of some concern in government circles. In writing on the prominence of NGOs in Bangladesh both White (1999) and Hossain et al (2002) suggest that the state could be regarded as in competition with the NGO sector for both donor resources and political legitimacy amongst the people. Writing specifically on education, they go further to infer that competition, particularly for political legitimacy, has acted as a spur for government primary expansion (Hossain et al, 2002, p. 12). Moreover, picking up observations by White, Hossain et al (2002) also tentatively speculate that 'the "threat of the positive example", from NGOs or other providers of education, may well provide the strongest spur to the quality reforms now so urgently required' (p. 23).

While BRAC's success may be viewed as motivating a competitive drive for both educational expansion and improved quality, concerns have been expressed regarding its potential impact on accountability. In contrast to private fee-dependent schools where 'short route' accountability (direct customer–service provider relationship) between parent and school is prevalent, NGOs are organisations – thus there is inevitably greater distance between management and client. The very success of NGOs in Bangladesh has given them access to substantial donor funding enhancing both their power and autonomy. In such circumstances to whom are the NGOs accountable? To take this argument to its extreme form a situation could be envisaged in which the role of a democratically elected state government in education is supplanted by a large NSP sector mandated through donor financing. Though this is clearly not the case in present-day Bangladesh, concerns have been expressed about the influence of NGOs on government policy and initiative. As Chowdhury et al (2004, p. 13) note: 'The large NGE [Non Government Education] sector in Bangladesh clearly fits the pattern of "gap filling" by non-state providers in response to state weakness. It is interesting to speculate however how far this gap filling is desirable in the long-run'.

While it may be interpreted that NGO provision of education in Bangladesh is relieving pressure on government commitment to education, it is also evident that NGO provision is by its very nature different in a range of areas: scale, approach, technical capacity and flexibility regarding employment conditions. The elements to which the success of NGO provision is attributed may not be replicable within the government system – a point similarly made by Jellema & Archer (1997) on the potential for upscaling successful non-formal education programmes facilitated by ACTION AID. It would appear then that, in general, NGOs provide a differentiated service tailored to the needs of specific groups. In contrast, governments seldom have the flexibility, resources, or relationships with the communities to respond to needs in a similar manner. As such, the issue of NSP by NGOs cannot be regarded as simply one of replacement of NGO activity by that of government. This does not however negate the important question of where NGO legitimacy is derived from and to whom they are ultimately accountable.

Where Now?

As has been shown, NSP in its myriad forms is already a major provider of education services in developing countries. It would also seem safe to conclude that the role of NSP in meeting educational demand will increase, though the nature and drivers of such growth will be country specific. For example, in countries with emerging middle classes one might expect the growth of private for-profit institutions, and, as a response to globalisation, particularly those that offer access to internationally recognised examinations. Of greater significance will be the role of NSP in attaining the Education for All fast-track initiative targets of reaching the last 10%, as well as meeting growing demand for secondary education (the United Nations estimates that since 1990 global secondary enrolment has risen by 3% per year [UNESCO, 2005, p. 11]). Assuming that per student expenditure is maintained at a constant level, both endeavours will require significant increases in funding. How then are governments with constrained financial resources and competing demands for national spending going to respond to this increasing demand for education without encouraging new partnerships in both finance and delivery?

In the coming years the challenge of educational provision in developing countries seems set to grow in complexity. Governments will not only have to confront the issue of the relative financing of education but also who is best placed to deliver. It is stressed this does not mean wholesale withdrawal of the state from elements of educational provision. As Grindle notes: 'government ministries and agencies are at the centre of service provision, whether they actually deliver the services or not ... Indeed, for non-traditional service provision to be any more than haphazard and stop gap, considerable regulation, oversight, and funding by government is required' (Grindle, 2004, p. 9). Future educational challenges do however suggest a changing role for the state in which the preoccupation with direct state provision is tempered and greater efforts are invested in ensuring the state becomes the national guardian of quality, equity, and efficacy. In effect the government must become an effective arbiter of outcomes and access across all educational providers.

The challenges of changing the *raison d'être* of state educational administrations are not insignificant particularly given the ideologically charged nature of this area. For some countries public acknowledgement of diversified national provision incorporating NSP may be politically difficult as it may be construed as a failure of the state to deliver on its education manifesto. At a more practical level protecting the entitlement of all children to an education of a defined minimum quality whether they attend state or non-state schools will be an exacting task. For state education administrations to be effective in this expanded role requires improved data collection, management and analysis as well as a culture of informed decision making based upon data use. Established national standards and improved educational management information systems (EMIS) are not of themselves enough. The critical task is not just identifying underperformance but addressing it. This presents additional challenges in situations where the school is not under direct control of the state. In order to exploit the potential of NSP to contribute to the looming challenges of educational delivery, state administrations will need to develop the apparatus through which they can monitor issues of access and performance for all schools as well as have the leverage and influence to promote desired outcomes. National governments have three basic realms through which to influence NSP: finance, legal regulation and information (see Table I). These are reviewed below.

While the need for regulations, particularly those that set out the performance standards against which schools should be measured, is undisputed, for state bureaucracies it does appear that invoking regulatory controls is the common first and often only line of response to NSP. All too often regulations pertaining to NSP are limited to the meeting of set criteria, often heavily biased towards physical attributes at start-up. The effectiveness of regulations, however well intentioned and formulated, is determined to a large extent by the capacity of any state to conduct competent inspections and engender or enforce compliance. Too often the proliferation of regulation proves detrimental in that it consumes inordinate amounts of time and diverts attention from in-school processes. As the Bangladesh Education Review citing a government report notes:

> Inspection does not serve to identify weaknesses in quality or to work out remedial plans. A 1992 survey found that inspection was only concerned with academic supervision in 10 percent of cases. Granting or renewing recognition was the major purpose of

inspection with 70 percent frequency. Another 15 percent dealt with enquiries about allegations. (World Bank, 2000, p. 68)

FINANCIAL: Financial incentives and conditions *Influencing NSP through financial mechanisms*	*Incentives* Tax incentives Voucher systems, student stipends Direct school budgetary support Indirect budgetary support: e.g. secondment of government teachers, provision of free textbooks Low-cost leasing of school facilities to NSP completely for times of low utilisation such as holidays/evenings Contracting out educational services to NSP *Regulatory tools* Fee caps Minimum capital provision requirements for NSP Contracts
REGULATION: Establishing minimum requirements *Pre-condition:* *Effective inspection and enforcement capacity*	*Incentives* Support in meeting minimum standards Access to national exams Unimpeded movement of students between state and non-state providers Support through access to inspection/advisory services *Regulatory tools* Accreditation through: minimum requirements: teacher qualifications, facilities available, class sizes, curriculum taught, textbooks used, etc.
INFORMATION: Promoting accountability through disclosure *Pre-condition:* *Effective EMIS* Effective disclosure mechanisms – easily interpreted by parents	Empowering 'consumers' through the disclosure of school performance as a means of enhancing accountability

Table I. Mechanisms available to government for the support, regulation and development of non-state provision.

Reliance on complex regulatory regimes, particularly in the face of a limited capacity to inspect, would not seem to hold the answer to promoting a coalescence of objectives and standards between state and non-state. Indeed there is evidence that such practices can actually prove counter-productive. Tooley & Dixon's (2003) research in India is testament to the pitfalls of a repressive regulatory regime that, rather than assures quality of service, promotes 'gate keeping' opportunities for corrupt officials (Tooley & Dixon, 2003, pp. 17-18).

It seems clear that regulatory regimes alone are unlikely to provide the state with the means by which it can assure standards. There is, therefore, a need to develop more subtle means through which the state can encourage NSP growth and build trust while retaining influence over national standards. A proven approach to encouraging desired outcomes is to use incentives, in particular monetary ones. The utility of creating a regime of financial mechanisms that incentivises desirable outcomes and dissuades others is that, when well constructed, it does not require the levels of policing and inspection that other regimes may require. However, while the developing financial/performance-related incentives may be relatively straightforward, the political implications of implementing them may not be. In this respect it is interesting to note that though the percentage of government funding for teacher salaries has risen from 70% to 90% in the last decade there has been no concomitant attempt on the government's part to link this to improved performance.

An area receiving significant attention in recent years, particularly since the publication of the World Development report of 2004 (World Bank, 2003) is the use of accountability mechanisms to promote improved public service delivery. A range of initiatives including the publishing of school performance in national tests and school inspection reports in the United Kingdom, disclosure of school budget information (see Reinikka & Smith, 2004, on Uganda), performance 'score cards' (see Karim, 2004, on Bangladesh), and the introduction of school voucher programmes in Chile and Columbia have all been undertaken to this end.

At the core of these initiatives is the desire to mobilise the public as end users to exact pressure on service providers to improve performance. The dramatic results of disclosure and accountability measures are evident, such as in Uganda, where the percentage loss of per student funding designated for schools was reduced from 80% to 20% largely as a result of a public disclosure campaign (World Bank, 2003, p. 63). However, such improvements are dependent on the collection, use and most importantly disclosure of information in a form that is accessible and whose relevance is clearly understood by the public. Neither of these tasks are particularly easy. Data collection and use is notoriously problematic in developing countries. Putting aside issues related to ensuring information is accessible, there are legitimate concerns about using information disclosure to generate momentum for enhanced performance, not least the fact that raw scores quantify outcome but these reflect as much the inputs into a school as the process that takes place within it.

Conclusion

In the light of financial and demographic realities it seems certain that governments will increasingly need to call upon other partners to assist in the financing and delivery of education. Changing attitudes to educational finance are already apparent. Bray & Bunly (2005) suggest that until recently the pervasive view, informed by successive international declarations of rights, has been that public education should be free of charge. However, this assumption has been challenged by research on tertiary education indicating free, state provision can still be iniquitous and therefore is not necessarily appropriate (Bray & Bunly, 2005, pp. 7-8). Debate regarding the extent to which private contributions to education should be related to anticipated individual returns (e.g. earning capacity in later life), and at what level of education such contributions should be sought continue – however this is only one element. The issue of NSP and reformulating the role of the state is broader than this.

It seems certain that in the coming years the division between state and non-state is likely to blur further with government schools requiring household contributions, state funds subsidising private education, and government and/or donors supporting NGO provision. Given existing levels of NSP and what Kitaev has aptly termed the 'disappearing difference' (Kitaev, 1999, p. 69) between state and NSP, it is perhaps time to explore the role of NSP from a more pragmatic viewpoint. For this to happen it will require politicians, policy makers, and educational planners to reflect upon their assumptions regarding NSP particularly with regard to the degree that they are informed (and possibly constrained) by the experiences of Western industrialised countries. As Bloom (2004), writing on non-state healthcare, notes:

> One characteristic of discussions about strategies for the provision of services to poor people has been the persistence of ideological debates about the relative roles of public and private sectors. These debates are strongly influenced by the experiences of the advanced market economies and often do not reflect the reality of countries where most poor people live. (Bloom, 2004, p. 4)

The task of a contemplative review of the relationship between state and NSP is perhaps both most challenging and pertinent for donors. In conclusion, it is perhaps worth reflecting on donor interaction with the two broad categorisations of NSP reviewed in this chapter, namely private fee-dependent schools and NGO schools. Regarding the former, the private fee-dependent sector has often remained 'off radar' (even when a prominent provider). Undoubtedly, this is partly due to the fact that donors traditionally interact at state government level, with the mandates of some precluding support other than through central government. In addition, dialogue can only take place if a representative and legitimate voice for private fee-paying schools is present. This, for a variety of reasons, is not always the case. However, despite these observations there is still a sense that private fee-paying schools (whether for the elite or the disadvantaged) have too often been regarded as the 'ugly sisters' at Cinderella's ball.

In donor-funded sector reviews the private sector has only recently begun to attract serious attention. Consequently discussion regarding the appropriateness of supporting in situ those students in fee-dependent schools (even when they are the most disadvantaged) is rare. In contrast, a much more accommodating attitude appears prevalent with regard to NGOs. In many instances they have rightly been lauded for their targeted and innovative initiatives that serve the more disadvantaged sections of society. Consequently donors have extended assistance and financial support often at significant levels, such as in Bangladesh. However worthy, there is an issue here for donors. It is important that their support does not intentionally or inadvertently bypass government education administration and create a parallel yet unconnected system of provision with unclear lines of accountability. For if governments are to take on the role of arbiters of quality, they must have access to the basic input and output data from all school types in order to have a truly comprehensive national EMIS. Only through such a system can national government manage the dynamic between state and non-state providers, take remedial action in the instances of underperformance, and promote greater accountability at local level.

References

Asian Development Bank (1995) *Report and Recommendation of the President to the Board of Directors on a Proposed Loan for the Private Junior Secondary Education.* Manila: ADB.

Asian Development Bank (2004) *Report and Recommendation of President to the Board of Directors on a Proposed Loan to the People's Republic of Bangladesh for the Teacher Quality Improvement in Secondary Education Project.* Manila: ADB. http://www.adb.org/Documents/RRPs/Ban/rrp-ban-26061.pdf

Bangay, C. (2005) Private Education: relevant or redundant? Private Education, Decentralisation and National Provision in Indonesia, *Compare*, 35(2), pp. 167-180.

Berger, M.C. (1996) Commentary on Finance, Management and Costs of Public and Private Schools in Indonesia. Do Local Contributions Affect the Efficiency of Public Primary Schools? *Economics of Education Review*, 15(4), pp. 399-400.

Bloom, G. (2004) *Private Provision in Its Institutional Context: lessons from health.* DFID Health Systems Resource Centre. London: Department for International Development.

Bray, M. & Bunly, S. (2005) *Balancing the Books: household financing in basic education in Cambodia*. Hong Kong: Comparative Education Research Centre, University of Hong Kong.

Bray, M. & Thomas, R.M (Eds) (1998) *Financing of Education in Indonesia*. Hong Kong: Asian Development Bank, Comparative Education Research Centre, University of Hong Kong.

Chowdhury, A.F., Delay, S., Faiz, N., Haider, I., Reed, B., Rose, P. & Sen, P. (2004) *Main Report on Non-state Providers in Bangladesh*. Birmingham: International Development Department, School of Public Policy, University of Birmingham.

Chubb, J.E. & Moe, T.M. (1990) *Politics, Markets and Schools*. Washington, DC: The Brookings Institution.

De, A., Majumdar, M., Samson, M. & Noronha, C. (2002) Private Schools and Universal Elementary Education, in R. Govinda (Ed.) *India Education Report: a profile of basic education*. Delhi: Oxford University Press.

Drèze, J. & Saran, M. (1993) *Primary Education and Economic Development in China and India: overview of two case studies*. Discussion Paper No. 47, Development Economic Research Programme, STICERD, London School of Economics, London.

Grindle, M.S. (2004) *First in the Queue? Mainstreaming the Poor in Service Delivery*. Princeton: Princeton University Press.

Hanushek, E.A. & Rivkin, S.G. (2004) Does Public School Competition Affect Teacher Quality? in C.M. Hoxby (Ed.) *The Economics of School Choice*. Chicago: University of Chicago Press.

Hossain, N., Sunrahmanian, R. & Kabeer, N. (2002) *The Politics of Educational Expansion in Bangladesh*. IDS Working Paper No. 167. Falmer: Institute of Development Studies, Sussex University.

Jellema, A. & Archer, D. (1997) Critical Reflections on Strategies for Including the Marginalised in Quality Education. Paper presented at the 1997 Oxford Conference, September.

Jimenez, E. & Lockheed, M.E. (1995) *Public and Private Secondary Education in Developing Countries: a comparative study*. World Bank Discussion Paper No. 309. Washington, DC: World Bank.

Karim, S. (2004) *Transparency in Education: report card in Bangladesh*. Paris: International Institute for Educational Planning, UNESCO.

Karmokolias, Y. & van Lutsenburg Maas, J. (1997) *The Business of Education: a look at Kenya's private education sector*. Discussion Paper 32. Washington, DC: International Finance Corporation.

Kingdon, G. (1996) The Quality and Efficiency of Private and Public Education: a case of urban India, *Oxford Bulletin of Economics and Statistics*, 58(1), pp. 57-82.

Kitaev, I. (1999) *Private Education in Sub Saharan Africa: a re examination of theories and concepts related to its development and finance*. Paris: IIEP.

Larbi, G., Adelabu, M., Rose, P., Jawara, D., Nwaorgu, O. & Vyas, S. (2004) *Main Report on Non-state Providers in Nigeria*. Birmingham: International Development Department, School of Public Policy, University of Birmingham.

Manzoor, A. (1993) *Primary Education for All: learning from the BRAC experience. A Case Study*, ed. C.J. Prather. Washington, DC: Abel.

Reinikka, R. & Smith, N. (2004) *Public Expenditure Tracking Surveys in Education*. Paris: International Institute for Educational Planning, UNESCO.

Rose, P. & Kadzamira, E. (2004) Non State Provision of Basic Education in Malawi: annex two, in E. Kadzamira, D. Moran, J. Mulligan, N. Mdirenda, K. Nthara, B. Reed & P. Rose (Eds) *Malawi: study of non state providers of basic services*. Birmingham: International Development Department, School of Public Policy, University of Birmingham.

Sakellariou, C. & Patrinos, H.A. (2004) *Incidence Analysis of Public Support to the Private Education Sector in Cote d'Ivoire*. World Bank Policy Research Working Paper No. 3231. Washington, DC: World Bank.

Salami, J. (1998) *Equity and Quality in Private Education: the Haitian paradox*. World Bank LCSHD Paper Series, No. 18. Washington, DC: World Bank.

Tooley, J. (2001) Serving the Needs of the Poor: the private education sector in developing countries, in C.R. Hepburn (Ed.) *Can the Market Save Our Schools?* Vancouver: Fraiser Institute.

Tooley, J. (2003) Private Schools Can Bring Education for All, *Financial Times*, 29 October, p. 15.

Tooley, J. & Dixon, P. (2003) *Private Schools for the Poor: a case study from India*. Reading: CfBT.

UNESCO (1995) Boom in Secondary Education, *Education Today*, No. 13, April-June, p. 8.

White, S. (1999) NGOs, Civil Society, and the State in Bangladesh: the politics of representing the poor, *Development and Change*, 30(2), pp. 307-326.

Wils, A., Carrol, B. & Barrow, K. (2005) *Educating the World's Children: patterns of growth and inequity*. Washington, DC: Education Policy and Data Centre, AED/US Agency for International Development.

World Bank (2000) *Bangladesh Education Sector Review. Volume Two*. Dhaka: The University Press.

World Bank (2003) *World Development Report 2004: making services work for poor people*. New York: Oxford University Press.

World Bank (2005a) *Education in the Democratic Republic of Congo: priorities and options for regeneration*. Washington, DC: World Bank.

World Bank (2005b) *World Bank Edstats*, http://www1.worldbank.org/education/edstats

CHAPTER 7

Universalising Elementary Education in India: is the private sector the answer?

SANTOSH MEHROTRA & P.R. PANCHAMUKHI

Introduction

In India, the state has been the main provider and financier of elementary education.[1] However, the private sector has always been present, and is a growing phenomenon. The objective of this chapter is to examine the private sector in elementary education in India and compare its characteristics with the government school system, drawing on a survey based on a representative sample in eight major states. Seven of the eight states account for three-quarters of the country's children out of school. These are mostly contiguous northern states: Rajasthan, Madhya Pradesh, Uttar Pradesh, Bihar, West Bengal, Assam, and Andhra Pradesh on the south-east coast. We also selected one relative high-achieving state, Tamil Nadu.

First, the chapter briefly presents an overview of enrolment in different types of schools based on all-India data (as opposed to just the eight states). Then it analyses private schools and government-run schools in the eight selected states. This section focuses on locational (urban/rural), gender and social equity in the coverage of private and government schools in these states. Next, the quality of school facilities in private and government schools in these states is examined, focusing first on the physical facilities and then on human resources. Following this, outcome and process indicators (e.g. working days, attendance rates, drop-out rates, out-of-pocket costs) in private and government schools are presented. The final section summarises the findings and briefly discusses some policy implications.

Significance and Characteristics of
the Private Sector in Elementary Education

We identify essentially four types of schools in India:

- government schools, including those run by local bodies;
- private schools, aided by the government;
- private unaided schools (recognised by government);
- private unaided schools (unrecognised by the government).

Government schools are wholly financed by each state's government. They have a uniform curriculum, timetable, school hours, and textbooks. Teachers are hired and allocated to individual schools by the department of education of the state. Government-aided schools in the private sector finance their own initial and ongoing capital costs but are given government funds to cover salaries of all teachers and recurrent spending on non-teacher inputs. In all other respects, they are similar to government schools, following the same curriculum, syllabus, textbooks, and eligibility criteria for teacher recruitment. Teachers in government and aided schools are part of the civil service, and salary scales are linked to the civil service pay structure. As long as these private schools are unaided, they set salaries independently of the government. Once they become government aided, salaries are based on government schoolteacher salary sales (Kingdon, 1996; Bashir, 1997).

Unaided schools are entirely self-financing. This sub-sector is highly segmented. At one end of the spectrum are the private schools patronised by the elite of the country, run (often but not always) by Christian missionary institutions and surviving from colonial times. This elite sub-sector has expanded enormously in response to the growth of the middle class. Then there is the rest of the unaided sector, which has grown largely in response to demand in the post-colonial period from an emerging lower middle and middle class. Much of the discussion in this chapter on unaided schools will be confined to this segment.

In the first category, the medium of instruction is almost always English and fees are so high that the schools can only be patronised by the upper, upper-middle and, increasingly, the nouveau-riche middle classes. In the second category, most schools offer English as a subject, while often advertising themselves as English medium (Probe Team, 1999; De et al, 2001; Majumdar, 2001; Nambissan, 2001). In this context, it is relevant that government schools do not normally introduce English until sixth grade, though this is changing (e.g. Uttar Pradesh now introduces it from fourth grade, and Kerala from third grade).

Unrecognised schools may often not even be registered by the government, and therefore, face no requirements or regulations whatsoever. They are required to be registered though some may not be in practice. In addition, they should meet certain minimum standards in order to be recognised by the government. In many cases, the state government may not even be aware of their existence. Since the unrecognised schools are not affiliated to the department of education nor registered with any agency, it is difficult to generate a master list of these schools (Agarwal, 2000). Given the mixed management and funding structure of private aided schools, it is the unaided recognised and unrecognised schools that can be referred to as purely private schools.

The lifecycle of a private school in India consists of different stages, starting as an unrecognised school, often converting to a recognised school after a few years, in some cases being accepted as a recipient of a government subsidy, that is, as a recognised aided school. Since independence, there has been a nexus between grants-in-aid, politics and private schools. In fact, in India elected members of local bodies (i.e. politicians) are often keen to start a private elementary school and to make it an aided school in their constituency; elected members of a state legislature strive to start a private college and make it an aided institution; while a member of the national parliament is often interested in starting a private university in his/her jurisdiction and getting it funded through the state government and the University Grants Commission. This vividly describes the Indian situation on how private educational institutions are keen to get the status of an aided institution. This also shows heavy dependence of private educational institutions on the government.

The purely private sector (unrecognised and unaided schools) is in urgent need of greater regulation, in order to improve quality in such schools. One important need for regulation arises from the urgency to contain the practice of converting private schools into government-aided ones, which drains government resources and subsidises those parents who are willing and able to pay (see Tilak & Sudarshan, 2000; Kingdon & Muzammil, 2003; Mehrotra et al, 2005 for an elaboration of this argument). Some changes have already occurred in this regard, for example, Uttar Pradesh is no longer converting unaided to aided schools. While at the primary level, the share in India of total enrolment in government-dependent private schools is 15% compared to 10.6% in other developing countries for which data exist, at the lower secondary level (called upper primary or junior in India), the share of such schools in enrolment is much higher than not only OECD but also other developing countries, at 10.8% (Organisation for Economic Cooperation and Development/UNESCO, 2002).

Since Indian states offer government subsidy without requiring any performance guarantees, the decision to convert unaided schools to aided schools has serious efficiency and equity effects. Since private unaided schools are mushrooming as a response to the dysfunctionality of government schools, it does not make sense for state governments to convert private unaided schools to aided schools.

Enrolment increased sharply in the 1990s, and is thought to be nearly universal. The gross enrolment ratio in the most educationally backward states, even in rural areas, is high: 93% in Andhra Pradesh, 92% in Bihar, 98% in Madhya Pradesh, and 103% in Uttar Pradesh (Srivastava, R., 2005).

The top priority now is to improve quality in government schools, rather than divert scarce government resources to the 'nationalisation' of private schools, which do not appear to be responding to excess demand, but to the justified parental perception that government schools are dysfunctional.

Historically, Kerala used private schools by aiding them, in order to expand access to schooling, as did Tamil Nadu. However, given the fiscal constraints of the state governments, this pattern may be difficult to replicate now. More importantly, access is less of an issue now, as enrolment has grown sharply in all states since the 1990s, including the poorest ones (Mehrotra et al, 2005).

Findings from Past Surveys on the Private Sector

Periodic surveys by the National Council for Research and Training (NCERT) (of 1973, 1978, 1986, 1993) enable us to establish that the private sector's share in the number of schools as well as enrolment grew over 1973-93. For primary schools in rural areas, the government school share in the *number of schools* remained roughly constant, at around 95%. In urban areas, however, while the government share declined, the private unaided schools' share in the *number of schools* went on increasing over those two decades (from around 10 to about 22% at primary level, and from 8 to about 31% at upper primary level). The share of private aided schools also declined, but less so (from around 18 to 10% at primary level, and from 22 to 17% at upper primary level). Only at upper primary level has the share of government schools increased in rural areas (from 80 to about 88%). However, it has declined in urban areas.

With respect to *enrolment*, the story is quite similar. At primary level, the government share in total enrolment remained at around 90% in rural areas, while the private unaided sector's share increased marginally. In urban areas, at primary level, the government sector's share in enrolment fell from about 63 to 50%; the private aided sector's share fell slightly from about 26-28% (28% for boys, 26% for girls) to about 22%. Meanwhile, the private unaided segment has gone on increasing its share: from 9% in 1973 to 27% in 1993 for boys, and from 8 to 23% for girls.

At upper primary level, the story is similar only in the sense that the share of private unaided schools in enrolment has gone on increasing, but mainly in urban areas, while in rural areas, the increase is marginal. Just as the share of government schools in terms of numbers of schools has increased, similarly, the share of government schools in enrolment has also increased in rural areas (from 60 to 69% for rural boys, and 53 to 66% for rural girls)[2] while that of private aided ones has declined slightly in rural areas. In urban areas, the increase in the share of private unaided schools in enrolment is sharp: from 11% for urban boys to 20%; and from 6% for urban girls to 17%.[3]

The NCERT survey does not cover unrecognised schools.[4] As previously mentioned, the real private sector in elementary and secondary education consists of two categories: (a) the private recognised schools not aided by government; and (b) the unrecognised schools (which, by definition, are private). State-wise data on the size of this private sector are available from the National Sample Survey Organisation (NSSO) (1998) survey (52nd Round, 1995-96). The data are available for the 16 major Indian states that account for most of the country's population. We analysed these data to take into account enrolment in unrecognised schools and to gauge the extent of the true private sector, and then ranked the states by the size of the real private sector in primary education in descending order (Panchamukhi & Mehrotra, 2005). Size was defined as the share of all children attending primary schools.

Several interesting phenomena were observed. Firstly, the states that account for the highest private enrolment are Andhra Pradesh, Bihar, Haryana, Punjab and Uttar Pradesh.[5] It is remarkable that over two-fifths of all children in Haryana, one in three children in Punjab and Uttar Pradesh, and between a fifth to a quarter of all children in Andhra Pradesh and Bihar go to private schools at the primary level. On the other hand, the share of the real private sector falls in all the major states slightly for the upper primary stage.

We know that while Haryana and Punjab have the highest per capita state domestic product (SDP) of any state, the remaining three have among the lowest SDPs per capita. Secondly, the states that have the lowest SDP per capita (Andhra Pradesh, Bihar, and Uttar Pradesh) are among the ones that account for two-thirds of the children out of school in India (along with Rajasthan, Madhya Pradesh, and West Bengal).

In addition, there is clearly a difference in the kind of clientele served by various types of schools. The majority of children in government schools are drawn from the poorest households, and are likely to be first-generation learners. Between the private aided and unaided, NSSO survey data suggest that most children are in private aided schools (except in a few states like Andhra Pradesh, Bihar, Haryana, Punjab, and Uttar Pradesh), which, as we saw, are largely like government schools. Private aided schools tend to be located in bigger villages and semi-urban areas, and thus, serve a slightly more prosperous clientele. By and large, the unaided high schools are increasingly serving the lower middle classes and the better-off farmers in rural areas in general (Bashir, 1994). In addition, private unaided schools are mushrooming in many urban and rural areas at the primary level (De et al, 2002a; Tooley & Dixon, 2005; Srivastava, P., 2005).

Methodology of Our Survey

Our survey was carried out long after the NSSO and NCERT surveys, in 1999-2000. Unlike the NSSO and NCERT surveys, our survey did not cover the whole country, but focused on the eight states specified above. In that sense, it was purposive. The states for our study, supported by UNICEF, were purposively selected because seven of them account for three-quarters of India's children out of school (i.e. Andhra Pradesh, Assam, Bihar, Madhya Pradesh, Rajasthan, Uttar Pradesh, and West Bengal). They are mostly located in the north and east of the country. In addition, the high-achieving state, Tamil Nadu, was selected, which, like other high achievers in terms of social indicators, is located in the south.

The sample selected within each state was a representative one of the state. The units for the study were the village in the rural areas and the 'urban enumeration area' (or UEB, a term used by the Registrar General of India documents) in the cities and towns. The survey was carried out during the second half of 1999 (over the academic year 1999-2000) and covered more than 120,000 households and a thousand schools spread over 91 districts in the eight states.[6] The rural sample was based on 34 districts, four per state for all states except Uttar Pradesh, which had a sample of six districts. The urban sample of 80 towns and cities was spread over 64 districts. While most towns and cities fell in a different set of districts, a few districts coincided with those covered under the rural sample. The sample size is fairly large and comparable with major national-level surveys.[7]

The sampling design involved a multi-stage stratified sampling technique to select districts and cities and sub-samples. For each of the districts selected as above in the rural sample, nine villages were selected for data collection. Villages were stratified before selection. Villages with less than 100 households were excluded in each of the districts, and the remaining villages were stratified into three sub-samples of large, medium, and small, based on the number of households per village. As in the case of the selection of districts, the random sampling technique was used to select three villages from each stratum to form nine villages per district. In all, 306 villages were selected in the eight states.

For the urban sample, similarly, the cities and towns were stratified according to population size into four categories (below 50,000; 50,000-199,999; 200,000-999,999; and above 1 million). Primary Census Abstract data were used to select the towns and cities randomly within each state. Four towns each in the first two categories, and one city each in the third and fourth categories, were chosen in each state.

Schools and teachers to be interviewed were not selected on a sample basis. All schools, formal or alternative, falling within the jurisdiction of a village or UEB boundary, were surveyed, irrespective of the type of management, level, or recognition status, thus capturing unrecognised schools as well. A teachers' schedule was used to interview all teachers. On average, three teachers per village or UEB were interviewed.

Focus group discussions were held with a select group of parents in each sample village in the rural areas. The discussions, on issues such as household spending on education, educational incentives and their effectiveness, the strengths and weaknesses of schools in the village, provided insights about the parents' perceptions and suggestions on the schooling situation.

The Survey in Eight Selected States: an analysis

This section examines data collected in our survey of the eight states in the year 2000. Detailed tables for each state can be found in Mehrotra et al (2005) and Mehrotra (2006).Throughout the following discussion, the comparative discussion of schools, that is, government, private aided, and private unaided (recognised and unrecognised), tries to distinguish between the situation in rural and urban areas. In these mostly northern states of India, at least 70% of the population lives in rural areas.

Coverage of Children: enrolment and regional equity issues

Our data for enrolment in the different kinds of schools (government, private aided, and private unaided) in rural and urban areas reveal that almost all the children in rural areas tend to go to government schools. However, this share is much smaller in Uttar Pradesh (73%), where over one-fifth of children are in private unaided schools, and in Tamil Nadu (74%), where private aided schools have always been important. In the remaining six states around 90% of children are in government schools.

In urban areas, however, the share of government schools drops dramatically in almost all states. According to our survey of 1999-2000, the share of government schools in urban areas in the educationally weakest states (Bihar, Madhya Pradesh, Rajasthan, and Uttar Pradesh) hovers at around half of all enrolment (except in Madhya Pradesh, where it is two-thirds). So, while the purely private sector remains a significant contributor to enrolment in urban areas, the private unaided share in total recognised school enrolment may have even grown compared to the 1995-96 NSSO survey.[8] In Uttar Pradesh and Rajasthan that share is a third, in Bihar over a quarter, and in Madhya Pradesh a fifth of all urban enrolment. Uniformly in *rural* areas of all less developed states, the share of children in private unaided schools was larger than in private aided schools. In *urban* areas also, in the backward states like Bihar, Madhya Pradesh, and Uttar Pradesh the percentage of children in private unaided schools was much larger than in private aided schools.

In urban areas, the role of private aided and unaided schools is quite significant. The proportion of children in such schools is even more than that in government schools in a number of states. This seems to suggest that private aided schools have grown particularly in urban areas, that is, we posit that they would have emerged as private unaided schools catering to the urban lower middle and middle classes before being converted to schools aided by the government.

Gender and Social Equity in Different School Categories

Do households prefer admitting their daughters in government schools that are apparently less costly than private schools? Of all enrolled boys, slightly more go to private unaided (i.e. fee-paying schools) than to private aided ones. Even more importantly, in urban areas, the percentage of enrolled girls in government schools is higher than in private ones in the educationally backward states. More enrolled girls (compared to enrolled boys) are in government schools; in other words, the share of girls enrolled in private unaided schools is correspondingly lower compared to boys. In urban areas, where private schooling has expanded faster than in rural areas, 65% of enrolled girls in Andhra Pradesh but only 57% of enrolled boys are in government schools. The corresponding shares for enrolled girls and boys in government schools in urban areas are: 57% vs. 50% in Bihar; 71% vs. 66% in Madhya Pradesh; and 56% vs. 44% in Uttar Pradesh. There was no such difference in the high-achieving Tamil Nadu or the other three states.[9] We have noted earlier that it is in urban areas that private schools have mushroomed, and this gender difference in parental decision making is pronounced in urban areas, but almost non-existent in rural areas.

How well represented are the constitutionally recognised socially deprived sections of the population, that is, the Scheduled Castes (SC), Scheduled Tribes (ST), and Other Backward Castes (OBC), in government and non-government schools? What is the relative role of government and private schools in enrolling boys and girls of lower castes and tribes?

Our eight-state survey reveals that a higher proportion of children from SC, ST and OBC groups were in government elementary schools, compared to children from upper castes. Of all enrolled SC children in Assam, 7% went to private aided schools, while of all enrolled upper caste children, 16% were in private unaided schools. The corresponding shares were 12.7% and 16.7% in Bihar; 15.2% and 22.6% in Madhya Pradesh; and 17.7% and 38.6% in Uttar Pradesh.

Some interesting contrasts emerge while comparing SC girls with upper caste girls. In Bihar, now well known for its caste-based oppression and violence (see, for example, Karan & Pushpendra, 2006), 76% of enrolled SC girls were in government schools, as compared to only 55% of upper caste girls. The corresponding shares are 80% and 66% in Madhya Pradesh; and 77% and 56% in Uttar Pradesh. Furthermore, while only 10% of all enrolled SC girls are in private unaided schools in Bihar, 21% of upper caste girls are. The corresponding shares are 15.5% for SC girls and 37% for upper caste girls in Uttar Pradesh.

In other words, a higher proportion of upper caste children are enrolled in non-government schools, compared to lower caste groups.[10] Private schools do not seem to be a factor favouring gender or social equity.

Facilities in Private and Government Schools: qualitative aspects of supply

Do private schools provide better physical and teaching facilities for children as compared to government schools? Physical facilities refer to the number of classrooms, and drinking water and toilet facilities. Teaching facilities, on the other hand, refer to the pupil–teacher ratio, experience and training of teachers, contractual status and suitable remuneration for teaching staff – all essential to ensure they pay adequate attention to their teaching responsibilities.

Physical Facilities

Classrooms. A primary school has five grades (1-5), and ideally there should be at least one classroom and one teacher per class. However, one must make allowance for the widespread phenomenon of multi-grade teaching at the primary level. Hence, running a primary school with two or more classrooms for five grades is still feasible, though far from optimal. Almost all the urban schools in the eight states in our survey have two or more classrooms. The majority of rural schools also have two or more classrooms (except in Assam). However, the proportion of rural schools with only one classroom is quite high in some states: Assam (63.5%), Tamil Nadu (35%), Andhra Pradesh (19%) and West Bengal (17%).

The problem of one-classroom schools seems largely confined to government schools. The share of government schools that are single-classroom schools is: Andhra Pradesh: 17% (rural) and 9% (urban); Assam: 32% (rural) and 2% (urban); Bihar: 11% (rural) and 10% (urban); Madhya Pradesh: 14% (rural) and 15% (urban); and Uttar Pradesh: 6% (rural) and 19% (urban).

Most of the private unaided schools – mostly located in urban areas – do not seem to have a space constraint in terms of classrooms. All of them have two or more classrooms. From the focus group discussions it emerged that parents are legitimately hesitant to send their daughters to upper primary schools if adequate space is not available in classrooms for the proper seating of boys and girls.

Drinking water and toilet facilities. In some states, participants of focus group discussions observed that incentives like midday meals would be ineffective as instruments to encourage children to attend school if drinking water and toilets were not available. Some participants observed that absence of these facilities has made each working day into a partial working day because children go home to drink water and do not return.

According to the survey, most schools have some drinking water facility, although in rural schools the absence of drinking water facilities is much greater than in urban schools in all states.[11] Nonetheless, a significant minority of rural schools have no drinking water facility: 9% in Uttar Pradesh

137

and Madhya Pradesh, 17% in West Bengal, 18% in Rajasthan, 19% in Assam, and the highest percentages were found in Andhra Pradesh (28%), Bihar (26%), and Tamil Nadu (35%). The problem of no drinking water facility was almost non-existent in private unaided schools in both rural and urban areas. A higher share of private unaided schools had a piped water supply, especially in urban areas.

Schools without drinking water are either government or private aided. The problem appears to be most serious in government schools, which have the largest share of schools with no drinking water facility. This is a widespread problem in rural government schools: 8% in Uttar Pradesh; 11% in Madhya Pradesh; 17% in West Bengal; 20% in Andhra Pradesh; 20% in Rajasthan; 22% in Assam; 28% in Bihar; and 38% in Tamil Nadu. In private unaided schools in every state (except Andhra Pradesh) drinking water was available even in rural areas.[12]

One of the reasons female teachers are not willing to be posted to rural schools is the lack of toilet facilities. What is remarkable from the survey is that in nearly all the states, more than half of the schools do not have a toilet facility for staff. The problem is most serious in rural areas. In all states (except West Bengal) the private unaided sector tends to have a higher proportion of schools with toilets for staff than government or private aided ones. Of all government schools 28% have toilets for staff in Andhra Pradesh, while 59% of all private unaided schools have them. The corresponding shares in Assam are 43% vs. 72%; in Bihar 14% vs. 27%; in Madhya Pradesh 18% vs. 52%; in Uttar Pradesh 19.5% vs. 52%; and in Tamil Nadu, 42% vs. 100%.

Separate toilet facilities for girls are an important consideration in the minds of parents when sending their daughters to school, especially to upper primary school (ages 12 to 14). In urban areas the share of schools with separate facilities for girls is low in states with the lowest girls' enrolment rate: Bihar (26%), Madhya Pradesh (27%), Uttar Pradesh (37%), and West Bengal (37%). The share of schools with separate girls' toilets does not exceed 61% in any state. Less than a fifth of rural schools in all states (except Rajasthan with 38%) have separate girls' toilets.

Many more private unaided schools in urban areas have separate toilets for girls than do government schools (45% vs. 22% in Uttar Pradesh; 61% vs. 41% in Rajasthan; 50% vs. 16% in Madhya Pradesh; and 32% vs. 15% in Bihar). More private aided schools seem to have separate toilets for girls than either government or private unaided schools.

Teachers

Single teacher schools. Usually rural schools have difficulty in finding teachers, since regular government teachers try to avoid a rural posting (Kingdon & Muzammil, 2003). Most teachers in government schools tend to have an urban background, and would go to great lengths (including bribing education ministry decision makers) to preclude a rural posting. Not surprisingly, the problem of single teacher schools is much greater in rural than in urban schools.

The problem is confined to government schools since their teachers are part of the civil service, wherein staff are transferable within the state from school to school. For example, 13% of government schools in Bihar and 11% of government schools in Uttar Pradesh are found to be single teacher schools. Nearly 17% of private aided schools in Madhya Pradesh are single teacher schools. The problem of single teacher schools is practically non-existent in private unaided schools.

Student–teacher ratios. According to the survey, the problem of high student–teacher ratios is predominantly a rural one. Urban areas generally do not seem to have the problem for presumably the reason mentioned above regarding teacher staffing. The second noticeable fact is that government schools in most states have higher student–teacher ratios than private schools, particularly in rural areas. This phenomenon is particularly noticeable for the less developed states where the comparable student–teacher ratios for government versus private schools are as follows: Bihar (56 vs. 25), Madhya Pradesh (31 vs. 18), Rajasthan (50 vs. 27) and Uttar Pradesh (51 vs. 34).

In fact, while high student–teacher ratios characterise the rural areas of all states, the ratio is not high in private unaided (or even aided) schools, except in the less developed state of Uttar Pradesh. In fact, by and large, the states with high shares of enrolled students in private unaided schools have quite reasonable student–teacher ratios in rural and urban schools, usually below 30:1. In government schools in rural areas, it is always over 40:1 (except in Assam). This might partly account for their attractiveness, relative to government schools, in these states.[13]

Pre-service training of teachers. Over 90% of all teachers in government schools are trained in both rural and urban areas (with the exception of Assam, West Bengal, and Madhya Pradesh).[14] On the contrary, the overwhelming majority of private unaided school teachers in both rural and urban areas in all states are untrained. The contrasts in the share of untrained teachers of all teachers in government schools versus private unaided schools are striking: 8.6% vs. 62% in Andhra Pradesh; 32.5% vs. 75% in Assam; 1% vs. 68% in Bihar; 18% vs. 74% in Madhya Pradesh; 5% vs. 52% in Rajasthan; 1% vs. 17% in Tamil Nadu; 5% vs. 64% in Uttar Pradesh; and 16% vs. 88% in West Bengal.

The proportion of untrained teachers is usually lower in private aided compared to unaided schools. However, untrained teachers account for a much higher share of the teacher force of aided schools than of regular government schools, which is presumably a historical legacy from the time that the aided schools were unaided schools.

Temporary teachers. The overwhelming majority of government school teachers are on the permanent payroll of state governments.[15] Private schools (especially unaided ones) generally hire teachers on a temporary basis more than government schools. This is particularly notable for private unaided schools in urban areas (with 41% of all teachers in West Bengal being temporary, 63% in Rajasthan, 87% in Madhya Pradesh, 69% in Bihar, and 100% in Andhra Pradesh). It is surprising that even in the case of private aided schools temporary teachers are a sizeable percentage in the less developed states of Bihar, Madhya Pradesh, Rajasthan and Uttar Pradesh, though it is an urban phenomenon here as well.

Teacher salaries.[16] The average salary of a teacher in private unaided schools is generally a fraction of government teacher salaries in all states. They are also generally less for private aided schools as compared to government schools. On average, in all states, a teacher's annual salary in government schools varied in 1999 between about Rs. 63,000 and Rs. 90,000 in rural areas, and about Rs. 76,000 to Rs. 106,000 in urban areas.

However, the salaries of teachers in private unaided schools are deplorable. In states like Bihar the annual salary of an elementary school teacher in private unaided schools was as low as Rs. 10,307, which amounts to monthly emoluments of less than even Rs. 1000 ($22)! Even in West Bengal, urban teachers in private unaided schools were very poorly paid. Their average annual salary was as low as Rs. 6698, which amounts to monthly emoluments of around Rs. 500! The situation is even worse in Assam. In rural areas of Assam, for example, private unaided schools paid less than Rs. 200 per month to their teachers and 50% of teachers received even less than Rs. 150 per month. In no state did teacher salaries at primary level in private unaided schools exceed 20% of the salary of government teachers.

Performance Indicators in Public and Private Schools

Working Days and Working Environment

According to UNESCO, a school must have a minimum of 180 working days in a school year. Our survey asked school management about the number of working days. It is interesting that of the eight selected states, only three (Bihar, Madhya Pradesh, and Rajasthan) reported total school days (on average for all schools) significantly higher than 180. Most other states reportedly had only around 180 school days or fewer.

In many states, the number of working days in private unaided schools is found to be greater than in government schools. This is true in rural areas for at least four states (Andhra Pradesh: 199 vs. 181; Assam: 178 vs. 163; Bihar: 217 vs. 199; Uttar Pradesh: 190 vs. 174 days, respectively). These are also the states where, as we have seen above, the private unaided sector accounts for a significant share of enrolment. Perhaps the fact that private unaided schools are seen by parents to be better functioning than government schools is a reason for the higher than average enrolment in such schools.[17]

In fact, using a representative sample in a recent survey for the World Bank of 20 states in India, Kremer et al (2004) came to the conclusion that the teacher absence rate is 25% on average. This was the second highest rate in a sample of eight countries studied (it was higher only in Uganda at 27%). It is interesting that the states that have better elementary education indicators have a lower incidence of teacher absence. Specifically, Kerala, Tamil Nadu, and Himachal Pradesh had the lowest absence rate, and Uttar Pradesh, Bihar, Chhatisgarh, Jharkhand, and Assam had higher than national average rates.

Attendance Rates

In all states, attendance rates in government schools are invariably lower than in private unaided schools in both rural and urban areas. The attendance rate for children was taken by head count by the surveyors on the day they visited the school (one day), as opposed to what was registered in the school records. In urban areas, this attendance rate was 84% in government schools vs. 91% in private unaided schools in Assam; 55% vs. 74% in Bihar; 64.5% vs. 87% in Rajasthan; 83% vs. 98% in Uttar Pradesh; 70% vs. 91% in West Bengal. By contrast, in the high-achieving state of Tamil Nadu, the attendance rate in government schools at 97.4% was higher than in private unaided schools at 89.8%.

Drop-out Rates

Generally, drop-out rates in government schools were found to be much higher than in private schools. This seems to suggest that private unaided schools take all precautions to retain children within the school (because parents in private schools are the stakeholders). The share of children dropping out in rural government versus private unaided schools was: Andhra Pradesh: 10% vs. 0.5% in private unaided schools, Assam: 9% vs. 6.7%, Bihar: 16% vs. 2.6%, Madhya Pradesh: 12% vs. 0.8%, Rajasthan: 17% vs. 1.1%, Tamil Nadu: 17% vs. 7%, and Uttar Pradesh: 10% vs. 3.5%.[18]

Cognitive Achievements

Our survey was not designed to examine cognitive achievements in either government or private schools. However, some studies bring out the differences in cognitive achievements of children studying in private and government schools in selected states of India. Some of the selected states in the literature are the same as those examined in the current study. For example, studies comparing cognitive achievement between private and public schools in India have been conducted by Govinda & Varghese (1991) in Madhya Pradesh, Bashir (1994) in Tamil Nadu, Kingdon (1996) in Uttar Pradesh, and Varghese (1994, 1995) in Kerala.

The Madhya Pradesh study [19] found that at the primary level, after controlling for student background characteristics, private unaided schools performed better than private aided schools. Both these types of private schools performed better than government schools in language (Hindi) and mathematics achievement tests among children of grades 4 and 5. Of the various school and teacher variables examined, the level of general education of the teacher emerged as a factor influencing pupil achievement but teacher training status was significant only in urban areas.[20] Possession of all prescribed textbooks was also significant. Varghese (1994) found a marginal advantage for private aided schools over government primary schools in Kerala. This was true in both language (Malayalam) and maths achievement tests.[21]

Bashir (1997) also notes that these studies (like the international ones [22] using single-level models, seemed to show that private schools were more effective. However, studies using hierarchical or multi-level models do not show a clearly positive effect in favour of the private sector in developing countries.[23] In fact, as Bashir (1997) shows, regardless of whether ordinary least squares (OLS) or multi-level models are used, the inclusion of peer group characteristics and certain school variables (which cannot be manipulated by policy) reduce, if not entirely eliminate, the private school advantage. These models tell us more about the possible variables that influence cognitive test achievement than the private–public comparison.[24]

Financial Burden of Schooling on Households by Management Type

By and large, the financial burden on households for children going to private unaided schools is much higher than for children going to government schools. The financial burden in urban areas (for all categories of schools) is much larger than in rural areas. In rural areas, the annual household cost of sending a child to a private unaided elementary school was, as a multiple of government school: 3.4 in Andhra Pradesh, and anywhere between 1.4 and 1.9 times in the rest of the states. In urban areas, the multiple was 3.7 in Tamil Nadu, and between 1.8 and 2.7 in the rest of the states.

When one compares the household expenditure per child with average per capita consumption expenditure (in 1999-2000), the magnitude of the burden borne by parents of sending children to school becomes clear. Sending *one* child to a primary school in rural areas can cost the family anywhere between 11 and 15% of its monthly per capita expenditure in the states under discussion here.[25] In urban areas, the monthly household expenditure on primary education per child as a proportion of per capita expenditure per month is even higher: ranging between 11% in West Bengal to 21% in Assam.[26] Even allowing for the fact that incomes are higher than consumption, these proportions are still forbiddingly high.

Conclusions and Policy Implications

A Summary of Findings

This chapter tends to confirm the analysis that the private sector has expanded particularly in those states of India that have the most dysfunctional government school system. Our analysis of national-level data showed that some of the latter states also tend to be the states with the lowest per capita income in the country, demonstrating the willingness of even poor parents to pay for schooling (even though the ability to pay may be lacking); in other words, demand for schooling remains high.

Our survey revealed that private schooling is gender biased in terms of enrolment against girls, who comprise a larger share of children out of school. Furthermore, it does not help to redress the bias against lower caste groups, in that lower caste groups, who have much lower enrolment rates than upper caste groups, are generally less likely to be enrolled in fee-paying schools than upper caste groups.

The survey of eight states enabled us to compare facilities, both in terms of physical infrastructure and human resources, between government and private schools. The problem of one-classroom schools is largely confined to government schools. Private aided schools do not have this problem. Similarly, most of the private unaided schools do not seem to have a space constraint in terms of classrooms.

Most schools in the selected states have drinking water facilities. Where they do not, the problem appears most serious in government schools, which are the largest share of schools without drinking water facilities. The problem of no drinking water facilities is non-existent in private unaided schools, in both rural and urban areas. In all selected states (except one), private unaided schools tend to have a higher proportion of schools with toilets for staff than government or private aided ones. Many more private unaided schools (and private aided ones) in urban areas have separate toilets for girls than do government schools.

The problem of single-teacher schools is confined to government schools (especially in rural areas), since they are the ones where teachers are part of the civil service and staff are transferable from school to school within the state. Government schools of most of the selected states have higher student–teacher ratios (well over 40:1 in most states) than private schools, particularly in rural areas.

While over 90% of government school teachers are trained, the overwhelming majority of private unaided school teachers in both rural and urban areas in all states are untrained. Untrained teachers also account for a higher share of teachers in private aided schools than in regular government

143

schools. Also, private schools (especially unaided ones) generally hire teachers on a temporary basis more than government schools; most government school teachers are permanent employees of the state governments. The average salary of teachers in private schools is much less than in government schools. When one combines these facts with the widespread known phenomena of teacher absenteeism in government schools, it speaks volumes for the inefficiency of the government school system. The well-paid, permanently employed, trained government teachers often do not turn up to teach; though, in some situations, one cannot blame them given that they are teaching a huge class, consisting of multiple grades, possibly in a single classroom school!

The reported school working days are much lower in government schools, and in many, actually fewer than the 180 days that pedagogues regard as the absolute minimum. Generally, the number of working days in private unaided schools is much greater than in government schools. This is one indication that despite having poorly paid, temporary, and untrained teachers, private unaided schools may still seem attractive to parents because they operate more regularly. The drop-out rates in government schools are found to be much higher than in private schools. In all states, attendance rates in government schools were usually lower than in private unaided schools, as per head count on the day of the survey, in both rural and urban areas.

Policy Recommendations

If universal elementary education is to be achieved, the efficiency and equity of the entire educational system has to improve – not just that of the public sector. There is no firm evidence in India of children in private schools achieving better learning. Second, our own examination of the data (Panchamukhi & Mehrotra, 2005) and other studies show that the taking over of private schools by the state has had adverse equity effects. Third, we know that unrecognised and recognised private unaided schools are almost totally unregulated, despite their considerable importance in terms of enrolment in several states. There are policy implications from each of these issues.

First, a national policy on private schooling articulated by the Central Government should emerge after a process of consultation. Second, transparent guidelines should be prepared at the state level for government education departments to regulate the operation of unaided schools.[27] Elsewhere (Panchamukhi & Mehrotra, 2005), in an analysis of 1995-96 NSSO data, we have established that the share of enrolled children attending private schools (both recognised and unrecognised) is much lower at upper primary level than at primary level. At upper primary level the share was under 10% in the majority of states; in no state did it exceed 25%; and in only five states (Haryana, Punjab, Andhra Pradesh, Uttar Pradesh, and Bihar) was it between 10 and 25%.

Furthermore, while the numbers of private schools would have only grown in the last decade, the problem of poor regulation is particularly serious in the seven major states where the share of private enrolment in total primary enrolment exceeds 10% (i.e. Rajasthan 10%, Kerala 15%, Bihar 19%, Andhra Pradesh 28%, Uttar Pradesh 33%, Punjab 34%, and Haryana 43%). It is these states where both the central and state governments need to take heed. If state governments are unwilling to take action, it should be initiated by the Central Government under the threat of sanctions.

The third issue regarding regulation is identifying its content. One has to distinguish here between recognised and unrecognised schools. Recognised private schools supposedly face a range of regulations, from teacher salaries and qualifications to class size, playground size, school facilities, advertising of positions, a joint school–government bank account (to pay teacher salaries in case the school goes bankrupt), a library, and so on. In reality these conditions are usually breached, through the payment of bribes (see, for example, Tooley & Dixon, 2005, based on a small sample of Hyderabad schools; Kingdon & Muzammil, 2003; Srivastava, P., 2005, a case study of Lucknow District). There is no easy solution through administrative means of solving the problem of corruption in the school inspection system.

The conditions and norms for recognition need to continue. They set a benchmark against which unrecognised schools can be judged. As De et al (2002b) point out, these norms appear to be providing a sort of benchmark against which unrecognised schools can measure themselves. Unrecognised schools tend to have an understanding with recognised schools so that the former schools can send their children to the latter to take board exams. If there were board exams at the end of the primary cycle (grades 1-5) in every state there would be an automatic, in-built accountability mechanism for all private schools, recognised and unrecognised (see Panchamukhi & Mehrotra, 2005, for this proposal). The discipline of market competition would then weed out the schools with the worst records and the poorest facilities, regardless of whether they were recognised or not. This would benefit children, parents and the entire educational system.

The final policy recommendation is that one element in the national policy on private schools could be that the 'nationalisation' of private schools, that is, the conversion of private unaided schools into aided schools, should be banned henceforth. We have established elsewhere, based on an analysis of NSSO survey data (Panchamukhi & Mehrotra, 2005), that the share of private aided schools in enrolment rises with level of education, from primary to upper primary to secondary. All existing private aided schools should only be provided aid under very strict performance criteria. Those performance criteria need to be clearly spelt out in the national policy/legislation, after a thorough evaluation of the international experience with respect to giving grants-in-aid by the state to private schools.

The fiscal deficits of state governments (at 5% of gross domestic product) are too high for scarce resources to be diverted to subsidising private schools, and making them dependent upon government aid. Already, the share of government-dependent private schools in India is much higher than in other developing countries, and certainly than in OECD countries (Organisation for Economic Co-operation and Development/UNESCO, 2002). Government resources have to be conserved to be used efficiently to improve quality in government schools.

The experience of the now industrialised countries demonstrates that while the private sector could play a supportive role in India's quest to universalise elementary education, the Indian state will need to be much more proactive in reforming the public school system. If the public system provided reasonable competition to the private sector, both recognised and unrecognised schools would have to put their houses in order. It was the public system which played the dominant role in universalising schooling in the now industrialised countries (see Sanderson, 1983; Stephens, 1998; Mehrotra & Delamonica, 2007, for a detailed discussion). The experiences of the high-achieving developing countries point in the same direction (see Mehrotra & Jolly, 1997; Mehrotra, 1998, for a detailed discussion). At the same time, the quality of schooling in the private sector could improve if the state took a more proactive regulatory role.

Acknowledgements

Thanks are due to Geeta Kingdon, N.V. Varghese, Jean Drèze, Vimla Ramchandran, and John Micklewright for comments on this chapter. The study was supported financially by the UNICEF India Country Office. Statistical assistance by Mario Biggeri and Ngindu Kalala is gratefully acknowledged.

Notes

[1] Elementary education consists of classes 1-8, of which 1-5 is primary, and 6-8 is upper primary or junior.

[2] Where the denominator is all rural boys in the first case, and all rural girls in the second case.

[3] What is also interesting is that the share of government and private aided schools in urban areas is roughly similar, that is, both are equally important in terms of enrolment, each accounting for around 40% of total enrolment in urban upper primary schools in 1993, though in 1973 they each had a share of around 45%.

[4] In other words, the analysis in the preceding three paragraphs refers only to the recognised schools.

[5] At primary level, the purely private sector's share in enrolment was: Punjab 43.3%, Uttar Pradesh 34.3%, Andhra Pradesh 32.5%, and Bihar 19.4%. The average for the 16 states was 15.5%. In upper primary education, the shares were: Andhra Pradesh 25.1%, Bihar 24.7%, Uttar Pradesh 22.5%, and Punjab 21.1%. The average share for the 16 states was 10.2%.

[6] There were 25 states in India in 1999, which were further divided into over 500 administrative districts. Each district had on average a population of about 2 million people. Uttar Pradesh had the largest number of districts, numbering 68. In fact, the eight states in the study are among the largest and most populous of the country. The analysis for Uttar Pradesh, Madhya Pradesh, and Bihar refers to these states before they were divided.

[7] In fact, the sample is much larger. For example, the National Family Health Survey had a sample of 3000 interviews of eligible women for states having a population of 25 million or less in 1991 and 4000 interviews for states having a population of more than 25 million.

[8] Unfortunately, in the analysis of the raw data the consultancy firm that conducted the survey for UNICEF did not distinguish between unrecognised and recognised private unaided schools.

[9] Others have come to the same conclusion, for example, Tilak & Sudarshan (2000) based on the National Council of Applied Economic Research (NCAER) Survey (1994); De et al (2002a) based on NCERT surveys, and the Probe Team (1999), based on their survey in Uttar Pradesh, Madhya Pradesh, Bihar, and Rajasthan.

[10] Ravi Srivastava (2001) comes to the same conclusion with respect to two districts in Uttar Pradesh.

[11] The source of water varied by location (rural vs. urban). The highest proportion of schools which had drinking water sourced it from a hand pump, others had a tube well, an ordinary well, or the water was brought from outside. Schools with piped water accounted for less than 10% of rural schools. In a desert state like Rajasthan water was brought from outside the school in over a third of the rural schools.

[12] That is, it was available from a hand pump/tube well/ordinary well, or piped water was available, or it was brought in from outside the school.

[13] The Probe Team also found that private schools had a better pupil–teacher ratio than government and aided primary schools. Even the multi-grade teaching, though common, was different: since classes were smaller, it was not obviously problematic (Probe Team, 1999).

[14] The relatively high share of untrained teachers in Madhya Pradesh is accounted for probably by the increase in para-teachers (additional teachers with lower qualifications hired locally) that occurred after the introduction of the Education Guarantee Scheme in early 1997.

[15] Only Madhya Pradesh has a significant proportion of teachers (23% in rural and 15% in urban areas) who are on temporary contracts, primarily because of the large numbers of new para-teachers hired to provide for the Education Guarantee Scheme.

[16] As reported by the teachers interviewed by the enumerators during the school survey.

[17] The Probe Team (1999) noted that there was a parental perception of private schools that their children would benefit much more from private schooling; they also *look* better (private schools are generally kept clean); and above all, they have an atmosphere of active teaching. When investigators visited the schools, students and teachers were almost always at work.

[18] In urban schools, there were similar differentials with respect to drop-out: Bihar: 18% in government schools versus 4% in private unaided ones; Madhya Pradesh: 22% vs. 6%; Rajasthan: 17% vs. 4%; Tamil Nadu: 17% vs. 3%; and Uttar Pradesh: 19% vs. 7%.

[19] It was based on a sample of 2159 students in 59 schools in five districts of Madhya Pradesh.

[20] Kingdon (1994) found that of the five teacher variables included, the teachers' average exam results in all external board exams taken – a proxy for teachers' cognitive skills – had a strong, statistically significant impact on pupils' achievement. Others, namely teachers' education in years, teachers' experience, and teachers' training in years, did not.

[21] The tests were administered to 3089 students studying in grade 4.

[22] See Jimenez et al (1991), Jimenez & Lockheed (1995), among others.

[23] As Bashir (1997) rightly points out, a major weakness of single-level models (OLS) is that the within-school variation (within the government and private schools) is entirely ignored, and the effect of pupil-level variables on individual outcomes cannot be ascertained. Models using school means alone cannot take account of situations where a pupil's outcome is influenced both by his/her socio-economic status and by the average socio-economic status of those children in the school. In the multi-level model (a slight misnomer since most used are two-level models), the pupil-level model consists of the regression of the pupil's test score on pupil characteristics. The school-level (second level) model then enables the regression to separate out the within-school factors from the between-school factors influencing achievement.

[24] Results of a 1999 assessment of primary pupils in five Latin American countries do not support significant effects associated with public and private schools and descriptive analyses indicate that private schooling contributes substantially to the segregation of students from different socio-economic backgrounds. Similarly, the PISA study in 2000 shows that students in private secondary schools come from households with higher socio-economic status than public school students in every country studied (Organisation for Economic Co-operation and Development/UNESCO, 2002).

[25] These figures are an average based on costs of all kinds of schools, government, private aided, and private unaided. Naturally the costs of private unaided schools are greater to the household than government schools. The shares in rural primary schools, where the majority of schools are government ones, are (in %): Assam 11, West Bengal 11, Madhya Pradesh 12, Rajasthan 14, Tamil Nadu 15, Uttar Pradesh 15, and Bihar 16.

[26] The shares in urban primary schools are (in %): West Bengal 11, Tamil Nadu 12, Madhya Pradesh 15, Bihar 17, Uttar Pradesh 19, Rajasthan 19, and Assam 21.

[27] Further, all unrecognised schools should be required to register with the state government, and the state government should be required to provide this list to the centre on an annual basis before funds for central schemes of assistance are released.

References

Agarwal, Y. (2000) *Public and Private Partnership in Primary Education in India. A Study of Unrecognized Schools in Haryana*. Delhi: National Institute of Educational Planning and Administration.

Bashir, S. (1994) Achievement Performance at the Primary Level in Public and Private Schools of Tamil Nadu, *Indian Education Review*, 29(3-4).

Bashir, S. (1997) The Cost Effectiveness of Public and Private Schools: knowledge gaps, new research methodologies, and an application in India, in C. Colclough (Ed.) *Marketizing Health and Education in Developing Countries*. Oxford: Clarendon Press.

De, A., Majumdar, M., Samson, M. & Noronha, C. (2002a) Role of Private Sector in Basic Education, in R. Govinda (Ed.) *India Education Report: a profile of basic education*. New Delhi: Oxford University Press.

De, A., Noronha, C. & Samson, M. (2002b) Private Schools for Less Privileged: some insights from a case study, *Economic and Political Weekly*, 28 December, pp. 5230-5236.

Govinda, R. & Varghese, N.V. (1991) *The Quality of Basic Education Services in India: a case study of primary schooling in Madhya Pradesh*. Paris: International Institute of Education Planning and New Delhi: National Institute of Educational Planning and Administration.

Jimenez, E. & Lockheed, M. (1995) *Public and Private Secondary Education in Developing Countries: a comparative study*. World Bank Discussion Paper No. 309. Washington, DC: World Bank.

Jimenez, E., Lockheed, E. & Paqueo, V. (1991) The Relative Efficiency of Private and Public Schools in Developing Countries, *World Bank Research Observer*, 6, pp. 205-218.

Karan, A. & Pushpendra (2006) Bihar: including the excluded and addressing the failures of public provision in elementary education, in S. Mehrotra (Ed.) *The Economics of Elementary Education in India*. New Delhi: Sage.

Kingdon, G. (1996) The Quality and Efficiency of Private and Public Education: a case study in urban India, *Oxford Bulletin of Economics and Statistics*, 58(1), pp. 57-82.

Kingdon, G.G. (1996) Private Schooling in India: size, nature and equity effects. London School of Economics, DEP no. 72.

Kingdon, G.G. & Muzammil, M. (2003) *The Political Economy of Education in India: teacher politics in U.P.* New Delhi: Oxford University Press.

Kremer M., Muralidharan, K., Chaudhury, N., Hammer, J. & Rogers, H. (2004) *Teacher Absence in India*, http://www.worldbank.org, accessed 1 September 2004.

Majumdar, M. (2001) Educational Opportunities in Rajasthan and Tamil Nadu: despair and hope, in A. Vaidyanathan & P.R. Gopinathan Nair (Eds) *Elementary Education in India: a grassroots view*. New Delhi: Sage.

Mehrotra, S. (1998) Education for All: policy lessons from high achieving countries, *International Review of Education*, 44(5-6), pp. 461-484.

Mehrotra, S. (Ed.) (2006) *The Economics of Elementary Education in India*. New Delhi: Sage.

Mehrotra, S. & Delamonica, E. (2007) *Eliminating Human Poverty: macro-economic and social policies for equitable growth*. London: Zed Books.

Mehrotra, S. & Jolly, R. (Eds) (1997) *Development with a Human Face: experiences in social achievement and economic growth*. Oxford: Clarendon Press.

Mehrotra, S., Panchamukhi, P.R., Srivastava, R. & Srivastava, R. (2005) *Universalizing Elementary Education in India: uncaging the 'tiger' economy*. New Delhi: Oxford University Press.

Nambissan, G. (2001) Social Diversity and Regional Disparities in Schooling: a study of rural Rajasthan, in A. Vaidyanathan and P.R. Gopinathan Nair (Eds) *Elementary Education in India: a grassroots view*. New Delhi: Sage.

National Sample Survey Organisation (1998) *Attending an Educational Institution in India: its level, nature and cost*. Report No. 439/52/25.2/1. 52nd Round, 1995-96. New Delhi: Department of Statistics, Government of India.

Organisation for Economic Cooperation and Development/UNESCO (2002) *Financing Education: investments and returns*. Analysis of the World Education Indicators 2002 edition. Paris: OECD.

Panchamukhi, P.R. & Mehrotra, S. (2005) Assessing Public and Private Provision of Elementary Education in India, in S. Mehrotra, P.R. Panchamukhi, R. Srivastava & R. Srivastava, *Universalizing Elementary Education in India: uncaging the 'tiger' economy*. New Delhi: Oxford University Press.

Probe Team (1999) *Public Report on Basic Education in India*. New Delhi: Oxford University Press.

Sanderson, M. (1983) *Education, Economic Change and Society in England, 1780-1870*. London: Macmillan.

Srivastava, P. (2005) The Business of Schooling: the school choice processes, markets, and institutions governing low-fee private schooling for disadvantaged groups in India. Unpublished doctoral thesis, University of Oxford.

Srivastava, R. (2001) Access to Basic Education in Rural Uttar Pradesh, in A. Vaidyanathan & P.R. Gopinathan Nair (Eds) *Elementary Education in India: a grassroots view*. New Delhi: Sage.

Srivastava, R. (2005) Review of Elementary Education in the Selected States, in S. Mehrotra, P.R. Panchamukhi, R. Srivastava & R. Srivastava, *Universalizing Elementary Education in India: uncaging the 'tiger' economy*. New Delhi: Oxford University Press.

Stephens, W.B. (1998) *Education in Britain, 1750-1914*. New York: St Martin's Press.

Tilak, J.B.G. & Sudarshan, R.M. (2000) Private Schooling in India. Paper prepared under the Programme Research in Human Development of the National Council of Applied Economic Research by United Nations Development Programme, New Delhi.

Tooley, J. & Dixon, P. (2005) An Inspector Calls: the regulation of 'budget' private schools in Hyderabad, Andhra Pradesh, India, *International Journal of Educational Development*, 25, pp. 269-288.

Varghese, N.V. (1994) *School Equality and Student Learning: a story of primary schooling in Kerala*. New Delhi: National Institute for Educational Planning and Administration.

Varghese, N.V. (1995) School Effects on Achievement: a study of government and private aided schools in Kerala, in National Council for Educational Research and Training (Ed.) *School Effectiveness and Learning Achievement at Primary Stage: international perspective*, pp. 261-288. New Delhi: NCERT.

CHAPTER 8

For Philanthropy or Profit? The Management and Operation of Low-fee Private Schools in India

PRACHI SRIVASTAVA

There has been an increased emphasis on the examination of private schooling in India in recent years. The impetus for its analysis is arguably based on the realisation that the private sector in India has become increasingly heterogeneous and is no longer the purview of middle-class and elite groups (Tilak & Sudarshan, 2001; De et al, 2002; Panchamukhi & Mehrotra, 2005; Tooley & Dixon, 2005a; Srivastava, P., 2006). The emergence of what I term, the *low-fee private* (LFP) sector, has marked a change in the nature of schooling provision for disadvantaged groups in India, which, as results of a previous study show (Srivastava, P., 2005), is operating in an increasingly marketised and privatised arena. This change necessitates an examination of schooling behaviours and patterns among traditionally low participating groups; the regulatory frameworks through which LFP schools function; and an understanding of the daily realities within which LFP schools operate.

The first two concerns are dealt with elsewhere (Srivastava, P., 2005, 2006). The purpose of this chapter is two-fold. The first is to give a brief account of the marketised schooling arena for disadvantaged groups in this study. The second, and more substantial point, is to provide an 'inside look' at some aspects of how LFP schools are managed and operated in Uttar Pradesh. Given that little is known about LFP schools, the discussion is intended as a descriptive analysis about their operation, specifically, their internal management structure and strategies, the challenges they face, and the motives of their owners. It is envisioned as a complement to some of the more macro-type accounts provided, for example, by Mehrotra & Panchamukhi and Tooley & Dixon in this book.

Research Strategy

This chapter presents results and analysis forming part of a larger household, school, and state-level study on LFP schooling in Lucknow District, Uttar Pradesh. Uttar Pradesh is classed as one of the most 'educationally backward' states in India, with a literacy rate of 57.4%, ranking it 31st of 35 states and territories (Government of India, 2001). At the same time, according to one estimate, it is the state with the second highest distribution of private school enrolments in elementary education in the country at 57.6% (Panchamukhi & Mehrotra, 2005, p. 236).[1]

The study's main aims were to analyse:

1. disadvantaged households' school choice processes and behaviours in relation to the LFP sector;
2. LFP school operation and management practices; and
3. the policy and regulatory framework applicable to LFP schools in principle and how they were applied to and mediated by LFP schools in practice.

Despite its emergence, the LFP sector has been neither officially defined by local education bodies nor operationally by researchers. For the purposes of this study, the LFP sector was defined as occupying a part (often unrecognised) of the highly heterogeneous private unaided sector. LFP schools were defined as those that: saw themselves targeting disadvantaged groups, were entirely self-financing through tuition fees, and charged a monthly tuition fee not exceeding about one day's earnings of a daily wage labourer at the primary and junior levels, and two days' earnings at the high school and higher secondary levels.

The discussion here is based on results at the school level. Fieldwork was conducted between July 2002 and April 2003 in 10 case study schools (five urban and five rural) in Lucknow District. Of these, two focus schools were chosen (one urban and one rural) for more intensive study using ethnographic-style techniques. Focus schools were chosen on the basis that they were the most successful competitors among the rural and urban groups, having the largest enrolments. The 60 household participants in the study were drawn from them.

Data collection spanned almost the full course of one school year. The most direct school-level data were collected through 30 formal semi-structured interviews with principals/owners of LFP schools. Each interview was designed to explore a specific topic comprising background information on the school, school responsiveness and parental involvement, and the policy context. In addition, data were collected through numerous informal interviews with principals/owners. Non-participant observation was employed to observe daily parent–school interactions. School policy and other documents were analysed for further data on school administration issues. A teachers' questionnaire was also distributed to all teachers at case study schools for data on teacher qualifications, teaching load, and salary. Finally, the 70 formal interviews with households and state officials, and observation and documentary data from the state level, were also used to triangulate evidence at the school level.

Disadvantaged Households and the Marketised Schooling Arena

The heterogeneity of the private sector has only recently been noted in the education discourse in India (Majumdar & Vaidyanathan, 1995; Tilak & Sudarshan, 2001; De et al, 2002), and to a limited extent. However, households in the study built a sophisticated picture of the schooling arena, which may seem jarring at first, given their limited experience with formal schooling and low educational levels, income, and occupational status.[2] A picture of an increasingly marketised and privatised school arena emerged, and extended to how disadvantaged households in the study saw their own positioning in the schooling market. Households in the study saw the greater private sector as highly differentiated, not only by the variable quality of schooling offered between and within different private school types, but also along lines of social class and various forms of advantage.

Their distinctions of the schooling market were made according to their perceptions of the target groups that different private school types focused on attracting. As compiled in Table I, household interviewees identified three types of private schools primarily along perceived school characteristics (medium of instruction and location) and perceived social status of clientele (level of parents' educational awareness, educational status, caste group, class group, and income level).

The typology reflected the households' conceptions of the ability and/or willingness of different groups to pay for varying ranges of perceived school quality and their level of educational awareness. Thus, the state sector, which was largely thought to offer the least satisfactory quality of schooling, was relegated by parents to groups from the lowest social status (as defined by respondents regarding educational awareness, economic class, and caste). It seemed to reflect a distinction that LFP clients in this study wanted to make about themselves. In particular, despite the fact that most households in the study belonged to lower socio-economic and caste groups themselves, some felt that part of the reason why schooling 'doesn't take place in state schools' was because it was attended almost exclusively by those groups.

A Window on LFP Schools

Given that little is known about LFP schools, the bulk of the chapter provides a descriptive analysis of LFP case study schools. The heart of the analysis centres on how LFP case study schools in Lucknow District operated in an increasingly marketised schooling arena, their management strategies, internal structures, and challenges.

	School type			
	State	Lowest Fee Charging	Low to Moderate Fee Charging	High Fee Charging
Rural interviewees' perceptions				
Perceived school characteristics	Hindi medium	Hindi medium	English medium	English medium
	Rural or urban	English taught as a subject Rural	Urban	Urban
Perceived social status of clientele	Least educationally aware Uneducated Some mixing of caste groups with a predominance of lowest caste groups	Educationally aware Uneducated to somewhat educated Lower classes	Educationally aware Somewhat educated Better off lower classes and some middle class	Educated Wealthy High caste Upper middle classes and elites
Urban interviewees' perceptions				
Perceived school characteristics	Hindi medium	Hindi medium	English or Hindi medium	English medium
	Rural and few urban	Urban and some rural	Urban	Urban
Perceived Social Status of Clientele	Not at all educationally aware Uneducated Poorest of society Lowest caste groups	Educationally aware lower classes	Educationally aware Somewhat educated Middle classes	Educated Wealthy High caste Upper middle classes and elites

Table I. Household-constructed typology of the schooling market.
Note: Data are from the 60 formal household interviews.

Case Study School Profiles

The LFP case study schools varied considerably on a number of school-related attributes such as: amount and types of fees charged, recognition status, building type (*pakka* or *kachcha*)[3], size and number of classrooms, available facilities (e.g. library, playground, toilets, drinking water), enrolment, and the number and qualifications of teachers. There was variance on all these attributes in rural and urban schools. The only exception was regarding building type in which all urban schools were *pakka*, whereas there was a mix of *pakka* and *kachcha* buildings in rural schools. There were a few attributes on which all schools in the study were similar: all were Hindi medium, recognised or seeking recognition with the Uttar Pradesh state boards, and family run. Unlike some high-fee schools, all case study schools were run as single operations rather than as part of a chain. Overall case study school profiles are presented in Table II.

Certain areas of variance and similarity between the schools were surprising. While some level of heterogeneity was expected, given that six of the ten schools were recognised through the Uttar Pradesh state boards and others were actively seeking recognition through them, the assumption was that they would all adhere closely to state norms. Therefore, it was surprising that recognised case study schools operated from premises ranging from a three-room open brick structure with a corrugated tin roof and no toilet facilities (School D), to a large multi-storied modern building with separate girls' and boys' toilets on every floor (Taj Nagar). The variance was in line with state-level findings that the application of formal requirements regarding recognition by government officials was selective and related to the payment of under the table 'fees'. Tooley & Dixon (2005a) found similar results in their study on Andhra Pradesh.

Finally, the fact that all schools were Hindi medium also challenged intuitive assumptions that the private sector is increasingly accessed because it is largely English medium. Such assumptions do not take into account the highly differentiated schooling market. Owners explained that the degree of English instruction at various school types within the private sector depended on the specific type of private schooling accessed and fee level. LFP case study school owners targeted their schools to a specific niche in the schooling market. They explained frankly that their schools could not be English medium as that would mean paying higher teachers' salaries, hence, charging higher fees, and ultimately, forcing them out of the LFP market niche to enter one in which they felt unable to compete. Parents were aware that the focus schools did not provide full English-medium instruction but provided more English-language instruction than state schools.

It is important to note the recurring categories of 'official' and 'actual' for enrolment and for the highest levels of instruction. These are directly related to how case study schools actually operated as LFP schools and mediated the formal regulations that they were supposed to adhere to.

(a) Rural schools

	Rural schools				
	A	B	C	D	Siyapur
Year first established	1994	1995	1998	1994	1984
Recognition status	Registered	Registered	Registered	Primary	Junior
Official enrolment	55	89	19	261	236
Actual enrolment	69	120	45	392	258
Highest official level	Primary	Primary	Primary	Primary	Junior
Highest actual level	High school	High school	High school	High School	Inter
Status of building	Donated by villager	Rent	Own	Own	Own
Number of classrooms	4	4	3	5	5
Toilets	No	No	No	No	No
Drinking water	No	Yes	Yes	Yes	Yes

(b) Urban schools

	Urban schools				
	E	F	G	H	Taj Nagar
Year first established	2000	1993	1977	1987	1991
Recognition status	Inter	Registered	Junior	Junior	Inter
Official enrolment	590	205	318	262	1089
Actual enrolment	137	347	318	276	1089
Highest official Level	Inter	Primary	Junior	Junior	Inter
Highest actual level	Inter	High school	Junior	High school	Inter
Status of building	Own	Own	Own	Own	Own
Number of classrooms	5	6	8	6	17
Toilets	Yes	Yes	Yes	Yes	Yes
Drinking water	Yes	Yes	Yes	Yes	Yes

Table II. Overall case study school profiles.[4]

Typical of schools in the LFP sector, case study schools operated to maximise their interests regarding profit maximisation and client retention, as well as recognition status. Thus, 'official' data were what schools presented in line with their recognition status, and 'actual' data were reflective of how they operated in practice.

Actual school enrolment varied from 45 for the smallest school to 1089 for the largest. Except for School E, G, and Taj Nagar, all actual enrolments exceeded official enrolments. This is because official enrolments only included students falling within the highest official grade level. School E was recognised and followed the common LFP school practice of 'affiliation', which entailed enrolling students in key high school and intermediate years from other unrecognised LFP schools for a fee, enabling them to take board exams. Taj Nagar did not follow this practice and School G did not operate beyond junior level.

Schools had increasing fee structures either by grade or by instruction level [5] (primary, junior, secondary, and intermediate). Official monthly tuition fees ranged from Rs. 25 to 130 at the primary level (rural mean = Rs. 40, urban mean = Rs. 99) and Rs. 30 to 145 at the junior level (rural mean = Rs. 57, urban mean = Rs. 106). Fee increments varied and were set by individual school owners. As expected, rural case study schools charged less on average than urban schools. However, the lowest urban school fees and highest rural school fees were roughly the same amounts for corresponding instruction levels. Effectively, official tuition fee amounts acted as guide prices and represented the maximum amount that a school could charge. Many parents employed a '*fee-bargaining* strategy' and negotiated a lower amount, thus not paying the full tuition fees. Furthermore, fee concessions for families with multiple children enrolled or those that could not afford the set fee were internally instituted in most case study schools.

The LFP Sector and the Schooling Market

Owners claimed that the impetus to start their schools emerged from their philosophies on the need to improve educational opportunity for disadvantaged groups in their communities. The catalysts were related to their overall beliefs about the educational needs of disadvantaged groups, and that:

> education is most important, it's a must. If we want to help raise
> the standard of poor children then at least our country will
> improve. It will become educated. (Co-owner, Taj Nagar)

However, as the discussion below will show, understanding their motives was not straightforward. The marketised arena in which the LFP case study schools operated necessitated a more nuanced understanding, reconciling owners' competing concerns for profit making and philanthropy. The significance of the LFP sector in altering the landscape for the delivery of schooling for disadvantaged groups is crucial to understanding the operational structure that LFP case study schools adopted. While owners did not officially express strong market ideologies guiding them, data indicated that the increased privatised and marketised educational context necessitated that maintaining and attracting clients was their prime concern. Thus, case study school owners managed their schools with an adept analysis of their market niche which most strongly manifested itself as: conflicting LFP sector/school self-concepts; the conceptualisation of disadvantaged parents as a specific LFP client group; and specific LFP school market strategies.

LFP School and LFP Sector Self-concepts

School owners not only distanced their LFP schools from state schools but distinguished them from high-fee schools by simultaneously conceptualising them in two discrete ways. Firstly, they expressly distanced their LFP schools from the state sector and from what they perceived as lower quality schooling, questionable teaching practices, and alleged casteism. Secondly, regarding high-fee schools, owners distanced their schools from what they described as extortionist fee practices which they claimed did not lead to better quality schooling compared with LFP schools in most cases. This contrasting self-concept was best articulated by one rural principal, keen to convey what set the LFP sector apart:

> First of all, they [LFP schools] are concerned with fees. [So] there is no casteism. Everyone, I mean all the kids sit in one class and it's not like, 'He's from this caste and he's from that caste'. And in some state schools it's like ... they [teachers] feel that those from backward castes remain backward, so those state school teachers have this feeling.
> ...
> And the private schools are looting.
> [What do you mean by looting?]
> I mean fees, fees according to their whimsy. You can charge whatever you like. Look in the cities. A kid is going to nursery school and it charges Rs. 3000-4000 for his admission. And he'll study the same thing, 'aa' to 'gya' [equivalent to 'A to Z' for the English alphabet] or how to behave ... how much can you teach a child in nursery anyway? (Principal, School C)

The practice of charging 'fees according to their whimsy' was attributed by this principal and other owners/principals to high-fee schools particularly in urban areas. This was despite the fact that, as we shall see, LFP case study schools also set their own fee structures and fee amounts, charging various extra fees at their discretion, even though this was contrary to state regulations. In the minds of case study school owners, what set LFP schools apart from high-fee schools was that fees charged by the latter were deemed unfounded and based solely from a profit/business perspective to maximise revenue margins without increasing educational return. Despite their own business motives (discussed below), most case study school owners sharply contrasted this to their own schools, which they conceptualised as performing a 'social service'. Therefore, from the perspective of case study school owners/principals, the distinction between high-fee and low-fee sectors was the former's 'aim to earn' or profit, versus the latter's social service or philanthropic ideal. The following is an excerpt from one co-owner stressing that distinction:

> We took that aim and opened this school: to educate children at low cost and give them a good education with good facilities ... And we maintain that aim to this day. We never had an aim to earn. This [running an LFP school] is very good work. I don't think there is any occupation more honourable in society than in education. Education is a temple that educates all the children of the state or nation ...There is no temple bigger than this. (Co-owner, School G)

Particularly significant is the fact that case study school owners restricted notions of nobility and holiness to LFP schools. Likening education at LFP schools to a temple and to the ancient Indian tradition of education as noble and holy is disjointed given the marketised nature of the LFP sector. It seems deliberately extended from the self-propagated concept of social service. It seemed that respondents' perceived lack of quality provision in the state sector and the 'exorbitant' fee practices of the high-fee sector overrode the eligibility of both school types to some conceived pedestal of nobility. Nonetheless, there were several inconsistencies in their reported self-concept as philanthropic, particularly since case study schools were essentially run as businesses.

Firstly, four case study schools were expressly opened for the gainful employment of their owners who could not find suitable employment elsewhere. Furthermore, while all owner teams included one individual who had previously worked in the education sector, one of the schools above and three others also had a partner who currently or previously managed a small business. Hence, at least four case study schools had strong incentives to engage in business-like practices and four had the background knowledge to do so.

Secondly, while all principals asserted to clients and outsiders that their schools did not make enough to meet school expenses and that they volunteered their own services, all except one confided that they actually earned sufficient revenue for expenses and, particularly in the urban group, to supplement or constitute their main income. While some owners invested part of this revenue into the school for maintaining existing facilities, building or buying new facilities, and installing new equipment, others seemed to use it primarily to fund their lifestyles. Therefore, the revenue could be constituted as profit, which while was not distributed to the managing society members [6] was similar to the profit claimed by owners of family-run businesses.

Finally, in contrast to their reported philanthropic ideal, some owners confided that their actual wish was to become part of the high-fee sector. However, since they did not have the capital to run a high-fee school and effectively compete in that sector, they were wary of losing the clients they already had, and thus, remained part of the LFP sector. Nonetheless, for example, School E's owners were contemplating experimentally rebranding the school as a medium-fee school in coming years. To this end, some expansion and redecoration work was underway at the end of the data collection period with a view to marginally increase fees for the 2003-04 year. The business-like mindset of case study school owners was further highlighted in their perception of disadvantaged households as a distinct client group and the market strategies they actively employed.

Perceptions of Disadvantaged Groups as a Client Group

Owners viewed the disadvantaged households accessing their schools as a distinct client group and targeted their schools accordingly. They perceived their client group as being illiterate or semi-literate, belonging to low socio-economic groups, and having very limited buying power regarding schooling. While owners felt that their client group was similar in educational and socio-economic status to that accessing the state sector, they felt the key distinction was this group's desire to access 'good' schooling and their ability/willingness (on the whole) to pay for it. This was also tied to assessments of this group's slightly higher economic resources, although the bases for these judgements were neither typically nor clearly articulated. Similar to household interviewees, owners/principals also stratified the school market for disadvantaged groups in accordance with the target group's perceived distinctiveness:

> Now, those who are well and truly poor, their children will go to the state sector. Those that are even a little ... suppose even if they're making Rs. 2000-2500 a month, he thinks, 'OK, we'll enrol them in a school that's a little bit better. Where fees are low and the schooling is good too'. (Co-owner, Taj Nagar)

This perception of the client group was remarkably similar to household interviewees' own conceptions of themselves regarding their place in the school market (Table I). In essence, households and school owners/principals in the study generalised the client group accessing LFP schools as unwilling to access the state sector but unable to access medium-fee or high-fee private sectors.

Market Strategies

Far from a concern for philanthropy, the market strategies adopted by case study schools were instituted to harness their overarching concern to maintain and expand their client base. The importance of adopting market strategies to compete for clients was captured by the oldest case study school, School G, whose target client group changed over its 26-year history from high-income to disadvantaged groups:

> At the beginning, when we first opened, we even got children from the IAS [Indian Administrative Service], IPS [Indian Police Service], engineers, and those from good backgrounds. We opened the school in view of their admission …But now lots of big 'hi-fi' schools have opened up so those families have money and everything, so they're diverted there. … there wasn't a single English medium [i.e. private] school. At elementary level there was one junior school [state] … So IAS and IPS families would go there and come here for the younger children because we were also nearby. Now we don't have a single child from IAS, IPS, or engineering backgrounds. (Co-owner, School G)

School G's experience was that the change in the schooling market was due to the emergence of large numbers of a range of private schools. This had a significant impact on the place that some schools occupied in the expanded schooling market. For example, it altered School G's focus to disadvantaged groups, a client group that was not previously accounted for in the market, as private schools were traditionally frequented by the elite and upper middle classes. Thus, despite the earlier assertion that their aim was to provide for disadvantaged groups without the 'aim to earn', in fact School G's strategy to rebrand itself as an LFP school was to capitalise in a niche where it could effectively compete and profit.

Rebranding was more complex than the traditional conception that schools in lower positions of the schooling market adopt strategies to elevate their place (Tooley, 1999). In this study, rebranding was bidirectional: from LFP to high fee (mainly aspirational) and from high fee to LFP (as above). The more typical aspiration to rebrand as a high-fee school and increase revenues (via a few years of medium-fee rebranding) was expressed by owners who felt that it would allow cream-skimming by altering intake through fee increases. Owners assumed this would have a positive effect on achievement results, confirming the school's status as a 'good' school in local school markets.

The prime motivation behind rebranding was to increase the school's competitiveness by developing its reputation as 'good', thus increasing its popularity. It had little to do with internal pedagogical or administrative changes regarding the delivery of schooling, but with raising the school's profile to attract more or different types of clients. Typically, this was by mimicking higher fee schools by, for example, planning to or actually constructing new buildings and facilities and naming schools to signify difference from the state sector (e.g. in English or with the words 'public school' [7] or 'Saint'). Case study school owners felt this would externally indicate that their school was 'good'. Some owners also considered mimicking the highest fee schools in Lucknow by operating a chain and opening multiple branches in the future. In fact, some case study schools experienced a loss of clientele if they failed to engage in mimicry even if the school produced good results on board exams. School D's co-owner described their experience:

> we taught them really well from the 1st to 8th. We gave them a really solid grounding, that, 'OK they're going to bring us results in classes 9 and 10' [state board exams]. However, when they all passed with first division in class 8 they immediately came asking for their TC [transfer certificate]: 'Sir, give me my TC. Sir, give me my TC'. I said, 'What's going on?' So they said, 'We want to study in class 9. They're going to put us in a good school. They'll enrol us somewhere, anywhere else'
> …
> Then I said, 'Mate, what's a good school and what's a bad school?'
> [So what did parents mean by a 'good school'?]
> According to parents a good school is one that looks good, that's all. That's what I think. …
> There were 14, seven left, seven stayed. (Co-owner and Principal, School D)

Nonetheless, this owner, like most others, believed that in order to expand their client base, LFP schools needed to provide some minimum standard in tandem with increasing the external look of the school. For case study schools, this mainly meant instituting few school holidays, having minimal teacher absences, and closely following the state curriculum.

The biggest strategic distinction between schools in the market niche for disadvantaged groups (state and LFP) was for LFP schools to follow through with contractual obligations to parents. Most case study school owners claimed that since parents procured educational services through a fee, LFP schools felt a sense of contractual obligation to provide a reasonable standard of schooling which would lead to building a solid reputation in the local market, and attracting and maintaining clients. As above, schools interpreted this as instituting rules and procedures that would contribute to the regular and timely provision of schooling, such as: strict discipline procedures, fixed daily timetables, minimal school closures, and regular teacher attendance.

Owners/principals claimed that they felt intense competition from other LFP schools in their immediate vicinity, particularly from more established ones. However, none felt any competition from the state sector, mainly due to the perceived inferior quality of schooling offered there. The degree of competition was reduced to two main factors: the number of LFP schools in their immediate vicinity (more pronounced for urban schools) and the fluidity of the LFP sector due to the ease with which parents could enter and exit LFP schools.

Thus, some case study schools offered even lower fees or more concessions than more established schools in a bid to attract their clients. School E, operating next to an established medium-fee school, capitalised on the latter's existing reputation by arranging to use its playground facilities in exchange for a fee. Thus, it compensated for a lack in its external package and recruited clients who could not afford to send their children to the medium-fee school, by riding on the coat-tails of the latter's reputation. Others opened their schools in their own communities to play up the characteristic of a 'home grown' school to win the confidence of community members and encourage enrolment.

Finally, most schools reported adopting aggressive marketing and recruitment techniques by door-to-door canvassing and inviting potential clients to school events. However, this canvassing was carefully balanced with playing up owners' higher socio-economic positions to maintain some power. Most owners adopted a paternalistic tone, convincing potential clients to access their schools to improve household economic returns in the future. Others only used door-to-door canvassing in areas outside the school's immediate locale, so as not to weaken their position in the local community by highlighting its dependence on local clients.

Having located their schools in a distinct place within the greater schooling market, case study school owners structured the internal operation of their LFP schools accordingly. This is highlighted in the following discussion.

The Inner Workings of LFP Case Study Schools

The internal structure of case study schools was hierarchical with the locus of control entirely in the hands of the owners. While in principle, state regulations outlined that all private unaided schools should be established and managed through a registered society [8] and, in the case of secondary schools, through a 'Committee of Management' (Section 16-A, Intermediate Education Act [Jain, 2001]), in practice, case study schools were run as the private operations of individuals or teams of family members who were the de facto owners. In nine of the schools, the principal was also the sole or part de facto owner. In the remaining case, School C, the principal was a very close family friend. In the six schools where de facto school ownership was in family teams, the most common arrangements were husband–wife or father–son. These family ownership and employment practices were contrary to the formal rules barring relatives of any member of the management as heads or teachers in junior schools and for any family to constitute a monopoly in the management of secondary schools.[9]

Internal Management Structure and Duties

The operational management structure in all case study schools reflected a top-down approach with the de facto owners carrying out functions necessary to the establishment and daily running of the school. Of interest here were those related to devising rules and procedures such as: setting school policy (and establishing latent philosophies); defining school visions (in the few schools that had one other than increasing school enrolment); devising school timetables; choosing curricula and teaching materials; setting the pedagogical framework; hiring and firing teachers and support staff; establishing fee structures and fee collection procedures; setting parent–teacher meetings (and sometimes conducting them); organising school events; establishing staff salary scales and hiring teachers; and overseeing salary payment.

The owners exclusively interacted with district officials and other recognised LFP schools to establish external rules and procedures used to mediate or fulfil requirements of the formal regulatory framework, such as: applying for registration; seeking information about the recognition process; negotiating affiliation with recognised schools for high school and intermediate students (for unrecognised schools or those that were not recognised beyond primary or junior level); following through with the recognition process; and making the necessary arrangements to ensure their students' eligibility in board exams. The dominant view in all case study schools was that a top-down management structure was necessary for their smooth functioning. In effect, this tight hierarchal structure promoted maximum control for owners and buffered them from certain official requirements regarding the management of their schools.

Only Taj Nagar and School G had middle managers acting as principals' assistants. These middle managers' authority did not extend to setting any policy or regulatory focus for the schools. Rather, their roles served as checks to maintain established school-specific rules and procedures, alerting the owners when action had to be taken to uphold them. Their tasks included: reporting teachers' punctuality; ensuring school timetables were followed; reporting student attendance figures; ensuring school records were updated; and distributing school notices.

Furthermore, while the formal rules highlighted the role of the managing societies, in practice they were little more than a loose collection of individuals who had close connections with the owners and very little input or involvement in the functioning of the schools. In one instance, the principal of School A, a co-owner with her husband, was not even aware of who the society members were. Thus, it was evident that the societies critical to the initial existence of case study schools remained muted entities and mere technicalities in their subsequent functioning with all internal and external management and administration related actions and decisions taken by the owners.

Admission and Enrolment Procedures

According to State Government rules, new admissions should not be accepted after 30 September of a given school year. Furthermore, only students with a 'transfer certificate' [10] from their previous school should have been accepted. Nonetheless, case study schools confided that the general procedure was to admit any student at any time of the year to expand their clientele. Since open admission and enrolment was common practice within the LFP sector, it not only fuelled competition between case study and other LFP schools, but provided them with a chance to increase their client and profit base year-round. Open admission without transfer certificates was standard procedure at LFP case study schools upon the payment of an admission fee, particularly in the primary and junior grades. For high school and intermediate, it was more difficult because of the stricter rules governing examinations.

Upon admission, case study schools claimed to administer a school-devised test to determine the grade level for enrolment. In most cases, children were placed according to the results regardless of age. However, one principal claimed that in some instances parents negotiated the grade level regardless of the child's previous schooling or skills:

> some parents come and say, 'No, you have to admit my child in the 5th class'.
> [Why?]
> That's just how they are. They say that you have to for my child ... when we've already taken the test and found that the child's not even ready for nursery.
> [Then what happens?]
> Well, we're caught in a difficult position, we're helpless. Either we admit the child. Like if our enrolment is low, and we have to fill up the number of children, then we'll take him. And if not, then we won't.
> [So do you take him in the 5th then?]
> We take them.
> [But then how is that child able to cover the material?]
> He's not able to cover it. It's immoral regarding that child's future. He won't be able to cover it. (Principal, School C)

Thus, keeping the motive of client retention and profit maximisation in mind, School C enrolled children in grade levels for which they were not prepared even though it felt it was unethical to do so, raising serious questions about the nature and quality of education provision and delivery.

Hiring Procedures and Conditions of Service

The detailed rules for appointing teaching staff (Jain, 2001) [11] and the establishment of the Secondary Education Services (SES) Board clearly outlined the hiring procedures and conditions of service, particularly for secondary schools. However, since recruiting teachers at LFP schools was difficult and staff turnover was high due to the low salaries offered, case study schools did not usually follow the detailed recruitment and selection procedures.

In fact, owners of recognised case study schools claimed that they usually spread notice of vacancy through word of mouth instead of advertising in newspapers as mandated, so that they could avoid the involvement of regional or state selection committees altogether. Furthermore, the disqualification rule (Rule 6, 1978 Rules) stating that no one related to the management could be appointed as a head or teacher at junior schools [12] was ignored by all case study schools. In each school, the principal and/or at least one teacher was either a co-owner of the school or a close relative (most commonly husband, wife, son, or daughter).

Similarly, at the secondary level, both recognised case study higher secondary schools (or inter-colleges) (Taj Nagar and School E) also made appointments on an ad-hoc basis, neither one recruiting teaching staff through the SES Board. In addition to conducting interviews and making offers on the spot, conditions regarding the dismissal of staff and salaries were also not followed. In fact, hiring procedures and conditions of service at all case study schools were often contrary to the formal rules despite the possible threat of punishment. Owners explained that it was important to establish close links with state departments, particularly for high schools and inter-colleges. They also claimed that they had to be prepared to pay an under-the-table 'fee' to hire independently.

Challenges Faced by Case Study Schools

Case study school owners identified three main challenges for the management and operation of their schools, which they claimed were typical of LFP schools: teacher staffing issues, fee collection problems, and low parental participation and interest.

Teacher Staffing

Owners/principals noted that, like other LFP schools, they were unable to offer salaries either consistent with the government scale (a condition placed on recognised schools) or higher (see Table III). All case study schools reported monthly teacher salaries far below the basic government scale for primary teachers, which at the time was Rs. 4500 to Rs. 7000. Monthly salaries ranged from Rs. 300 to Rs. 2000, which in some cases were even lower than the earnings of parents accessing their schools. As a result, the schools experienced high staff turnover, difficulty in recruiting motivated teachers, and some had problems compelling teachers to perform duties outside of class time. Owners/principals claimed that their inability to raise salaries was related to fee collection problems as a good proportion of parents did not pay the required fees either on time or in full.

(a) Rural schools

	Rural schools				
	A	B	C	D[+]	Siyapur[+]
Number of teachers	4*	4*	4*	6	9*
Number of class sections	6	11	7	11	11
Overall school student–teacher ratio	17:1	30:1	11:1	65:1	29:1
Number of trained teachers	0	0	0	0	0
Qualifications range	Inter BA MA	Inter BA	BA BSc.	Inter BA	Inter BA BSc.
Salary structure by qualification (Rs. per month)	Inter: 500 BA: 600 MA (owner): claims not to take a salary	Inter: 300 BA: 400	BA: 600 BSc: 1000	Inter: 650 BA: 1100 to 1150	Inter: 950 BA: 1050-1150 BSc: 1150 Owner: 3695

(b) Urban schools

	Urban schools				
	E[+]	F	G[+]	H[+]	Taj Nagar[+]
Number of teachers	5	10*	13	10	22*
Number of class sections	12	12	10	12	16
Overall school student–teacher ratio	27:1	35:1	24:1	28:1	50:1
Number of trained teachers	0	1	0	0	4

Qualifications range	Inter BA	BA B.Ed. MA	BA	BA	BA BSc. B.Ed.
Salary structure by qualification (Rs. per month)	Inter: 500 BA: 600	900+ 100/year experience at school Max. 1900	800 to 2000 by exp. at school	700 to 1500 by exp. at school + cash incentives	BA: 500 B.Ed.: 800 BSc.: 1000 + 100/years experience at school Max. 2000 Owners jointly: 7250

*Denotes that at least one owner undertook teaching responsibilities.

Table III. Teacher profiles in LFP case study schools.[13] Note. +Denotes a recognised school. School E and Taj Nagar were recognised until intermediate; School D until primary; and Schools G, H, and Siyapur until junior.

Several points must be noted about reported teachers' salaries and profiles. No school reported increasing salary by instruction level even though they all operated beyond primary regardless of recognition status. The two factors contributing to salary increases were qualifications and years of experience at the current school. Prior teaching experience did not affect salary levels. Salaries reflected a ranking of qualifications, with intermediate-pass teachers earning the least and those with a B.Sc., not a teacher training qualification, earning the most.

Only five of the total eighty-seven case study schoolteachers were trained, despite the fact that in recognised schools all teachers should have been. Teachers' qualifications ranged from intermediate pass to postgraduate, with most teachers being university graduates. Although six schools were recognised, only Taj Nagar had trained teachers. School F had a trained teacher but was unrecognised.

Owners/principals, particularly from recognised schools, stressed that they did not hire more trained teachers because they were in short supply. They used the *shiksha mitra* [14] government initiative launched for state schools as justification for employing untrained teachers at LFP schools. They further justified employing untrained teachers by claiming that teacher training qualifications were not good predictors of how well a teacher would teach, and relied on their own judgement instead. Owners/principals felt the problem was more acute in rural areas because not only did trained teachers prefer to work in the state or high-fee sectors because of higher salaries, they were also less willing to travel daily. They attributed these factors to mid-year teacher attrition and frequent staff turnover. Only one owner/principal expressed a concern of the above factors adversely impacting on children's schooling.

Owners/principals managed the low number of teachers either by operating multi-grade classes or double shifts. This was the case in all schools except School G and Taj Nagar. They employed teachers subject-wise, explaining why the number of teachers exceeded the number of class sections to be taught. While the highest overall school student–teacher ratio was 65:1 at School D, the largest class size at any school was 46 at Taj Nagar compared to the state's recommended maximum class-size indicator of 40. Similarly, while the smallest school student–teacher ratio was 11:1 at School C, the smallest actual class size was eight at the same school.

All the owners felt that it was important to strictly control teaching activities to prevent teachers: going off task; recruiting students as clients for private tuition thereby not delivering full lessons in class (similar to alleged behaviour of state teachers); or frequent absenteeism. Participants believed the above would adversely affect their school, whose reputation partly depended on teacher behaviour, causing parents to exit. However, they maintained that they had leverage over their staff through the threat of immediate dismissal unlike state school principals.

For example, while owners were aware that most teachers supplemented their meagre wages through private tuition, most banned teachers from providing private tuition to students of their own school. School H's co-owners went as far as banning parent–teacher meetings, and conducted meetings with parents themselves. Taj Nagar installed a CCTV-style remote monitoring device in every class which was bought with part of the school's revenues. The co-owners felt that it put a stop to teachers who would otherwise 'hang around the stairs in the halls and chatter'. All owners/principals felt that by 'keeping a tight control on them', teachers performed according to set expectations.

All owners saw themselves as education experts, whether or not they had prior professional experience in the education sector. None reported involving teachers in discussing pedagogical approaches, teaching strategies, or course agendas, and there were no reported or observed joint staff meetings for school target-setting. This raises fundamental questions about how case study schools could expect commitment from teachers when they were not offered adequate salaries, uninvolved in the school's teaching ethos, and in one case were held in blatant contempt:

> what's it to the teacher? ... They can work for two days and leave. They can go back to the village and start begging again. What's it to them? A person who is of no or low standard ... How can I say it, they should feel some responsibility towards the school ... But teachers don't co-operate like that. (Co-owner, School E)

Problems with Fee Collection

All owners/principals claimed their challenges were rooted in problems with fee collection, claiming that approximately 10-15% of tuition fees were left unpaid at the end of every school year. Given their clientele's limited financial resources, owners/principals were not surprised by this outcome, but they all stressed its negative consequences on the running of their schools. They attributed fee collection problems to a sharp distinction between parents who valued education and were educated to some level, and those who were not. They concluded that this difference was displayed in their fee-paying behaviour, claiming that those who were educated and 'understood the value of education' were regular with their payments while those who were not, were irregular. However, some owners/principals were more cynical. They felt that some parents who were irregular only claimed to have financial constraints but actually wanted a 'free ride'.

In rural areas particularly, owners/principals suspected that this minority of parents would send their children to medium-fee or even high-fee schools if they were available, and regularly pay fees in order to access what they felt parents thought was a 'truly' good school. In these cases, owners/principals felt that financial constraint was not the issue, rather timely and full fee payment was related to how these parents assessed the value of the schooling offered at the LFP schools they accessed. Effectively, owners/principals felt that this minority of parents withheld payment because they judged the value of schooling at LFP schools not to be worth the fee charged.

Given that fee collection was presented as a major challenge in running their schools, owners/principals were asked why students with outstanding fee payments were not expelled. They claimed that this was for two reasons: 1. a profit/business motive: as long as students were enrolled and attended, the school could hope to recover at least part of the outstanding fees; and 2. a philanthropic motive: it was unfair to expel students because parents refused or were unable to pay. Most owners/principals unofficially subscribed to the profit/business motive in informal interviews, but cloaked it as the philanthropic motive in formal interviews. Some, like Siyapur's owner, further claimed that students were not expelled because it did not affect his cost–benefit analysis since the number of teachers was kept constant unless there was a substantial increase in enrolment:

> If 10 kids are giving fees and if four are not the giving type, then [they] keep studying. Suppose I'm strict like, 'If you don't bring the fees then I won't let you sit'. If I don't let them sit in class it's not like there's any extra benefit for me. For me those same 10 kids whose fees I'm getting, those are the fees that will continue to come. When there's no extra benefit and that teacher is teaching those 10 kids, he'll teach those four too. So what's the problem? Let them study with them too.

...
This way at least I have the hope that, 'OK, the Rs. 600 that they owe me, maybe he'll give it, if not today then tomorrow'.

Low Parental Interest and Participation

Finally, low parental participation and interest in their schools was considered a main challenge by owners/principals. This was attributed by them to their clients' low education levels and inexperience with schooling. Most owners/principals stressed that parents only approached the school if they were concerned with fees and were far less likely to approach them on educational matters. This was also consistent with most parents' assessments of their level of participation. Household interviewees claimed they either felt ill-equipped to contact the school about educational concerns because of their own inexperience, or did not see the need for parental involvement unless they had a fee-related query or a specific complaint.

Owners/principals claimed that this lack of involvement did not contribute to a dynamic school environment. Nevertheless, none of them instituted platforms for participation such as parents' school committees or parent–teacher groups. These were limited to infrequent parent–teacher meetings and a few school events. Therefore, it is hardly surprising that some owners/principals claimed turnout was low at special functions and events to encourage parental involvement.

Furthermore, most owners/principals felt that parents' inability (or presumed unwillingness) to pay fees led to their hesitation in approaching the school. At the same time, however, none of the owners welcomed interference in any aspect of their schools. This was consistent with the hierarchical management structure which limited parents' roles to end-users, in line with the owners' desire to buffer schools from unwanted parental requests. Nonetheless, owners' characterised parents as simply procuring a service without assuming any responsibility beyond paying (or attempting to pay) fees and sending their children to school. Furthermore, they felt that the impetus for parents to regularly send their children to school was economic rather than educational – parents did not want their money to go to waste. Ironically, having set up such a client–provider structure, owners then complained that parents acted in ways asserting that responsibility for schooling was entirely the school's, particularly since it was part of the private sector.

Both parties continually shifted the responsibility of schooling to one another: owners/principals stressed that parents needed to provide a home environment conducive to learning and be more involved at school; and parents claimed that the school should provide all instruction and attention. From the schools' perspective it seemed that this shifting of responsibility was related to their wish to maintain some power in the household–school relationship. As the following discussion will show, interviews and observations indicated that this relationship was changing due to the increasingly marketised schooling arena and households' increase (though limited) in bargaining power.

Changing Household–School Power Dynamics and School Responsiveness

The study revealed that the increasingly marketised nature of schooling for disadvantaged groups prompted some shift in household–school power dynamics at LFP case study schools. This was related to both parties' awareness that the very existence of LFP schools depended on disadvantaged groups accessing them, as fees were their only source of funding. The key for case study schools was to attract new clients and maintain their existing client base, given expected attrition due to household schooling patterns and engagement strategies such as 'fee bargaining' and 'fee jumping'. In short, fee bargaining was used by parents to negotiate a lower amount of tuition fees. 'Fee jumping' was a strategy whereby parents paid only a few initial months of fees and exited to another LFP school at the end of the year with a substantial outstanding balance. Therefore, the funding structure of case study schools (as other LFP schools) attributed some power to a group that was traditionally marginalised in formal education, or who otherwise accessed the state sector which tended to be dismissive of them (see Probe Team, 1999; Balagopalan & Subrahmanian, 2003). In this limited sense, marketisation through the LFP sector seemed to prompt a shift in household–school relationships favouring clients.

Since parents were aware that the school relied on their money to survive, this attributed some bargaining power to them. As household interviewees claimed, paying fees signified the right to question principals about schooling practices. Furthermore, it entered them into a contract with the school, which indicated that in line with other market behaviour in India, they could negotiate prices through fee bargaining. This realignment was also transmitted across observed household–school interactions where there was often an unexpected level of banter and humour (sometimes bordering on chiding) directed by parents to owners.

This is not to say that households were on a higher or equal footing with case study school owners, but nonetheless, it challenged the assumption that interactions would typically mirror parents' social positioning vis-à-vis school owners of higher socio-economic class. For example, in some instances, washerwomen or *riksha*-pullers who otherwise served school owners accessed their schools. In such cases, owners claimed that school interactions with these clients were on very different terms than in other circumstances.

Most owners/principals claimed that they felt a shift. For example, Siyapur's and Taj Nagar's owners felt that parents were too demanding or did not show 'proper respect' for teaching staff. In addition, most owners/principals explained that it was not uncommon for them to defend their actions to parents who would sometimes come to the school and question certain behaviour towards their children. They construed this assertive action by parents as a marked change in traditional household–school relationships, and contrasted this to a perceived golden era when parents did not question school practices with the understanding that power rested with the school. Many owners claimed that they were unnerved by this change in parents' attitudes and behaviour and that it hindered their work, rendering the school powerless.

Thus, it seemed that the act of paying fees seemed to empower parents in a limited sense. Empowerment, in the context of increased choice, has been defined by Goldring & Shapira (1993) as 'the parents' role in exercising control within a school, typically through decision-making. ... Empowerment, usually through decision-making forums, is accompanied by sources of power and influence' (p. 398). Here, empowerment was not realised through increased decision making, but by exercising some control resulting from increased bargaining power through the act of fee paying. The resulting influence of this empowerment in affecting the operation of LFP case study schools must be stressed, as it led to the establishment of certain mechanisms (e.g. fee mechanisms below) in response. Thus, school responsiveness was a combination of the reactionary or pre-emptive actions taken by LFP case study school owners, in view of this household–school relational shift, and resulted in certain internal structures that were instituted to cope with clients' increased bargaining power. In essence, it promoted an increased marketised and consumerist approach to schooling.

In the interest of maintaining and expanding their client base, case study schools, at the very least, had to be seen to be responsive to parents' concerns. Therefore, the crux of the analysis rested on whether schools responded to parents' concerns or whether they only *seemed* to do so. From the school's perspective, it can be argued that it should receive complete information about parents' concerns for it to be truly responsive. This would require LFP case study schools to actively seek out such information and for parents to clearly articulate it. However, none of the schools reportedly did so. Thus, responsiveness could only be judged by how clearly, strongly, and frequently parents articulated their concerns independently. Data indicated three areas of parental concern: treatment of children by school staff, educational issues, and financial concerns.

Owners/principals claimed that educational concerns were voiced the least. Therefore, they stressed that it was more difficult to address issues regarding special educational needs, attainment, or pedagogical concerns. Nonetheless, most claimed that if parents presented specific educational concerns they would make further inquiries with teachers. However, School H's co-owner and principal insisted that his first step was to assuage parents by convincing them of the school's practice, even if parents did not see visible results of progress:

A lot of parents say: 'My child has been coming to school for two years and he can't even recognise the letter "A"'. So you should just forget about that. The more you think that he can't recognise 'A', or he can't recognise '1, 2, 3' in mathematics, it will have no effect on his education. A routine is being created for him. That's more important. That he comes here, studies – and about the things that he doesn't understand – if you tell him instead that he has a lot more to learn right now, then he'll get much better results. Rather than saying in front of him or coming and telling me that he's not learning anything, he's been coming for two years, or for five years, this won't lead to any improvement in the child. ... So they should take care that ... however much he understands and whatever marks he gets, he should never be forced to bring very high marks. It's more important to create an interest in schooling.

Thus, rather than addressing questions about basic attainment levels, School H downplayed the importance of students excelling. The co-owner and principal stressed that specific pedagogical instructions or suggestions by parents would not be accepted, since that would undermine the school's position and its educational practices:

I never say anything to the teachers. Whatever complaints our parents have, I try to convince them, I try to convince parents to what extent we are right in what we are teaching, and to what extent we are wrong, where they are wrong in their thinking, and how our thinking is different. We try and explain that to them more than anything. If we get any instructions [from parents] like that [about schooling practices], then we never pass them on [to the teachers]. That just means that we have no teaching ability if parents come here and guide us and we go tell the teacher, meaning that I'm just sitting here on this chair for nothing.

In other cases, despite claims to the contrary, it seemed that certain schools responded only half-heartedly to parents' educational concerns (as they did not actively seek these out), exerting their power by ignoring or dismissing them. Additionally, they claimed that it was difficult for schools to be responsive to educational needs that were neither clearly articulated nor brought up at all. According to owners/principals, some parents voiced concerns regarding children's treatment at school such as hitting. Interviews and observations revealed that most schools responded defensively, staunchly maintaining their positions and actions. Ultimately, responsiveness in LFP case study schools was best analysed by examining those concerns most frequently and clearly articulated – financial.

Responsiveness to Financial
Concerns: school fee mechanisms

LFP case study schools responded most directly to changing power dynamics when households attempted to exert bargaining power by employing fee-bargaining or fee-jumping engagement strategies. While Tooley & Dixon (2005b) claim from their study on similar schools in Hyderabad that 'private schools might show "concern for the poor": through their own philanthropic provision of free or subsidised places' (p. 20), the analysis here suggests that LFP case study schools instituted fee concessions and other fee mechanisms in an attempt to exert their bargaining power and maintain and expand their client base (see Table IV).

Fee mechanism	Corresponding engagement strategy	Leverage
Flexi-fees	Fee bargaining	Parents
Fee concessions	Fee bargaining	
Fee setting	Fee bargaining	Schools
Extra fees	Fee bargaining & fee	
Withholding	jumping	
documentation	Fee jumping	

Table IV. Fee mechanisms at LFP case study schools.

Some fee mechanisms were instituted in response to parents' leverage in bargaining power, while others were instituted pre-emptively in anticipation of these engagement strategies. While the flexi-fees and fee concessions mechanisms resulted from a greater degree of household bargaining power in an open and fluid LFP market, the others were expressly instituted to exert schools' power in response to household fee-bargaining and fee-jumping engagement strategies.

Furthermore, responsiveness to and the power dynamics surrounding actively voiced financial concerns were connected to a host of factors such as: principals' perceptions of their clients' ability to pay fees; schools' self-interest in maintaining and attracting clients; schools' interests in meeting expenses and increasing revenue; parents' assessment of the relative importance of different fees regarding their perceived immediate effect on their children's education; parents' perceived degree of entitlement to negotiate the timing and amount of fee payments; and parents' financial constraints.

Flexi-fees

The flexi-fees mechanism emerged because owners acquiesced to the fee-bargaining strategy and to repeated parental pressure to adopt a more flexible

177

fee collection approach without late fines. Owners claimed that even though this led to decreased profit margins, they did it to maintain their client base:

> If they are very adamant and the amount is Rs. 100 or 200 then we adjust the amount of fees owed because if we argue with them then they won't send their children to school here the next year. If the child studies here then it's to our benefit. That's how it is. We think of the business point a little bit here. (Co-owner, School E)

While fees should have been paid on the first of every month (or on 'Fees Days' in some schools), in practice, many parents paid according to their own schedules. The flexi-fee mechanism enabled these LFP schools to cope with fee bargaining by making arrangements for households to pay late without fines and usually with a 10-15% discount. Flexi-fees were appropriate for LFP schools since it was impossible to institute a payment scheme for advance payment of a full year's fees (as in high-fee schools), or successfully institute late payment fines (as in medium-fee schools).

(a) Rural schools

	Rural schools				
	A	B	C	D	Siyapur
Concession	3 children's tuition fees for the price of 2	2 for 1½	3+ = 1 child free	3 for 2	3+ = 1 child free

(b) Urban schools

	Urban schools				
	E	F	G	H	Taj Nagar
Concession	3+ = Rs. 20 off per child	3 for 2½ 4 for 3	2 for 1½ 3 = 2	Nursery to Primary: Rs. 25 off per sibling Junior: Rs. 50 off per sibling	Rs. 20 off per sibling

Table V. Fee concessions at case study schools.

Fee Concessions

Superficially, fee concessions may appear to be quite similar to flexi-fees. However, there was one main difference. Fee concessions were established by the school in advance, and in most cases, were expressly used as a marketing tactic when attracting clients. Furthermore, while flexi-fee discounts ranged in amount and applied only to those households that voiced financial concerns, fee concessions were instituted with definite and fixed amounts and as a matter of overt school policy. They were available to all applicable clients; however, a few urban case study schools were selective on household income. Reported fee concessions are presented in Table V.

Fee concessions applied to households that sent multiple children to the same school. Owners maintained that they were instituted to make it more affordable for parents to access their schools, thus increasing and retaining their clients. They explained that while some potential revenue was lost, this was necessary to offset some fee bargaining and was recouped by fee setting and extra fees. Furthermore, they felt that the likelihood of households accessing the school for a longer period increased if all children were enrolled in the same school.

Fee Setting

In anticipation of fee bargaining and to recoup some money lost through flexi-fees and fee concessions, many schools instituted the fee-setting mechanism. This involved marking up tuition fees slightly higher than the amount schools would like to receive, knowing that they would later offer a 10-15% discount to those that fee-bargained. As such, schools appeared to respond to parents' financial concerns while actually maintaining their interest and power. Since not all parents demanded flexi-fees or were eligible for fee concessions, the school effectively expanded its profit margin. In this sense, fee setting can be seen as a mechanism to maintain the appearance of responsiveness. Leverage in bargaining power remained with schools while parents felt that they exerted some power over them.

Most owners justified fee setting in terms of household engagement strategies, claiming that it was a way to recoup fees that would otherwise be lost. They further asserted that increasing revenue margins each year was necessary to meet recurrent expenses. Proposed fee increases were not substantial because LFP case study schools were aware that there was a market cap prohibiting them from setting fees beyond a certain threshold. It was delicately balanced to ensure that potential clients were not alienated and existing ones did not exit to another LFP school. Thus, it required knowledge honed into the local market and the school's existing and potential client base. Given competition in the local school market, LFP case study schools took stock of the minimum revenue required to pay school staff, building maintenance and facilities, and other school-related expenses before setting a fee. They also took into account a 10-15% loss from fee bargaining and fee jumping. While parents could employ fee bargaining on the new fees, the fee-setting mechanism ultimately mediated the power shift and schools maintained leverage.

Extra Fees

Instituting fees in addition to monthly tuition fees was another way that schools attempted to exert bargaining power (presented in Table VI).

	A	B	C	D	Siyapur
Admission/ Registration Fees (Rs.)	10	50	10	40	50
Exam Fees (Rs.)	Nursery and Kindergarten: 5 Grades 1-8: 10 Grades 9 & 10: 15	30	25	10	30
*Period of Collection of Exam Fees	H Y	Q H Y	H Y	H Y	H Y
Other Fees (Rs.)	–	–	–	–	–

	E	F	G	H	Taj Nagar
Admission/ Registration Fees (Rs.)	150	250	150	200	1 month fees + 150
Exam Fees (Rs.)	30	20	15	25	50
*Period of Collection of Exam Fees	Q H Y	Q H Y	H Y	H Y	H Y
Other Fees (Rs.)	–	High school computer course: 70	Games fees: 20 Electric fees: 20	High school technical-vocational short courses: 50	–

Table VI. Extra fees at case study schools.
Period of collection is abbreviated as follows:
Q = Quarterly, H = Half-yearly, Y = Yearly.

All owners/principals stressed that they were unable to charge as many different types of extra fees as their higher fee counterparts because of their market niche. They explained that high-fee schools charged extra fees for: sports, various activities, and extra tuition. Assessing their market niche, most owners only instituted admission and school exam fees. Unlike tuition fees, extra fees were non-negotiable and not subject to concession (with a few exceptions). Once again, owners asserted that full collection of these fees was crucial to offset fee-bargaining and fee-jumping costs.

In absolute terms, admission fees in the rural schools were lower than those in urban schools but they still represented one or two months' tuition fees per child at the highest level of education offered, except in Schools A and C. For urban schools, admission fees represented on average between one and a half to nearly three times the tuition fees at the highest level. Owners/principals explained that this high amount acted as an insurance against lost fees from new admissions that may engage in fee jumping later on. Schools felt that initial admission and exam times were when they had the most bargaining power, since this was when households were most sensitive to the negative consequences of withholding payment. As a result, parents would pay a premium (within a limit) for their children's schooling. Owners/principals felt that, unlike for tuition fees, households would make the necessary financial arrangements by saving, using reserve money, or borrowing.

From the perspective of most owners/principals, parents placed hierarchical value on the importance of different fees. Siyapur's owner, for example, felt that parents saw tuition fees as peripheral, whereas fees that were considered 'official' or 'necessary' were not bargained or forfeited. For example, just as school exam fees and board fees for necessary documentation were seen as serving a specific purpose with immediate negative consequences to their children's schooling if unpaid, so were admission fees, without which the desired school could not be accessed. Thus, in such instances, schools could adopt a staunch collection policy and felt that parents would make the necessary financial arrangements to make payments.

On the other hand, some owners felt that some parents did not see the relevance of paying tuition fees because they did not understand their role in meeting school expenses. Instead, they felt that parents saw tuition fees as directly contributing to school owners' coffers, hence, a peripheral cost. In short, owners claimed that to some parents, paying tuition fees on time and in full was perceived as advisable rather than obligatory. In contrast, this did not hold for fees considered absolutely essential by parents, even if admission and exam fees were little more than administrative add-ons instituted to cover part of the shortfall in tuition fee collection.

Withholding Documentation

Withholding official documentation was discriminately used for students in key years and was the mechanism by which case study schools had the greatest degree of leverage. As evidenced through the ease with which parents could enter and exit LFP schools, the LFP sector was quite fluid. LFP schools readily admitted students in years that were not board examined or that were in the middle of an instruction cycle without the required transfer certificates. Thus, the mechanism of withholding documentation most readily applied to students completing the primary and junior cycles (classes 5 and 8) and high school and intermediate cycles (classes 10 and 12) as they would require transfer certificates or other official documents such as 'admit cards' for board exams.

This mechanism was used as a last resort with those parents who owners thought were going to fee jump at the end of the year, as they neither paid fees for more than three months nor approached the school and fee bargained. While the threat of withholding documentation did not automatically guarantee recouping all fees due, it was the only way the school could recoup the majority of overdue fees by exerting maximum pressure and power over households who knew that taking exams hinged on these documents. As Taj Nagar had the highest number of intermediate and high school students, withholding documentation was most often used there compared to other case study schools.

For Philanthropy or Profit?

LFP schools are portrayed in the existing literature as one of two ways: either as 'engaged in philanthropy towards the poorest families' (Tooley & Dixon, 2005b, p. 21), or as ill-equipped 'teaching shops' out to make a profit and dupe otherwise unsuspecting and vulnerable parents:

> The so-called public schools [15] are increasingly becoming commercial ventures and even the rural areas are falling prey to the idea of their 'excellence' ... Some urgent steps are therefore, needed to discipline the petty teaching shops to save students as well as teachers from exploitation. (Singh, 1995, p. 140)

Empirical results from this inquiry demonstrate that it would be hard to characterise LFP schools as entirely one or the other. While there was a definite financial motive for case study school owners to open their schools, owners couched their operation as a desire for social service and a response to the failing state sector. On this point, if, as many studies indicate, the quality of state schooling requires serious attention and improvement (Probe Team, 1999; Dyer, 2000; Govinda, 2002; Balagopalan & Subrahmanian, 2003; Srivastava, R., 2005), then perhaps LFP schools can, in principle, provide an alternative to this sector for some disadvantaged groups. However, given some of the concerns about the nature and quality of school provision highlighted above (e.g. enrolling students in years for which they are not prepared; minimal standards of quality performance; disinterest in promoting student excellence), and in the absence of longitudinal data assessing school quality across LFP and state sectors, it is premature to make such claims.

What is evident is that the way that LFP case study schools were managed and run, highlighted increasing market forces in the schooling arena for disadvantaged groups. With vested interests in the survival and profitability of their schools, owners were keen to capitalise on their schools' reputations by mimicking certain practices of high-fee schools while simultaneously distancing LFP schools from the state and high-fee sectors. Although owners may have had some motive for 'social service' and philanthropy, especially in cases where LFP schools were opened in their own communities, increasing market forces prompted a more immediate daily concern for client retention and profit maximisation. Thus, as exemplified by fee mechanisms, not only were LFP case study schools adept at instituting internal mechanisms to mediate household–school relationships and maintain their leverage, they were also acute analysts of their market niche identifying strategies from which to capitalise. One thing is clear – whether LFP schools are operating for profit or philanthropy, we are only at the beginnings of understanding the impact of LFP schooling on the educational opportunities of disadvantaged groups.

Notes

[1] The figure for Uttar Pradesh refers to enrolments in elementary education (primary plus junior) in recognised and unrecognised private unaided schools through a survey carried out in eight states by researchers for UNICEF. They compared UNICEF survey figures with data for a further eight states from a household survey of 1998 by the National Sample Survey Organisation.

[2] An overview of the households: 55% belonged to Other Backward Caste or Scheduled Caste groups (ranked as the lowest official caste groups in India); 80% earned below the minimum annual taxable income of Rs. 50,000; mean rural income: Rs. 26,018; mean urban income: Rs. 41,768; 84% fathers: manual labour, small farming, or low skilled jobs; 83% mothers: housewives (of those who worked all but three engaged in domestic or manual labour); 51% of parents either had no formal education or only some primary schooling.

[3] *Pakka* literally means 'solid' and in this context refers to a permanent structure made of, for example, brick. *Kachcha* refers to temporary structures.

[4] Siyapur and Taj Nagar are the pseudonyms for the rural and urban focus schools respectively. 'Year first established' refers to the first year that the school was operational and not the year in which it became an 'official' school, that is, registration or recognition. 'Official' and 'actual' enrolments refer to enrolments on the books versus those children who were actually taught at the school. 'Official' and 'actual' levels of instruction refer to the highest level of instruction the school is officially supposed to provide and those that were actually provided.

[5] In Uttar Pradesh, elementary education comprises the primary (classes 1 to 5) and junior (classes 6 to 8) levels and secondary education comprises the secondary (classes 9 and 10) and intermediate (classes 11 and 12) levels.

[6] According to state regulations, a school cannot be technically owned by an individual. It must be established and registered by a managing society. In practice, data revealed that for case study schools the society existed on paper only and had little or no involvement in the actual management or operation of the LFP case study school.

[7] The term 'public school' was used here to refer to established, elite independent schools as in the British system and not publicly managed schools.

[8] Schools should have been registered and operated through a registered society consistent with the Societies Registration Act, 1860 and the U.P. Societies Registration Rules, 1976. Reference for Act and rules: Jain (2001).

[9] As per the Uttar Pradesh Recognised Basic Schools (Recruitment and Conditions of Service of Teachers and Other Conditions) Rules, 1975; Uttar Pradesh Secondary Education [Services Selection Board] Act, 1982; Uttar Pradesh Intermediate Education Act, 1921. These can be found in Jain (2001).

[10] This is an official school record for every student.

[11] For reference: Uttar Pradesh Basic Educational Staff Rules, 1973; Uttar Pradesh Recognised Basic Schools (Recruitment and Conditions of Service of Teachers and Other Conditions) Rules, 1975; Uttar Pradesh Recognised Basic Schools (Junior High Schools) (Recruitment and Conditions of Service of Teachers) Rules, 1978; Uttar Pradesh Junior High Schools (Payment of Salaries of Teachers and Other Employees) Act, 1978; Uttar Pradesh Basic Education (Teachers) Service Rules, 1981; Uttar Pradesh Recognised Basic Schools (Junior High Schools) (Recruitment and Conditions of Service of Ministerial Staff and Group 'D' Employees) Rules, 1984; Uttar Pradesh Secondary Education [Services Selection Board] Act, 1982; and the Uttar Pradesh Secondary Education Services Selection Board Rules, 1998. These can be found in the *Uttar Pradesh Education Manual* (see Jain, 2001).

[12] Rule 6, Uttar Pradesh Recognised Basic Schools (Junior High Schools) (Recruitment and Conditions of Service of Teachers) Rules, 1978 (see Jain, 2001).

[13] These data were collected at several points during the research process at each case study school through formal interviews, a staff questionnaire for principals and teachers, informal and formal conversations with principals, and school records. Since the information was considered sensitive, this was done in order to match respondents' replies over the course of the research process. Some participants presented conflicting information. These were questioned. None of the principals allowed teachers to reveal their salary or qualification data on the questionnaire. Principals' questionnaire responses were typically inflated compared to verbal structured interview responses to the same questionnaire. When asked why, principals commented that this was to make sure their paperwork was consistent but that they did not mind

revealing the 'actual' results verbally. Presented here are the 'actual' data as reported by principals.

[14] *Shiksha mitras* were hired through a government initiative and were intermediate-pass 'para-teachers' recruited for state schools (particularly in rural areas and for classes 1 and 2) to cover the shortfall of teachers. These were temporary 10-month positions.

[15] The reference to 'public school' here is the traditional British notion of independent or private schools.

References

Balagopalan, S. & Subrahmanian, R. (2003) Dalit and Adivasi Children in Schools: some preliminary research themes and findings, *IDS Bulletin*, 34(1), pp. 43-54.

De, A., Majumdar, M., Noronha, C. & Samson, M. (2002) Private Schools and Universal Elementary Education, in R. Govinda (Ed.) *India Education Report: a profile of basic education*, pp. 131-150. New Delhi: Oxford University Press.

Dyer, C. (2000) *Operation Blackboard: policy implementation in Indian elementary education*. Oxford: Symposium Books.

Goldring, E.B. & Shapira, R. (1993) Choice, Empowerment, and Involvement: what satisfies parents?, *Educational Evaluation and Policy Analysis*, 15(4), pp. 396-409.

Government of India (2001) *State of Literacy. Provisional Population Totals. Census of India*. India, Series 1, Paper 1 of 2001, Chapter 7. http://www.censusindia.net/results.html (accessed September 2003).

Govinda, R. (2002) Providing Education for All in India, in R. Govinda (Ed.) *India Education Report: a profile of basic education*, pp. 1-20. New Delhi: Oxford University Press.

Jain, R.K. (2001) *H.S. Nigam's Uttar Pradesh Education Manual: an encyclopaedia of education laws in U.P. from primary education to higher education* (5th edn). Allahabad: Alia Law Agency.

Majumdar, M. & Vaidyanathan, A. (1995) *The Role of Private Sector Education in India: current trends and new priorities*. Thiruvanthapuram: Centre for Development Studies.

Panchamukhi, P.R. & Mehrotra, S. (2005) Assessing Public and Private Provision of Elementary Education in India, in S. Mehrotra, P.R. Panchamukhi, R. Srivastava & R. Srivastava, *Universalizing Elementary Education in India: uncaging the 'tiger' economy*. New Delhi: Oxford University Press.

Probe Team (1999) *Public Report on Basic Education in India*. Oxford: Oxford University Press.

Singh, I. (1995) Restructuring School Education, in I. Singh (Ed.) *School Education: some reflections*, pp. 139-149. New Delhi: S. Chand & Company.

Srivastava, P. (2005) The Business of Schooling: the school choice processes, markets, and institutions governing low-fee private schooling for disadvantaged groups in India. Unpublished doctoral thesis, University of Oxford.

Srivastava, P. (2006) Private Schooling and Mental Models about Girls' Schooling in India, *Compare*, 36(4), pp. 497-514.

Srivastava, R. (2005) Review of Elementary Education in the Selected States, in S. Mehrotra, P.R. Panchamukhi, R. Srivastava & R. Srivastava, *Universalizing Elementary Education in India: uncaging the 'tiger' economy*, pp. 31-124. New Delhi: Oxford University Press.

Tilak, J.B.G. & Sudarshan, R. (2001) *Private Schooling in Rural India*. Working Paper Series, No. 76. New Delhi: National Council for Research and Training.

Tooley, J. (1999) *The Global Education Industry: lessons from private education in developing countries*. London: Institute of Economic Affairs.

Tooley, J. & Dixon, P. (2005a) An Inspector Calls: the regulation of 'budget' private schools in Hyderabad, Andhra Pradesh, India, *International Journal of Educational Development*, 25, pp. 269-285.

Tooley, J. & Dixon, P. (2005b) Is There a Conflict Between Commercial Gain and Concern for the Poor? Evidence from Private Schools for the Poor in India and Nigeria, *Economic Affairs*, 25(2), pp. 20-26.

CHAPTER 9

Private Schools and Political Conflict in Nepal[1]

MARTHA CADDELL

The Maoists are trying to demolish all the 'big buildings', to make the education landscape flat and then they will start building again. What can we private schools do? (Private school principal, Kathmandu, June 2005)

Please, brother, think that you are in a jungle. At any time you could be killed. (President, Nepal Teachers' Association, April 2004)

Introduction

These two quotes are emblematic of concerns and fears faced by the teaching profession in contemporary Nepal. The first is the words of the owner and principal of a private school in Kathmandu who has received numerous threats and repeated visits from Maoist-affiliated student activists. His refusal to make payments to them or to close his school led to him being punished in front of his students, forced to do sit-ups with a garland of shoes placed around his neck. Traumatic as this appears, teachers in Kathmandu work in relative security compared to those in schools outside the Kathmandu Valley, in provincial towns and rural areas. Teachers in government and non-government schools face pressure from state and Maoist forces to comply with demands. School buildings may be commandeered as army barracks, students and teachers may be forced to attend Maoist-led programmes. As the NTA official quoted above noted, teaching has become incredibly dangerous, with threats on life and livelihoods coming from all quarters.

At the time of this study, private schools in most areas had been forcibly shut down, with those who continued to defy demands made by Maoist forces likely to see property bombed or face personal attacks. The demands of the rebels were multi-fold, focused on the government, private school entrepreneurs and, indeed, parents themselves. As the then leader of the Maoist-linked student group highlighted:

> if government schools had good facilities and were providing a
> high-quality education then there would be less demand for
> private schools, and less scope for profit-oriented businessmen to
> open schools. Currently opening 'boarding schools' seems to be
> the dream business (*sapanako byaapaar*), with middle-class people
> feeling compelled to send their children to private schools if they
> wish to give them a chance of a good education. (Parajuli, 2000,
> my translation from the Nepali)

Behind these snapshots of the frontline experiences of teachers working in the context of Nepal's de facto civil war, lie conceptual and practical challenges around the relationship between private and state education provision of relevance in more peaceful contexts. Most significant for this chapter is how schooling – and private schooling in particular –emerged as a focus of violent conflict. Understanding this, however, requires engagement with the educational as well as political context in contemporary Nepal. Popular and political debate around the content of schooling and the modalities for its delivery encompasses concerns of learners, parents, teachers and school owners as well as the interests of political activists. Quality and effectiveness concerns are thus intertwined with issues that extend beyond the specific sphere of education, to wider issues of political positioning and posturing.

Such political conflicts and tensions that surround private schooling are relatively invisible in the international education policy arena. Rhetoric of 'partnership' between the state and private sector dominates discussion, limiting the extent to which the frequently conflict-fuelled nature of such relations can be explored. Certainly there is increasing recognition and examination of private/non-state actors as crucial players in the movement towards Education for All (EFA) (Education for All, 2000; Rose, 2005a, pp. 153-154). Possibilities for initiating public–private partnerships to enhance learning opportunities for students from across the socio-economic spectrum are being explored and advocated by key agenda-setting agencies. Yet, it could be argued that the discourse around 'new and revitalised partnerships' to aid the pursuit of EFA (1990, 2000) contributes to the masking of underlying tensions and cultural, even ideological, differences in how private provision is perceived and engaged with. Private schooling is often highly contested in terms of the aspirations providers play on, as well as how it is promoted and engaged with vis-à-vis government provision of education.

In exploring these issues, this chapter draws on interview-based and ethnographic research conducted in Nepal since 1999. Particular emphasis is given to research conducted in 2003-05 to explore the process and implications of the negotiations between private school associations, the

Ministry of Education and Maoist-affiliated organisations. The focus of these later blocks of research was primarily on Kathmandu-based interviews and school visits, with brief fieldtrips to schools and education offices in districts in western Nepal.

It is important to flag from the outset the limitations to the study which arose from the context of the conflict. Where it was possible to go and who I was able to meet and talk to were somewhat constrained. Most crucially, with the Communist Party of Nepal (Maoist) and affiliated organisations declared 'terrorists' by the state, it was not possible to interview directly key leaders of the student union involved in negotiations. Consequently there is some reliance on documented demands and accounts of negotiations from other parties involved in the process. It should also be noted from the outset that this chapter captures a particular snapshot of the conflict and its impact on private schooling, particularly in the early years of the conflict and the process of negotiations in 2003-04. At the time of writing the situation remains dynamic and volatile.

Drawing on this material, the chapter explores the disjuncture between the relative silence on private provision evident in the education and development policy arena and the extensive and, at times, heated popular and political debate about private schooling that echoes around many Southern countries – including Nepal. Following this, it examines how private schools have emerged as a focus for campaigning by political parties and, in more recent years, a particular focus of attention for the Maoist forces in their efforts to wage and win a 'People's War' against the monarchy and state forces. Exploring this violent conflict between state and Maoist forces in Nepal provides a sharpened focus for highlighting more widespread concerns, casting the political debates around private schooling into stark relief.[2]

Exploring the Debates:
private schools and the pursuit of EFA

Consideration of private sector involvement in schooling remains only partially explored in relation to the EFA agenda. Calls for greater focus on partnerships with non-state actors resonate through much of the EFA literature, as the search for mechanisms for expanding provision of schooling opportunities continues (Education for All, 1990, 2000; Rose, 2005a, pp. 153-154). However, the extent of practical and conceptual engagement with such calls remains limited. In part debate is constrained by the widespread acceptance that education at primary level should be free, a position enshrined in the Universal Declaration of Human Rights. Despite brief flirtations in the early 1990s by agencies such as the World Bank with the possibility of promoting a market approach to primary education and charging fees (Daniel, 2004), this has returned as a largely incontestable position. Discussion and engagement with the concerns of the private sector is consequently of limited concern to international agencies working in the field of primary schooling.[3]

Conceptual challenges associated with defining and engaging with the diversity of the private sector are the focus of some debate. The range of schools from elite establishments to 'budget' private schools (Tooley & Dixon, 2005b) including those catering for poor, rural populations makes it difficult to speak in any meaningful way of the private sector as a monolithic category. Similarly, divisions between state and private schooling are not clear-cut. Private schools may run outreach programmes for poor children (Day-Ashley, 2005); government schools may offer two tiers of tuition within the same school, charging children who choose to take 'private'/English-medium classes.[4] Schools, including many in Nepal, may run with some government support, yet have a number of teachers funded from community sources or through the payment of tuition fees.

Understanding regulatory frameworks and the shifting relations between state, market and the somewhat amorphous concept of 'community participation' in schooling forms a related area of debate. Concern at level of international educational planning and at country-level programme development has, in recent years, focused on promoting decentralisation and the need to extend greater decision-making powers to sub-national bodies and to communities. Consideration of the private sector has, in many respects, become subsumed under this conceptual umbrella, with liberalisation of the education market enmeshed with the emphasis on the political and developmental advantages of greater and broader participation. Yet, states that are unable to provide quality schooling to their citizens are also those that are likely to have difficulty in enforcing quality controls and other regulations on non-state providers (Rose, 2005b, p. 2). Engaging with critical questions about the role of the state, as both the initiator of engagement with the private sector and as enforcer of any regulations developed, requires consideration. Again, however, there is a need to look beyond the rhetoric to the actual practices of regulation of private schools and the relationship between the multiple layers of the state and different private institutions (see, for example, Caddell, 2005a; Tooley & Dixon, 2005b).

Difficulties associated with how issues around schooling choice and the role of the private sector can be meaningfully compared in a cross-country context have also constrained exploration of the private sector. Debates have tended to centre on quality comparisons focusing on the effectiveness and efficiency of private/government schools on the basis of completion rates and exam results. While it may be possible to consider questions of relative 'quality' of private/government schooling provision provided in terms of exam results, more amorphous, contextually specific considerations associated with student and parental aspirations, assumptions about private education and citizenship and so on prove difficult to engage with in the context of educational policy and programme development at an international level. Questions around *perceptions* of relative educational quality and the opportunities proffered by private schooling are integral to understanding the dynamics of the sector (see, for example, Harlech-Jones et al, 2005; de Regt & Weenink, 2005), yet prove difficult to translate directly into action-oriented policy or statements of international comparability. But, as the Nepal case will further explore, wider concerns around the content of private schooling, the aspirations it feeds on and promotes and the ability to meet those aspirations are key to a deeper and more politically engaged conceptualisation of the sector.

A further area of debate focuses on the charitable or social motives of private school owners – and the tensions that exist between such interests and the market-oriented, fee-based mode of operation (Rose, 2005a; Tooley & Dixon, 2005a; Srivastava, this volume). In part such debate highlights the difficulties associated with talking of an undifferentiated 'private sector'. Yet it also opens up a more explicitly normative, value-based set of debates which tend to be masked by the depoliticised rhetoric of partnership and the promotion of EFA.

This diverse array of debate around private schooling highlights the need for further investigation and the development of the field conceptually and in terms of detailed case study material. While decisions around private schooling provision have considerable significance for learners and their families and are a source of considerable debate in specific locales, this needs to be reflected further in policy and academic arenas. This chapter offers a contribution towards this. Through the Nepal case material it highlights the need for a broader and more politicised view of private schooling to be explored, one that encompasses but looks beyond efficiency and effectiveness debates and how the private sector can contribute to the pursuit of EFA. Questions around the role of schooling as an individual or social good (Colclough, 1996; Psacharopoulos & Patrinos, 2002), about whether formal education should be a government responsibility or opened to market forces, and what the content of that education should be are not 'dead issues'. Rather, they are the subject of ongoing political debate, and, in the case of Nepal, are fuelling one front of attack in the Maoist's 'People's War'.

Private Schools and Educational Aspiration in Nepal

The history of schooling provision in Nepal since the 1950s is one of ongoing tensions and continual reinterpretation of the relative significance of state and non-state actors as education providers. It is also a story of educational aspirations and the shifting nature of the divide between those able to pursue their schooling dreams and those thwarted in their efforts.

Private Schooling in Historical Context

The opening – and closing – of space for non-state, community and private provision of schooling has historically been highly politicised, highlighting the promotion of a particular vision of Nepali citizenship, development, and the 'educated person' (Pigg, 1992; Skinner & Holland, 1996; see also Caddell, forthcoming). Each shift in political regime has been followed by the revision of the education system, as the incoming regime attempted to reinforce its vision of the idea of the Nepali nation-state through re-articulating the relationship between the state, schools, and 'the people'. At times education policy has been used to maintain divisions, as under the Rana oligarchy (1846-1950), when formal schooling was explicitly denied to all but the ruling elite. In contrast, the mushrooming of schools in the decade following the overthrow of the oligarchy was presented as emblematic of the new government's openness and more inclusive vision of citizenship (e.g. National Education Planning Commission, 1955). At other points it has served to promote national unity, as with the introduction of the National Education System Plan (1971) and the nationalisation of all schools under the Panchayat system (1962-90).

The role of non-state schooling within this broader education arena has oscillated. In the post-1950 period the expansion of schooling was largely community led, with schools established through local support for teachers. In addition a number of large, elite-oriented private schools were established in Kathmandu, run predominantly by missionaries. As the state infrastructure was strengthened and expanded its reach throughout the 1960s and 70s, attempts to regulate and control the sector were introduced, culminating in the dramatic, yet relatively short-lived, nationalisation of schooling under the National Education System Plan (NESP).[5] With increased political and economic liberalisation apparent from the mid-1980s and culminating in the restoration of multi-party democracy in 1990, space for the expansion of the education market again emerged.

Democratic Education? Private Schooling Post-1990

In the post-1990 period, private schooling expanded at a dramatic pace, both in terms of numbers and in relation to the student base it was directed at. The dream of educational opportunity, and the employment and development opportunities associated with this, was bought into by an increasingly broad spectrum of the population. In part, this arose from a sense of optimism that multi-party democracy would lead to greater equity and opportunity for previously marginalised groups. Secondly, and more significantly, with educational opportunities opened to all through the expanded government school system, the search for ways of differentiating achievement and ensuring best advantage for young people intensified. Being educated would not, in and of itself, ensure status and employment. Rather the prestige of the school attended became increasingly significant as a marker of social standing and differentiation based on economic class (Liechty, 2003, pp. 212-216).

For example, English-medium instruction emerged as an important source of differentiation and is emblematic of the aspirations that the private sector plays on. The use of the English language in private schools – even of a very poor level – connects students to a wider international project and proffers a greater potential for mobility than is offered by the government schools (Harlech-Jones et al [2005] highlight similar concerns in relation to private schooling in northern Pakistan). It also differentiates between private schools. Broadly, the better the level of English instruction, the higher the school fees will be (Liechty, 2003, p. 213). This is a skill that the population of Kathmandu – and beyond – are willing to pay for. As Liechty notes, 'English proficiency is simultaneously the key to a better future, an index of social capital, and part of the purchase price for a ticket out of Nepal' (Liechty, 2003, p. 213).

Here we see the various strands of the private school dream intertwine. With rapid socio-political and economic change in the country throughout the 1990s, education has emerged as a focus for parents anxious and uncertain about how best to provide for their children in an environment dramatically different to that in which they grew up. Providing the best schooling that they can afford is a key concern for parents across the country, be it the Kathmandu middle class or rural farmers who see their children's future dependant on engagement with a wage economy. The close connection in popular discourse of ideas of education, development, and mobility reinforces such concerns (Pigg, 1992; Caddell, 2005b). Private schooling – whether at elite institutions or 'budget' schools in bazaar towns – is seen by parents as a way to mediate the risks of an 'unknowable "modern" future' (Liechty, 2003, p. 216; see also Lal, 2002).

The owners and principals of private schools frequently play on these concerns. Even for 'budget' schools in rural areas, the selling of a particular dream of a modern, developed future and enhanced employment opportunities was a key focus for student recruitment. Rural private schools examined as part of this study focused their marketing strategy on door-to-door advertising, with principals emphasising that attending their institutions would offer the opportunity for students to become 'doctors or engineers', allow children to move away from the village, and converse with foreigners (Field notes, 22 February 2000). Some attempted to promote a unique selling point that further enhanced these ideas. Particularly highly prized was the presence of teachers from 'outside' – from Darjeeling or Kalimpong (who consequently warranted higher salaries than their Nepali counterparts) or, for one particularly sought after-school in the district, the presence of volunteers from the United Kingdom.

But to what extent are these aspirations and dreams met? In parallel with the rise in pressure and interest in private schooling emerges a concern about what opportunities actually exist for those who complete their studies.

The expansion of education opportunities has proved something of a contradictory resource. On the one hand it is setting up apparent opportunities and encouraging hopes and aspirations. Yet, on the other, it establishes further barriers to success and sustains and reinforces inequalities. The existence of a de facto multi-tiered education system (Nepal South Asia Centre, 1998) means it is not sufficient to be educated – students have to be educated in the right place. Parents across the country may be spending as much as they can (or more) to send children to private, English-medium schools to give them as much chance as possible of getting a job or going for further study. Yet, despite this investment, students' aspirations are, in the main, not met. Budget private schools, with poor facilities, unqualified and underpaid teachers, are unlikely to provide education which will open the livelihood choices that the marketing efforts of their principals suggest. The dream of being a doctor or engineer can only be realised by a select few.

Attempts at Regulation: state–private sector relations

Such diversity within the sector is in part a reflection of the limited regulation of the market and the lack of controls on both the number of schools established and the quality of the facilities and tuition they provide. Attempts to integrate private school registration into wider educational planning processes have not been widely implemented. Whilst there is discussion of the importance of school mapping as a basis for determining government school construction and private school registration, this is only selectively applied. Similarly quality control concerns find little space for practical implementation in the work schedules of district education officers. In part, this is due to difficulties faced by staff in conducting their work more generally owing to difficulties associated with travel in the districts (compounded by the current conflict) and general pressures on government staff time (Caddell, 2005a). In Kathmandu for example, there are estimated to be around 1000 private schools – some registered, others not. For the district education office staff to engage in any meaningful way with these institutions whilst also tackling the pressing needs of the government schools seems an impossible task.

In addition, guidelines on the need for specific facilities, staff qualifications and so on are selectively applied by local officials, with the smoothing over of applications through 'bribery' commonplace. Private school proprietors realise they must maintain a cordial relationship with the district authorities to make the daily life of the school easier and prevent unnecessary intrusion into their activities. Doing so can make official registration and the designation of the school as an exam centre for district exams easier, all things which may encourage people to send their children to the school. As one principal noted: 'If we make them happy, then they [district officials] will be happy and not harass us' (Field notes, 3 March 2000). He explained that during the registration process he had to take district officials to the local inn for meals and drinks and employ one of the district officer's relatives as a teacher (see Tooley & Dixon [2005b] and Srivastava's chapter in this book for similar evidence from Indian schools).

Over the last decade, however, the issue of relations between the state and private schools has emerged as a key area of political concern at national level. As a result of the actions of the Communist Party of Nepal (Maoist), popular and political pressure for tighter controls on the sector has increased. Private school associations have emerged as significant political players, engaging in discussion with the government, the public and directly with the Maoists. Private schools have had to reconsider how they operate, what they teach and the fees they charge. The remainder of this chapter explores how private schooling has become a focus of such violent political conflict and the implications this has for how we engage with the concept of partnership between the state and the private sector. In beginning to respond to this, however, it is important to situate the Maoists' engagement with schools within the wider context of the populist and party political posturing and action of the mainstream parties in the post-1990 period.

Political Parties, Popular Debate and Private Schools

Given the historical importance attached to the position of the school in the community, activities in schools provide a useful 'jumping off' point for populist political campaigns to promote particular interests, with interest groups able to tap into the widespread concern of parents to provide educational opportunities to their children. In the 1990s, schools became increasingly drawn into the sphere of party political struggles, with teachers, education officials, and students aligning themselves with particular parties. Initially, political parties were particularly interested in using schools as a national network through which to spread their message and to build up a local support base. Student unions and teacher unions were directly linked to political parties, and in effect, worked as campaign groups for the party as opposed to defending the interests of the groups they purported to represent.

A particularly overt linkage between political structures and the school is seen in how the school is used as a recruiting ground for party members, with teachers and students actively sought out by activists. Recruitment focuses in particular on the secondary level, although involvement in primary classes is not unheard of. During the early 1990s in particular, when formal party structures were yet to be developed at the Village Development Committee level, the network of schools across the country became a key site through which to spread the message of particular parties. This led to a period of what one former teacher referred to as 'over-freedom', with students in particular believing that democracy meant that no one could tell them what to do. Accounts of this period tell of students refusing to be taught by teachers of particular political parties and of teachers being subjected to physical attack because of their political affiliation.

195

In addition, private schools, of both primary and secondary levels, frequently came to be associated locally with one or other political group, determined largely by the owner or principal's affiliation. One private school principal, for example, explained that there are 'no Communists in this school. Only Democrats send their children here', and referred a nearby rival school as a 'communist school' (Field notes, 18 April 2000).[6] Such distinctions appeared to impact on how some parents decided which school to send their children to. Supporters of Leftist parties tended to send their children to the so-called 'communist school' and Congress supporters avoided it. Such choice, however, was only open to those living in more urbanised areas where a range of schools was on offer. Even in these areas, the ability to choose is only open to those who have the financial capital required for private education.[7]

Despite political posturing around the inequities of schooling provision by all the major political parties throughout the 1990s, the dual calls for greater regulation of the private sector and the improved quality of state provision meant little in terms of action for change in classrooms or district education offices. So why, then, did the period from the late 1990s and the early years of the twenty-first century see a flurry of activity around private schools?

Battlefield Schools:
Maoist action against private schools

Since 1990, the Communist Party of Nepal (Maoist) has been demanding that the country be declared a republic, a position more vociferously and violently pursued since February 1996, when the party began waging an underground, guerrilla-style war. The scale of attacks and reprisals escalated dramatically following the declaration of a state of emergency by the government in November 2001 (see Maharjan, 2000; Thapa, 2002; Gellner, 2003; Hutt, 2004 for discussion of the movement and government response). The Maoists appear to view schools both as a site for gaining support for their activities and – as a particularly salient symbol of the state and of the abuse of state power – as a legitimate target of insurgency activities. Schools are also considered an important recruiting ground for the movement, a site where disaffected young educated people can be targeted and persuaded of the importance of the Maoists' activities and disciplined into the order and practices of the movement. Indeed, in his pronouncements on education, Comrade Prachanda, one of the key strategists of the movement, recognised students 'as the "reserve force" in a future "mass uprising"' (Bhattarai, Binod, 2001).

While the education sector as a whole is open to the attention of the Maoists, both militarily and politically it is the position of private schooling (and its juxtaposition with government provision) that has been a key focus of action. Calls to 'set fire to the educational supermarket' (*Nepali Times*,

1 April 2005) have been accompanied by specific calls for changes to the management and content of private schooling. Demands include the reduction of school fees; the removal of reference to the monarchy in school activities, including the singing of the national anthem; the end to Sanskrit teaching; the prevention of 'western influence' in teaching; and, ultimately, the nationalisation of schooling. Significantly, however, the focus of demands also extends beyond schooling-specific concerns to encompass broader concerns of the movement. For example, in a statement in 2000, the leader of the Maoist-affiliated student union, the All Nepal National Independent Students' Union (Revolutionary) (ANNISU(R)), linked school closures to demands for the return of land occupied by India, the involvement of the International Monetary Fund and World Bank in development efforts, and the pervasiveness of Hindi films as well as to schooling-specific concerns (Parajuli, 2000). Strike action in January 2003 drew attention to demands for the terrorist label to be lifted, in order to allow the ANNISU(R) to take part in student union elections.

Opposition is frequently couched in terms of the pervasive inequality in the education system. As Parajuli of the ANNISU(R) notes: 'In the current context one can see "unequal education" being provided, yet "equal competition" in the form of the SLC [School Leaving Certificate] exams' [8] (Parajuli, 2000). Challenges made by the insurgents thus highlight specific areas of school content considered antithetical to the Maoist position. In doing so, they draw attention to perceived inadequacies of the state – both as education provider and as source of security – and to highlight the disjuncture between aspirations and the realities of schooling and livelihood opportunities.

In a similar vein to the discussion of political parties there has, of course, been a similarly strong populist dimension to the Maoists' choice of schools as a site for promoting their position and challenging the state, particularly in the early years. Specifically, this has served to highlight the movement's ability to pick up on interests of the local community that are not being effectively addressed by other organisations, including the mainstream political parties. Demands to return school fees, a central feature of Maoist actions in schools, are thus designed to gain popular support and to situate the movement firmly on the side of 'the people' in opposition to the elitist 'state'. Other blatantly populist measures which dominated early action of the Maoists included the call for students to get a 50% discount on transport costs, entry to cinemas, and hospital bills, and access to cheaper kerosene for cooking. Such moves are clearly designed to increase students' support for the movement (Parajuli, 2000).

Further issues such as corruption in public office and the high cost of schooling have been the subject of much debate by the mainstream parties, but little change in practice is evident. Thus, to be seen to be actively addressing these issues sets the Maoists apart from other groups.[9] Teachers and school owners have been subject to extortion [10] and to pressure to

197

change the content of the school curriculum, including any mention of King Gyanendra or the monarchy and the singing of the national anthem. Demands have also been made to allow Maoist students to speak to pupils and to distribute recruitment literature in the school. Those who do not comply have been faced with humiliation in front of their students, such as having shoes tied round their necks and being made to do sit-ups in front of the students (Field notes, 24 June 2005). Other responses have been more violent in nature, involving the dousing of school principals in kerosene, physical abuse, and the abduction of teachers (e.g. Bhattarai, Binod, 2001).

In many areas the complete closure of private schools has been enforced. Those who have not complied with shut-downs and other demands risk being subjected to bombing of the premises.[11] In part, shut-downs are a means of highlighting concerns specifically related to schooling and the failure of the government to address the inadequate state of education in the country. Yet strikes also highlight wider inadequacies of the state, in particular its inability to provide security to its citizens. The government has urged schools to open, promising to ensure the safety of students and teachers. However, this claim did not lessen the widespread fear of violence and schools remained closed. Indeed, in many cases, parents have been directly threatened and warned not to send their children to school on strike days. This threat was later extended to a more generalised call to stop sending children to private school, particularly in areas outside the Kathmandu Valley.

Some school staff in Kathmandu reported that they had been able to engage in a degree of discussion with the Maoists over the payment of 'donations' (in essence a form of protection money). They negotiated a reduction in the amount handed over after explaining the social principles of the school and presenting its financial records. In the main, however, there appears to be little differentiation in terms of how non-state schooling is treated by the Maoists. Schools with explicitly social service mandates, including long-established missionary schools and institutions run by non-governmental organisations (NGOs), have been targeted and closed. Reports from eastern Nepal suggest that so-called 'community schools' – handed over to local management committees by the government – have also been subject to action, with demands being made for management committees to close schools unless they deliver a document saying that the contract with the government has been annulled (report in *Samaya*, 18 August 2005, translated in *Nepali Times*, 19 August 2005).

So what is the alternative being promoted? Baburam Bhattarai, one of the leaders of the Communist Party of Nepal (Maoist) has stated: 'the old reactionary system must be demolished [in order to build] anything new and progressive' (cited in Bhattarai, Binod, 2001). Schooling, from the Maoists' perspective, should be in the hands of the state, but in the process of revolution the form that the state itself takes must also be transformed. Thus, considerable broader changes have to be accomplished before a new model for schooling can be introduced. As the private school principal whose quote appeared at the start of the chapter noted, the Maoists appear to want to flatten the education system and squash the private schools (Field notes, 24 June 2005).

Recently, glimpses of what an alternative Maoist-approved school may look like have begun to emerge. According to NGO personnel working in western areas of the country, the Maoists claim to be moving from an 'era of destruction to an era of construction' (f/n: April 2004). For the education sector this appears to constitute the closure of all private schools, the application of pressure on teachers to attend and teach regularly in class, and the reorienting of the school calendar, curriculum and extra-mural activities. Indeed, there are reports that the Maoists are running 'model' schools and implementing a new curriculum in the districts of Rukum, Rolpa, and Salyan (Shahi, 2005).

In many respects, the structure of the provision seems similar to the state-sanctioned schooling, with the replacement of royalist or 'old' nationalist material with activities that promote Maoist visions of the Nepali state. Instead of the King's birthday being celebrated, Mao's birthday provides a focus for a school holiday. Commemoration of the martyrs of the democracy movement is replaced by veneration of those comrades killed in the People's War. In the formal curriculum the alternative vision appears in more 'everyday' ways such as the alliteration used for alphabet learning (e.g. 'chha for chhapamaa'r [guerrilla]) and display of weapon capture figures in discussions of pie charts (Shahi, 2005). The extent of the institutionalisation of these changes is, as yet, difficult to gauge.

Negotiations between Private Schools, State and Maoists

The Maoists' focus on education has served to highlight and exacerbate the tensions between the government and the private schooling providers, as well as casting into starker relief the differences and divisions within the private sector. This final section of the chapter examines the impact the conflict is having on such relations through a focus on the process and outcomes of negotiations between private school organisations, the Ministry of Education, and Maoist-affiliated groups.

Space for Negotiation

The pervasive use of school strikes, including the threat of permanent closure of private schools, has played a significant role in bringing the conflict into the homes of the Kathmandu middle classes. While the frontline battles and violence remain in rural areas, remote from the urban population's everyday frame of reference, the closure of schools taps directly into concerns about their children's future opportunities. This concern meant that the government had to at least be seen to be doing something about the problem, with representatives of a parents' group, the Nepal Parents Organisation, as well as the private school groups themselves calling for action.[12]

By late 2002, against this campaign of continued violence and an expanded focus on private schools, pressure was building for talks to take place. In December 2002, an indefinite school closure was called by the ANNISU(R), with the strike to be enforced until their 13-point list of demands was met by the government. Again, demands from the Maoist side encompassed issues beyond an education sector focus, including broader political demands as well as specific calls for the end of the teaching of Sanskrit as a compulsory component of the secondary curriculum, and assurances that education would be totally free to students and that private schools would be nationalised.

At this stage the possibility of talks had become more complex, as the Maoists had (in October 2001) been classed as a 'terrorist organisation' by the Nepali state. Nonetheless, with their livelihoods at risk, the private school organisations sought to initiate dialogue through the involvement of human rights organisations and other indirect routes to contact the Maoists. There followed a somewhat convoluted set of meetings, brokered by human rights organisations. Negotiators from the government and the largest private schools organisation, the Private and Boarding Schools Organisation of Nepal (PABSON), were unable to publicly declare that they had met with the Maoists face to face, however a series of meetings between the three sides took place in the Nepali month of Mangsir (November-December 2002). The result of negotiations remained largely inconclusive. The private school organisations claimed that they were under attack from both the government's attempts to introduce new tax and regulatory processes, and the Maoists' threats of closure and violence. The Ministry of Education was relatively powerless to act, given the broader government position on treating the Maoists as terrorists. While ANNISU(R) negotiators agreed to postpone the closure if demands to reduce fees and to introduce a Code of Conduct for private schools were met, it was recognised by all sides that this could only be a temporary solution. And, as it has transpired, strikes, calls for the closure of private schools, and violence against property and people have continued.

Implementing Changes: Ministry responses and the PABSON Code of Conduct

After the indefinite strike of 2002 was called off, attempts were made to find practical ways of implementing the new government regulatory framework introduced in the 7th Amendment of the Education Act (HMG, 2002) and the PABSON Code of Conduct (Private and Boarding Schools Organisation of Nepal, 2002). From the PABSON side, a fee structure for private schools has been developed, with schools differentiated in terms of the facilities they provide and were graded A-D accordingly. As well as providing an indicator of what fees should be levied, this formulation also complied with the Maoists' demand to reduce the level of those charges, cutting fees by between 10 and 25%.

From the government side, efforts have increased to ensure private schools comply with the regulatory structure (introduced in May 2002) aimed at meeting Maoist and broader popular demands to control the growth and quality of the sector. This requires schools to identify themselves as either trust schools (public or private) or institutional schools. In the case of public trust schools, the land and building are owned by the government, with other facilities and salary costs met by the community. For private trusts, all the physical facilities, building and land are provided by an individual or group of private investors. While they operate as trustees of the school, they cannot make a profit from it. Further, if they decide to stop operating as a school, then the land and buildings must be handed over to the government. For those who opt for the third option – institutional schools – schools remain the property of the investor, however this comes with a requirement to register the school as a private company and comply with the tax requirements levied by the Ministry of Finance. In addition, registration with the Ministry of Education is also required and a tax of 1.5% of school income is levied to contribute to a fund to improve rural government schools.

While the offer to develop and implement these frameworks was key to the withdrawal of the ANNISU(R) strike threats, the limited support for them from schools and the sense they were imposed under duress has meant they remain, in late 2005, largely unimplemented. As one school principal explained, the whole agreement is 'hogwash', a result of the government saying yes to all parties, but not having any means to enforce the implementation of change (Field notes, 23 June 2005). The school fee structures are regarded by principals of the more expensive schools as unworkable. The proposed cuts in charges would, they feel, result in them not being able to operate the institution. For schools towards the budget end of the spectrum, the fee structure is largely irrelevant as they have to undercut competitors to attract students. Consequently, the agreement remains only on paper and the lack of implementation serves to fuel the anti-private-school action of the ANNISU(R) and mainstream leftist student groups. Similarly, there has been little movement on the registration of schools as companies, with principals and owners refusing to pay tax and reluctant to enter into any agreement that could see their property commandeered by the state.[13] Many school owners expressed sentiments similar to those of a school principal who described such moves as the 'extortion of more money from private schools' (Field notes, 24 June 2005).

What Basis for State–Private Sector Partnership?

While drawn into discussions as a result of the pressure brought to bear by the Maoists, the tensions between the government and private school organisations remain, and indeed, have been exacerbated. The nature of the interaction highlights the lack of trust between them and the limited space there is for any 'partnership' to develop around the conflict or wider educational concerns. Engagement with the state as a source of security (by allowing army or police to 'protect' schools) risks incurring further attacks from the Maoists. For the government to engage with the extent of the demands made on private schools, it must divert attention and resources from its work in the state education sector. Furthermore, in recent years, trust has been further eroded by the uncertainties created by the King's takeover of direct executive powers. The question of who 'the government' is and the level of negotiation that is possible in the current political climate further erodes any possibility of productive partnership.

The process of negotiation and the agreements and codes of conduct that emerged from it demonstrate a selective engagement with the other party. PABSON, for example, wish to generalise the problems they face, shifting focus away from private schools specifically and involve other parties in the negotiations (interviews with PABSON officials, 21 January 2003, 23 June 2005). Thus, the PABSON Code of Conduct makes efforts to stress links with the government curriculum and textbooks and the need to take guidance from the Education Act and Regulations on such issues as salaries for staff and fees to be collected. Yet, there remains a strong feeling among private school activists that they have been left in the lurch by the government and are paying the price for government failures to address educational disparities and the broader problems arising from the Maoist conflict. This led to the somewhat farcical situation in July 2003 of private schools affiliated to the two main organisations – PABSON and National Private and Boarding School Organisation of Nepal (NPABSON) [14] – calling an indefinite strike themselves to draw attention to the limited government engagement with their plight.

With this perceived lack of support, private school organisations such as PABSON and NPABSON are seeking assistance from other sources, including the international community. In such efforts to gain support and widen engagement with the difficulties they face, they are drawing on the internationally sanctioned rhetoric of EFA, the right to education, and the need to promote schools as 'zones of peace' (e.g. UNICEF, 2005). A further example of the selective use of the idea of educational partnerships is evident here, with the private school associations incorporating elements of the global social agenda into their position statements, on the one hand, while striving to maintain their market position on the other.

A Distraction from the Real Issues?

There is a strong sense in which the current debates and action around the private sector in Nepal are something of a sideshow to the wider tensions in the education sector. Focusing on regulation and fees, for example, does little to address the issues of the divergence in student exam performance or the unmet aspirations of the vast majority of children and their parents. Engaging in talks and producing amendments to the Education Act and codes of conduct creates a façade of change and action, but changes little at the level of the school. Parents have not seen a reduction in the fees they pay, disruption to schooling has not ceased, and crucially, there has been no evident improvement in educational quality for students at either government or private schools. The broader issues around schooling content and purpose raised by the Maoists (and indeed in much popular and political debate) remain unaddressed.

A key area which remains unresolved, and which undermines any possibility of meaningful partnership between the government and private sector, is the difficulty of engaging with the tensions between profit-oriented and service-oriented motivations for operating private schools. In part, these debates are masked by the vested interests of the private school organisations, which, in the main, represent the wealthier educational enterprises as opposed to the more explicitly social service-oriented NGOs and charity institutions. Protecting their own business and profits remains key, with the discourse and rhetoric of educational quality and the provision of a social good used as both a marketing tool, and to counter the government's demands for tax payments and so on. Schools appeal to the private interests of parents and students to attract their custom, but in doing so, also engage with the philanthropic rhetoric of providing a social service in the context of a dysfunctional state alternative. Disaggregation of the private sector has tended to focus on the facilities offered, fees charged, and the exam results obtained as opposed to any wider concern with the content or quality of education in any broader sense. In turn this contributes to (and is reinforced by) the delimiting of popular debate on education. There is much to be gained by the private sector in maintaining a sense of antagonism and competition between the government and private schools – perceptions of government failure fuel private enrolment. The building of any meaningful partnership, thus, remains difficult and poses conceptual and practical challenges that remain unresolved.

Finally, there is much to be learned from the various elements of the interaction between the state and private sector and, crucially, from the interplay with parental and student aspirations and expectations. The expectations learners and parents have of schooling and the educational decision-making processes they engage in arise from particular dynamics of the relationship between state and private schooling. Discussion of schooling reform, whoever the provider may be, has to actively engage with and address these concerns. That should not mean simply playing on fears and the sense of education as the only mechanism to mediate an uncertain future. Rather it requires an active and honest dialogue about what diverse schooling opportunities can lead to in terms of individual and societal 'goods'.

Conclusion: partnerships in conflict

So where does this discussion take us in terms of understanding the role of private schools and their relationship with the state and the possibility of 'revitalised partnerships' in the pursuit of EFA? The case of the Maoist conflict in Nepal and the impact it is having on education provision, and private schools in particular, is an extreme one. But it casts into sharp relief issues of relevance for broader policy-oriented and academic engagement with non-state education provision. It highlights the multiple layers of engagement that take place around schooling provision and the key points where breakdown of trust and partnership can occur – from thwarted student aspirations to empty political posturing around education reform.

Further, the Nepal case highlights the need to open space for discussion beyond debate about appropriate and effective regulatory mechanisms and the categorisation of schools. Fundamental questions around the role of schooling as an individual or social good, whether formal education should be a government responsibility or opened to market forces and so on, remain pertinent. The actions of the Maoists demonstrate that there are groups who are prepared to use violence to advance their belief that 'education should be a government responsibility' (Bhattarai, Babiuram, 2001). The content and management of schooling, and indeed, the outcomes and livelihood opportunities it can lead to, are more contested than the EFA-focused approach that dominates international education policy suggests. Critically engaging with such concerns is crucial if conceptual space is to be created within which to understand private schooling–state relations and in deepening our understanding of the social and political context (and content) of schooling more broadly.

Notes

[1] This chapter draws upon a previous article 'Private Schools as Battlefields: contested visions of learning and livelihood in Nepal' published in *Compare*, 2006, 36(4), pp. 463-480.

[2] The core ethnographic research this chapter draws on was conducted from September 1999-December 2000. Additional blocks of interviewing and observation-based research were carried out in 2003, 2004 and 2005. The author gratefully acknowledges the support for this research work provided by the Economic and Social Research Council in the form of a Research Studentship and Postdoctoral Fellowship and by The Open University through a Faculty of Technology Research Grant.

[3] Although discussions of the potential of public–private partnerships in other areas of education, notably higher education, are receiving increased attention.

[4] Several cases emerged during fieldwork in Nepal of government-funded schools offering a private stream for those who could afford it. This usually consisted of students being taught in English and using English-medium

textbooks, but being taught in the same building and by the same teachers as those in the 'non-private' stream.

[5] Notably, the elite missionary schools such as St Xavier's and St Mary's in Kathmandu were able to continue to operate relatively autonomously.

[6] Supporters of the Nepali Congress often used the terms 'Communist' and 'Democrat' in referring to the main conflicting political positions. This is a result of the attempts made by the party to capitalise on the party's connection to the Jan Andolan, the democracy movement of 1990, with slogans such as 'Congress means multi-party democracy' and 'multi-party democracy means Congress' being propagated (Hacchetu, 2000, p. 14).

[7] In the context of a tripartite struggle between the King, the political parties and the Maoists in the period since 2001, the Palace has also emerged as a player in this arena. A revised curriculum emphasising the role of the monarchy has been ordered and schools have been requested to send students and teachers to pro-royalist rallies. Similarly, state security forces have made use of schools in rural areas as army barracks and so on.

[8] The School Leaving Certificate is the key school-based examination, held at the end of Year 10.

[9] The radical actions of the Maoists appear to have forced others wishing to gain attention for their political demands to adopt more hardline positions. In 2002, for example, six communist-affiliated student unions engaged in a forced lock-up of private schools in the Kathmandu Valley.

[10] There appears at times to be a degree of flexibility in the approach taken by some of those making demands – a number of institutions that view themselves as operating more of a 'social service' than a private business reported that they offered to show the Maoist representatives the accounts and documentation concerning who was donating to the school and who was benefiting from it. Some then saw the demand for protection money dropped or the sum reduced.

[11] Indeed many of the largest (and most expensive) schools in Kathmandu have been subjected to attacks, including the bombing of a Little Angels-affiliated school in Chitwan and the destruction of Galaxy School's fleet of buses and school office in central Kathmandu (Field notes, 23 June 2005, 18 January 2003).

[12] At the time of the initial pressure for strikes a multi-party system was still in place and concern about voter support in planned elections was a factor in pushing this issue further up the political agenda.

[13] NPABSON has recommended that its members go to the Company Act. PABSON has not made any general call, but is instead pushing for schools to be recognised as distinct from private companies through the development of an Act focused on 'service-oriented professions' (Field notes, 21 January 2003).

[14] NPABSON was formed as the result of a split in the main PABSON grouping.

References

Bhattarai, Baburam (2001) *Charter of Maoist Demands*. Reproduced and translated in *Nepali Times*, 16 February 2002.
http://www.nepalnews.com.np/ntimes/feb162001/nation.htm#Maoistdemands

Bhattarai, Binod (2001) A Classless Society? *Nepali Times*, 43, 18 May.

Caddell, M. (2005a) Listening to Local Voices? International Targets and Decentralised Education Planning in Nepal, *International Journal of Educational Development*, 25(4), pp. 456-469.

Caddell, M. (2005b) 'Discipline Makes the Nation Great': visioning development and the Nepali nation-state through schools, in V. Benei (Ed.) *Manufacturing Citizenship: education and nationalism in Europe, South Asia and China*, pp. 76-103. Oxford: Routledge.

Caddell, M. (forthcoming) Education and Change: a historical perspective on schooling, development and the Nepali nation-state, in K. Kumar & J. Oesterheld (Eds) *Education in Modern South Asia: social and political implications*. Delhi: Sage.

Colclough, C. (1996) Education and the Market: which parts of the neo-liberal solution are correct? *World Development*, 24(4), pp. 589-610.

Daniel, J. (2004) The Price of School Fees, *Education Today Newsletter*, July-September. Paris: UNESCO.
http://ww.portal.unesco.org/education/en/ev.php_url_ID=32496&URL_DO_TO PIC&URL_SECTION=201.html

Day-Ashley, L. (2005) From Margins to Mainstream: private school outreach inclusion processes for out-of-school children in India, *International Journal of Educational Development*, 25, pp. 133-144.

Education for All (1990) *World Declaration on Education for All: meeting basic learning needs*. New York: Inter-Agency Commission.

Education for All (2000) *Education for All: framework for action*. Dakar: Inter-Agency Commission.

Gellner, D. (Ed.) (2003) *Resistance and the State: Nepalese experiences*. New Delhi: Social Science Press.

Hacchetu, K. (2000) Nepali Politics: party–people interface. Paper presented at the 16th European Modern South Asian Studies Conference, Edinburgh, 5-9 September.

Harlech-Jones, B., Baig, M., Sajid, S. & ur-Rahman, S. (2005) Private Schooling in the Northern Areas of Pakistan: a decade of rapid expansion, *International Journal of Educational Development*, 25, pp. 557-568.

HMG (2002) *Education Regulations (7th Amendment)*. Kathmandu: Ministry of Education and Sport.

Hutt, M. (Ed.) (2004) *Himalayan 'People's War': Nepal's Maoist rebellion*. London: C. Hurst & Co.

Lal, C.K. (2002) Re-educating Revolutionaries, *Nepali Times*, 123, 13-19 December.
http://www.nepalnews.com.np/issue123/stateofthestate.htm

Liechty, M. (2003) *Suitably Modern: making middle class culture in a new consumer society*. Princeton: Princeton University Press.

Maharjan, P.N. (2000) The Maoists' Insurgency and Crisis of Governability in Nepal, in D. Kumar (Ed.) *Domestic Conflict and Crisis of Governability in Nepal*, pp. 163-196. Kathmandu: Centre for Nepal and Asian Studies.

National Education Planning Commission (1955) *Education in Nepal: report of the National Education Planning Commission*. Kathmandu: Bureau of Publications.

Nepal South Asia Centre (1998) *Nepal Human Development Report 1998*. Kathmandu: NESAC.

Nepali Times (2005) Targeting Schools, 241, 1 April. Translated from original article published in *Samaya*, 31 March 2005.

Private and Boarding Schools Organisation of Nepal (2002) *Private and Boarding School Organisation of Nepal: Code of Conduct*. Kathmandu: PABSON.

Parajuli, D. (2000) Why is There a School Strike? *Kantipur*, 13 December.

Pigg, S.L. (1992) Inventing Social Categories through Place: social representation and development in Nepal, *Comparative Studies in Society and History*, 34(3), pp. 491-513.

Psacharopoulos, G. & Patrinos, H. (2002) *Returns to Investment in Education: a further update*. World Bank Policy Research Working Paper 2881. Washington, DC: World Bank.

de Regt, A. & Weenink, D. (2005) When Negotiation Fails: private education as a disciplinary strategy, *Journal of Education Policy*, 20(1), pp. 59-80.

Rose, P. (2005a) Privatisation and Decentralisation of Schooling in Malawi: default or design? *Compare*, 35(2), pp. 153-165.

Rose, P. (2005b) *Workshop on Non-state Providers of Basic Services*. http://www.idd.bhm.ac.uk/service-providers

Shahi, S.J. (2005) A Class of Their Own, *Nepali Times*, 261, 19-25 August. http://www.nepalnews.com.np/ntimes/issue261/nation.htm

Skinner, D. & Holland, D.C. (1996) Schools and the Cultural Production of the Educated Person in a Nepalese Hill Community, in B.A. Levinson, D.E. Foley & D.C. Holland (Eds) *The Cultural Production of the Educated Person: critical ethnographies of schooling and local practice*, pp. 273-299. Buffalo: SUNY Press.

Thapa, D. (2002) The Maobadi of Nepal, in K.M. Dixit & S. Ramachandran (Eds) *State of Nepal*. Lalitpur: Himal Books.

Tooley, J. & Dixon, P. (2005a) Is There a Conflict Between Commercial Gain and Concern for the Poor? Evidence from Private Schools for the Poor in India and Nigeria, *Economic Affairs*, June, pp. 21-27.

Tooley, J. & Dixon, P. (2005b) An Inspector Calls: the regulation of 'budget' private schools in Hyderabad, Andhra Pradesh, India, *International Journal of Educational Development*, 25, pp. 269-285.

UNICEF (2005) *UNICEF Humanitarian Action: Nepal summary for 2005*. http://www.reliefweb.int/rw/RWB.NSF/db900SID/HMYT-6D6SPW?OpenDocument

Oxford Studies in Comparative Education

Series Editor: David Phillips

Lessons of Cross-national Comparison in Education, ed. David Phillips, 1991

Education and Economic Change in Eastern Europe and the Former Soviet Union, ed. David Phillips & Michael Kaser, 1922

Something Borrowed, Something Blue? A Study of the Thatcher Government's Appropriation of American Education and Training Policy, Parts 1 & 2, ed. David Finegold, Laurel McFarland & William Richardson, 1992

Key Issues in Educational Development, ed. Terry Allsop & Colin Brock, 1993

The University and the Teachers: France, the United States, England, Harry Judge, Michel Lemosse, Lynn Paine & Michael Sedlak, 1994

Developing Schools for Democracy in Europe, ed. John Sayer (with others), 1995

Aspects of Education and the European Union, ed. David Phillips, 1995

School Choice and the Quasi-market, ed. Geoffrey Walford, 1996

Global Perspectives on Teacher Education, ed. Colin Brock, 1996

Education and Change in the Pacific Rim, ed. Keith Sullivan, 1998

Education and Privatisation in Eastern Europe and the Baltic Republics, ed. Paul Beresford-Hill, 1998

Education for Reconstruction: the regeneration of educational capacity following national upheaval, Nina Arnhold, Julia Bekker, Natasha Kersh, Elizabeth McLeish & David Phillips, 1998

Processes of Transition in Education Systems, ed. Elizabeth A. McLeish & David Phillips, 1998

Comparing Standards Internationally, ed. Barbara Jaworski & David Phillips

The Education Systems of the United Kingdom, ed. David Phillips, 1999

Education in Eastern Germany Since Unification, ed. David Phillips, 2000

Opening Windows to Change: a case study of sustained international development, ed. John Sayer, 2002

Faith-Based Schools and the State: Catholics in America, France and England, Harry Judge, 2002

Can the Japanese Change Their Education System? ed. Roger Goodman & David Phillips, 2003

The InstitutionS of Education, William K. Cummings, 2003

The Challenges of Education in Brazil, ed. Colin Brock & Simon Schwartzman, 2004

Educational Policy Borrowing: historical perspectives, ed. David Phillips & Kimberly Ochs, 2004

New Approaches to Vocational Education in Europe, ed. Regina H. Mulder & Peter F.E. Sloane, 2004

Political and Citizenship Education, ed. Stephanie Wilde, 2005

Partnerships in Educational Development, ed. Iffat Farah & Barbara Jaworski, 2006

School History Textbooks Across Cultures, ed. Jason Nicholls, 2006

Education's Abiding Moral Dilemma, Sheldon Rothblatt, 2007

Reforming Teaching Globally, ed. Maria Teresa Tatto, 2007

Private Schooling in Less Economically Developed Countries, ed. Prachi Srivastava & Geoffrey Walford, 2007

The Changing Landscape of Education in Africa, ed. David Johnson, 2007

Further details of all volumes in this series can be found at
www.symposium-books.co.uk
and can be ordered there, or from
Symposium Books, PO Box 204, Didcot, Oxford OX11 9ZQ
orders@symposium-books.co.uk

Notes on Contributors

Modupe Adelabu is Senior Lecturer at the Department of Educational Administration and Planning, Obafemi Awolowo University, Ile-Ife, Nigeria. Her major research area is on policy issues related to education, including the state's role in education, teacher education, and poverty and gender related issues in education particularly in rural areas. She has published 27 articles in both national and international journals. Dr Adelabu has been involved in consultancy work for the World Bank, Universal Basic Education Commission in Nigeria, United Kingdom Department for International Development and other international agencies.

Colin Bangay is a senior education specialist with the British Council. He is currently on a two-year secondment to the World Bank Institute where he is working on issues of governance, decentralisation and non-state provision. Mr Bangay has worked extensively throughout Africa and Asia as teacher, researcher, consultant and resident project manager. His interest in non-state provision stems from experiences in Indonesia (where he was team leader on the Asian Development Bank-funded Private Junior Secondary Education Project) and project work in Bangladesh.

Martha Caddell is Lecturer in Development Studies at The Open University. Her research has focused on international education policy, donor coordination and frameworks for aid delivery, and citizenship and schooling. Recent work has focused on the impact of the de facto civil war in Nepal and the impact this has had on the education sector and on development efforts more broadly. She is also involved in the EU-funded Nepali Language Resources and Localisation for Education and Communication (NELRALEC) project, which aims to enhance Nepali-medium access to information technology through support for software localisation and language engineering. Dr Caddell teaches on The Open University's Global Development Management programme.

Pauline Dixon is International Research Coordinator at the E.G. West Centre in the School of Education at the University of Newcastle. She has worked and studied with Professor James Tooley for the past five years. She is the author and co-author of numerous studies and journal articles on private education in the developing world. Dr Dixon's interests range from the regulatory environment in which private schools catering for low-income families function, to researching alternative and innovative methods of pedagogy and e-learning for the poor.

Igor Kitaev was born in Moscow in 1960. He graduated as economist from the Moscow State University of Foreign Relations in 1982 (MA, BA) where he continued his Ph.D. research on the economics of developing countries. As a government expert he took part in many international events, including the 1990 Jomtien Conference on Education for All. As a staff member of the International Institute for Educational Planning of UNESCO in Paris, he has written many studies on educational finance, in particular on private education in developing and transitional countries.

Keith M. Lewin is Professor of International Education at the University of Sussex and Director of the Centre for International Education. He has worked widely in sub-Saharan Africa and Asia on education and development projects over the last 30 years for development agencies and national governments. Recently he has been working on plans to finance expanded secondary schooling in Uganda, Tanzania, and Rwanda, and has completed regional studies for the World Bank Secondary Education in Africa programme. His books include *Financing Secondary Education in Developing Countries* (International Institute of Educational Planning, with F. Callods, 2001); *Researching Teacher Education: new perspectives on practice performance and policy* (UNESCO, 1997); and *Educational Innovation in Developing Countries* (Macmillan, 1991). He currently directs the Department for International Development Research Consortium for Educational Access, and is President of the British Association of International and Comparative Education.

Santosh Mehrotra was Regional Adviser, Regional Centre for Asia, United Nations Development Programme, Bangkok, and is now with the Planning Commission of the Government of India in New Delhi. Earlier, he was Senior Policy Adviser to the Human Development Report. He also led UNICEF's research programme on developing countries at Innocenti Research Centre, Florence. After gaining his Ph.D. at Cambridge (1985), he was Associate Professor of Economics, Jawaharlal Nehru University, New Delhi (1988-91). Since then he has been 14 years with the UN, as a human development economist. His research interests have spanned industry and trade issues, the impact of macro-economic policy on health and education, the informal sector, and the economics of health and education. His books include: *India and the Soviet Union: trade and technology transfer* (Cambridge University Press, 1990); *Development with a Human Face. Experiences in Social Achievement and Economic Growth* (Oxford University Press, 1997, with Richard Jolly); *Universalizing Elementary Education in India: uncaging the 'tiger' economy* (Oxford University Press, 2005, with P.R. Panchamukhi, R. Srivastava & R. Srivastava); *The Economics of Elementary Education in India*

(Sage, 2006). Two co-authored books are to be published in 2006: *Asian Informal Workers. Global Risks, Local Protection* (Routledge, with Mario Biggeri), and *Eliminating Human Poverty: macro-economic policies for equitable growth* (Zed Press, with Enrique Delamonica).

P.R. Panchamukhi is one of India's earliest and best known education economists. He is a former Adviser, Planning Commission and Director, Indian Institute of Education, Pune. His major works are on economic reforms in the social sector among India's less developed regions. Dr Panchamukhi recently retired as Director, Centre for Multi-disciplinary Research, Karnataka.

Pauline Rose is Senior Lecturer in International Education at the University of Sussex. Her research from a political economy perspective relates to international and national educational policy and practice including in areas of non-state provision, decentralisation, and community participation. This work focuses on concerns for out of school children with respect to poverty and gender in particular. Dr Rose has led large multi-site collaborative research projects in sub-Saharan Africa and South Asia, funded by the Department for International Development, Rockefeller Foundation and others. Part of this work has been published in a co-authored book on *Schooling for All in Africa: costs, commitment and gender* (with C. Colclough, S. Al-Samarrai & M. Tembon, Ashgate, 2003), as well as in a number of journal articles. She is currently leading the education sector component of a research project analysing inter-sectoral collaboration for service delivery, as part of the Economic and Social Research Council's Non-Government Public Action Programme.

Prachi Srivastava is Lecturer in Education at the University of Sussex with the Centre for International Education and the Sussex School of Education. After obtaining her doctorate from the University of Oxford, she was awarded the Economic and Social Research Council Post-Doctoral Research Fellowship, which she undertook at the Department of Educational Studies, University of Oxford (2005-06). There, she co-organised the seminar series, 'Private Schooling in Developing Countries' with Professor Walford, from which most chapters in this volume are drawn. Her work on 'low-fee private' schooling in India led to an invited report by the Government of India, and to a number of book chapters and articles in press and under review. She is currently involved with the Consortium for Educational Access at Sussex, and is also working on a small study funded by the European Science Foundation on social capital and attitudes towards immigrants in Europe. Dr Srivastava has worked for NGOs in Albania, Bosnia-Herzegovina, and Kosovo where she also served for the United Nations Administration Mission in Kosovo. Her main research interests are: privatisation of education in economically developing countries; marketisation of educational reform;

school choice and social disadvantage; and applications of new institutional theory to educational governance.

James Tooley is Professor of Education Policy at the University of Newcastle and Director of the E.G. West Centre. He has just completed directing a two-year study of private schools catering for low-income families in Asia and Africa funded by the Templeton Foundation. James Tooley has also directed studies for the International Finance Corporation – the private finance arm of the World Bank – which included a global study of investment opportunities for private education in developing countries, which led to his book *The Global Education Industry,* now in its second edition (Institute for Economic Affairs, 1999). Professor Tooley has undertaken considerable consultancy work for the IFC, World Bank (International Bank for Reconstruction and Development), UN, UNESCO, and Asian Development Bank Institute on private education in developing countries. He is author of *Reclaiming Education* (Continuum, 2005) and co-editor of *What America Can Learn from School Choice in Other Countries* (Cato Institute, 2005).

Geoffrey Walford is Professor of Education Policy and a Fellow of Green College at the University of Oxford. His research foci are the relationships between central government policy and local processes of implementation, private schools, choice of schools, religious-based schools and qualitative research methodology. His books include: *Life in Public Schools* (Methuen, 1986), *Restructuring Universities: politics and power in the management of change* (Croom Helm, 1987), *Private Schools in Ten Countries: policy and practice* (Routledge, Ed., 1989), *Privatization and Privilege in Education* (Routledge, 1990), *City Technology College* (Open University Press, 1991, with Henry Miller), *Doing Educational Research* (Routledge, Ed., 1991), *Choice and Equity in Education* (Cassell, 1994), *Researching the Powerful in Education* (UCL Press, Ed., 1994), *Educational Politics: pressure groups and faith-based schools* (Avebury, 1995), *Affirming the Comprehensive Ideal* (Falmer, Ed., 1997, with Richard Pring), *Policy, Politics and Education – sponsored grant-maintained schools and religious diversity* (Ashgate, 2000), *Doing Qualitative Educational Research* (Continuum, 2001), *Private Schooling: tradition and diversity* (Continuum, 2005) and *Markets and Equity in Education* (Continuum, 2006). He was Joint Editor of the *British Journal of Educational Studies* from 1999 to 2002, is Editor of the annual volume *Studies in Educational Ethnography,* and has been Editor of the *Oxford Review of Education* since January 2004.